THE THEORY OF BEING

THE THEORY OF BEING

*Practices for Transforming Self and
Communities Across Difference*

*Edited by Sherry K. Watt,
Duhita Mahatmya, Milad Mohebali,
and Charles R. Martin-Stanley II*

Foreword by Parker J. Palmer

STERLING, VIRGINIA

COPYRIGHT © 2022 BY STYLUS PUBLISHING, LLC.

Appendix D, The Practice of Asking Open and Honest Questions.
Copyright 2021. Used by permission of the Center for Courage &
Renewal. See www.CourageRenewal.org.

Published by Stylus Publishing, LLC.
22883 Quicksilver Drive
Sterling, Virginia 20166-2019

Library of Congress Cataloging-in-Publication Data
The CIP data for this title has been applied for.

13-digit ISBN: 978-1-64267-364-7 (cloth)
13-digit ISBN: 978-1-64267-365-4 (paperback)
13-digit ISBN: 978-1-64267-366-1 (library networkable e-edition)
13-digit ISBN: 978-1-64267-367-8 (consumer e-edition)

Printed in the United States of America

All first editions printed on acid-free paper
that meets the American National Standards Institute
Z39-48 Standard.

Bulk Purchases

Quantity discounts are available for use in workshops and
for staff development.

Call 1-800-232-0223

First Edition, 2022

To bell hooks,
who taught us about truth telling, love, and liberation;
may your teachings always live through our work.

To all in our past, present, and future learning community
(our families, friends, students, colleagues, and our
research team members) where our Being is enriched.

CONTENTS

LIST OF FIGURES

LIST OF TABLES

In *The Theory of Being: Practices for Transforming Self and Communities Across Difference*, Sherry K. Watt and her colleagues promise to lay out a process that will enable constructive dialogue around the issues that drive us apart, both individually and collectively. As you will see, they deliver on that promise, with a focus on difficult dialogues about race and its intersections with sexual orientation, religion, and disability. In doing so, they take us on a deeply human journey, a journey from which we can learn much about living more fully into the human possibility.

The dialogue process described in this book is rooted in real-life experience and sound theory, tested and proven in practice, and illustrated with compelling stories. It's a process that works for individuals and groups, one that can help us find our way through the complex, conflicted, and high-stakes era in which we live and emerge more unified on the other side.

The process was developed in a university setting, but it reaches far beyond the groves of academe. No matter what sector of our shared life you care about—family, education, community, business, politics, religion, or any other—thriving depends on forging creative relationships with each other across our divides.

We cannot erase our differences, nor should we want to. Most of those differences can be held as paradoxes, as "both/ands" rather than "either/ors." *Paradox* means being able to disagree and stay in dialogue, recognizing that tensions between ideas and feelings can pull us open to a larger view of the world. The ability to hold paradoxes is an antidote to polarization when either/or thinking—as in "my way or the highway," "right or wrong," "this or that"—seem the only options. Holding our differences as paradoxes will enlarge and enhance our lives if we have enough patience, empathy, and stamina to stay the course.

What we need is a process that allows us to rediscover and return to our common bonds as we explore our differences. That's where "the theory of

Being" comes in. Connecting with each other across our divides begins with a deep dive into the one thing we share beneath all of our differences. I'm referring to the great aquifer of being—of *human* being—that is the primal well of our individual and collective lives. Science tells us that we are 99.9% identical in our genetic makeup. But we too often forget that we are 100% identical in our shared "human beingness."

Being is a hard thing to talk about because it's the medium in which we all live, and there is no conscious, self-reflective life for us outside of it. We're like the fish in David Foster Wallace's (2008) story:

> There are these two young fish swimming along and they happen to meet an older fish swimming the other way, who nods at them and says "Morning, boys. How's the water?" The two young fish swim on for a bit, and then eventually one of them looks over at the other and goes "What the hell is water?" (para. 1)

Wallace goes on to say, "The immediate point of the fish story is . . . that the most obvious, important realities are often the ones that are hardest to see and talk about" (Wallace, 2008, para. 2).

Being is one of those important realities, arguably the most important. That's why I'm grateful to the writer Annie Dillard (1982) who found language that allows us to visualize the aquifer of *being* and how it holds us together:

> In the deeps are the violence and terror of which psychology has warned us. But if you ride these monsters down, if you drop with them farther over the world's rim, you find what our sciences can not locate or name, the substrate, the ocean or matrix or ether which buoys the rest, which gives goodness its power for good, and evil its power for evil, the unified field: our complex and inexplicable caring for each other, and for our life together here. This is given. It is not learned. (pp. 94–95)

As Dillard says, this unified field is "given," not "learned." But what *can* be learned are the individual and group protocols that can open up and take us into the depths of our shared *being*. That's what this book is designed to help us do.

The pages that follow are rich with practices that allow us to be present to each other in our diversity and our conflicts without losing touch with the connective power of our shared humanity. To whet your appetite, I'll say a few words about practices that I can vouch for, based on the work I've done for 40 years.

In the field of group process, I don't know of any practice that makes more space for shared *being* to emerge than a ground rule that makes participation in the dialogue purely invitational, never a "share or die" event. When you create a space that people can occupy without being pressured to participate, people are more likely to participate.

A second practice that helps make it safe for shared *being* to emerge is the prohibition against trying to fix, save, or advise people in the kinds of dialogues described in this book. When *being* emerges in our midst via our stories, what it wants most is to be seen and heard. It quickly goes back into hiding when we respond to it as something broken that needs to be fixed, or something that needs to be altered in order to fit our version of truth.

A third practice flows naturally from the second: deep listening. When we are in a conversation where fixing, saving, and advising are allowed, we have no reason to listen to speakers with care. All we need to do is listen long enough to hear something that seems off to us, so we can jump in and set that person straight. Our advice may be offered with good intentions, but the result is usually to make the speaker feel unheard, uncomfortable, and even judged.

But when "fixing" is prohibited, we can listen with care since we're not spending half of our mental energy wondering how we're going to respond. And as we do so, we realize how much we have to learn from another person's witness to their own life, their own *being*.

Our listening becomes more active when we engage in a fourth practice that helps frame the dialogue process described in this book: addressing people who have spoken with open and honest questions. That may sound easy, but it isn't, because so many of us have figured out how to ask questions that are advice in disguise.

"Have you thought about seeing a therapist?" is not an honest, open question! But if we ask a question intended to help "hear the speaker into deeper speech"—such as, "You said you felt angry at that moment. Can you say more about the nature of your anger, where it came from, and where it took you?"—we are honoring the speaker by helping them mine their own experience more deeply (Your Dictionary, n.d.).

If you, the reader, have been holding the question of how to conduct constructive dialogue around the issues that drive us apart, both individually and collectively, now you are also holding a treasure trove of answers in your hands. We have much to learn from Sherry K. Watt and her colleagues, and much to learn from the great diversity of folks with whom we can walk while never losing sight of our shared "human being."

This is just the trailhead: let the walk begin!

References

Dillard, A. (1982). *Teaching a stone to talk*. Harper & Row.

Wallace, D. F. (2008, September 19). Plain old untrendy troubles and emotions. *The Guardian*. See https://www.theguardian.com/books/2008/sep/20/fiction

Your Dictionary. (n.d.). *Nelle Katherine Morton*. http://biography.yourdictionary.com/nelle-katherine-morton

PREFACE

You must
Be the thing you see:
You must be the dark snakes of
Stems and ferny plumes of leaves,
You must enter in.

—John Moffitt, *Living Seed*

Being With the Year of 2020

The sun is shining! It is the start of a spring day in Iowa. Out of the gray clouds bursts the sun. The sky has been dreary. The rain and snow have been falling. The trees have had no buds. The grass has hints of green through the brown as it wakes from its dormancy. I (Sherry) walk over to the huge sugar maple tree in my front yard. As I stand by the tree, I can feel the sun streaming through the branches. I look up, and it surprises me—there are red buds of leaves on the tree! I smile and immediately take a picture. I then stood next to her, and I said, "Well hello, lady." I placed my hand on one of her branches, and I took a deep breath in and closed my eyes. I needed to feel that sturdy branch and imagine her deep roots. I needed to be grounded. I needed to feel the hope of normalcy that comes from seeing a maple tree that blooms every spring despite what is living or dying around her.

It is March of 2020; the coronavirus is already killing thousands of people daily in the United States of America. Two months from now, a worldwide racial reckoning will emerge after the barbaric murder of George Floyd under the knee of a police officer in Minneapolis, Minnesota. The publicized murders of Breonna Taylor, Ahmaud Arbery, and countless racially motivated deaths of Black people over centuries finally come to a brighter light—and to public discussion—the undeniable pandemic of institutionalized racial violence. As an African American woman, I feel the isolation and powerlessness of generations in a particularly infuriating way. All exacerbated by political polarization.

This perfect storm gained more energy with the insurrection on January 6, 2021, mounted by White supremacist and antigovernment extremists in the United States Capitol. American democracy is being used to foment dissent by manipulating divisions and peddling lies that feed distortions of humanity. And these divisions and distortions continue to be fueled by political extremism, American exceptionalism, and a toxic mix of neoliberal and capitalist ideology, to name a few.

As I wrote the preface for this book, I was waking up to the reality that I am living in a moment in history that will have long-lasting social, economic, political, and global consequences. As the unprecedented uncertainty continued to multiply exponentially, I started to feel hopelessness, despair, and frustration. I felt at a loss as to how to move forward with the work for equity and justice. In this tailspin of two pandemics and widespread divisiveness, I wondered how our research might contribute to an individual's ability to build stamina for the many difficult conversations that we need to have to heal as a national and global community.

Why Us? Why Now?

Rather than being consumed by the feelings of hopelessness and anger, my Multicultural Initiatives (MCI) Research Team pondered how our work might support meaningful dialogue when a community is working together to take action to change racial inequity and other injustices. Since early 2000, our research has explored the ways in which individuals, organizations, and communities can work together to continuously evolve responsive, inclusive, and equitable practices that value social and cultural differences. Even before the death of George Floyd, our team discussed the various ways that our process of inquiry provided a framework for transformative learning and made a unique contribution to community efforts that seek to make fundamental social change. Collectively, we wanted our research to help communities move beyond the bewilderment that we felt in the face of 2020 events and toward meaningful, sustainable action.

Over the course of 20 years, the MCI Research Team evolved the theory of Being. The theory teaches about Being and the ways to build stamina to be present in authentic and meaningful dialogue as a collective (program, community, unit, organization, society) where conflict is inherent. Being is the practice of aligning thoughts, feelings, and actions when facing conflict. The theory of Being includes personal, relational, and community practices that support individuals and communities to better withstand the difficult dialogues necessary to transform systems of structural inequity. This book describes and offers applications of Being to help the reader understand and apply the theory's principles and practices. *Ways of Being* can shift how individuals, groups, communities, and/or organizations react when working through conflict. The practices invite an openness to controversy while facilitating deeper reflection.

Language is the place of social struggle and it's never settled. We have chosen to capitalize Being, as well as Difference, not to claim power of trademark or ownership, but to orient ourselves as authors and you, the reader, to pause and to explore these concepts. Our approach gazes at the ideals of Westernized ways of being and inherently that focus leads us to acknowledge power or power-evasive uses of the English language. Our Western culture idolizes doing and evidence of action-based outcomes. Instead, Being invites an attention to process and being *while* doing. Our view of Difference does not center on othering, but rests on the belief that difference is a natural and valued reality of the human experience.

About This Book

The purpose of this book is to describe what emerged during our research process, namely the theory of Being, which reconsiders the ways in which we react and relate to Difference. Difference is "having dissimilar opinions, experiences, ideologies, epistemologies and/or constructions of reality about self, society, and/or identity" (Watt, 2013, p. 6). Current renditions of civil discourse often involve a sterilization of difference while simultaneously growing "otherness, borders, separateness" (Brown, 2017, p. 133). Difference is inherent to the human condition. How leaders "make meaning" of and relate to it is steeped in "long and vast patterns" (Patel, 2015, p. 58) of how education has functioned in replicating systems of oppression and dehumanization. The interlocking relationship between the oppressed and the oppressor gives rise to obstinate problems that manifest inequity among those who have been historically centralized and valued (e.g., White, male, upper social class) and those who have been marginalized and devalued (e.g., People of Color, women, lower social class; Freire, 1970). To disrupt this process of replication, we must find productive ways to engage in difficult dialogues. A difficult dialogue is "a verbal or written exchange of ideas or opinions between citizens within a community that centers on an awakening of potentially conflicting views of beliefs or values about social justice issues (such as racism, sexism, heterosexism/homophobia; Watt, 2007, p. 112).

How to Use This Book

This book is divided into four parts plus an epilogue. All lead authors are current, affiliated closely with or past MCI Research Team members. When writing their chapters, the authors were encouraged to Be with the theory and the idea of Being. They were asked to lead with heart, acknowledging that an understanding of the theory of Being is strengthened by heartfelt sharing. In the chapters, heart might be a story, a reflection of the authors' writing processes, or quotes and phrases that invite the reader to draw upon their own Being (e.g., thoughts, feelings, or actions). From here, the authors guide readers through a conflict that called them to apply specific *ways of Being* practices. Each chapter includes applications (Appendix F) to encourage the reader to further explore and reflect on the theory of Being. While writing this book, we "lived into" an idea that Being is countercultural. As higher education conscious scholar–practitioners, our reflex is to write from our heads about what we do. Less often, we write about the turmoils and triumphs that surround our process. We have leaned into the messiness of the process of Being. Our hope is that through sharing our stories readers get to know our team and our team's process to arrive at an in-depth understanding of the theory.

Part One introduces the theory of Being, including a personal story by Sherry K. Watt to show how Being practices can show up outside the classroom, in real life. This part presents the foundational tenets, tools, terms, and components and discusses how we arrived at the theory. We describe *ways of Being* and explain how the theory can be used to traverse difficult dialogues across socially and politically controversial Difference, specifically across various organizational contexts within higher education.

Parts Two, Three, and Four explore *ways of Being*. Part Two describes the authors' relationship with the theory of Being and how the authors used the theory in a conflict, as well as experiences that can emerge as leaders employ *personal ways of Being*. The chapters explore specific outgrowths of Being such as wrestling with empathy, shame, and silence. Part Three highlights *relational ways of Being* and shares the authors' experiences with challenges in interpersonal communication when facing resistance in a classroom or observing boundaries in social relationships. The authors discuss how Being practices help sustain active authentic relationships with others during these conflicts while centering their exploration of communication, resistance, and boundaries. Part Four focuses on applications of *community ways of Being* featuring a group in conflict. The Authors consider the complexity of social identities and socialization in our relationships to ourselves, others, and broader communities (e.g., collegiate department, campus, professional organization/discipline). Particularly, when trying to create inclusive organizational practices that result in cultural change that is "deep and pervasive" (Kezar & Eckel, 2002, p. 296). The authors explore their relationship to truth, otherness, and research.

The epilogue offers a closing reflection on the strengths and limitations of the theory of Being as well as a thematic summary of the various types of its applications exemplified and woven throughout each chapter.

Our Hopes for the Readers

The primary audience for this book is higher education leaders and leaders-in-training including student affairs professional staff, campus administrators, higher education and student affairs faculty, and undergraduate and graduate students. We are speaking to leaders and educators who strive to be conscious scholar–practitioners (Watt, 2015). A conscious scholar–practitioner is a leader who is relational, collaborative, aware of the broader context of personal, social, political, and ethical commitments and who grounds his/her/their work in research, theory, and experiential knowledge (McClintock, 2004). We expect that this book will be used in diversity, equity, and inclusion courses. We also believe that this book will be used as a common read (*a third thing*) for organizations such as divisions of student life or academic colleges. Though the content of this book focuses on higher education settings, we suspect that it will resonate with any public- or private-community organizing efforts. We also believe there are applications of the theory in both professional (such as work) and private (such as familial) settings. The principles and practices of the theory of Being can go beyond the confines of social controversy. Leaders can also consider using *ways of Being* to support any process of change or when deciding on a new direction for the organization—particularly when the success of the initiative depends heavily on how well a community can discuss and ultimately align their personal and professional practices to achieve a goal.

Applying the theory of Being aligns well with the large selection of publications that center on strategies for critical dialogues (e.g., Shaffer & Longo, 2019), books that interrogate racism (e.g., DiAngelo, 2018; Kendi, 2019; Oluo, 2019; Singh, 2019), and strategies for thinking and leading that call for vulnerability, courage, and trust-building (e.g., Brown, 2018; Center for Courage & Renewal & Francis, 2018; Jana & Freeman, 2016; Palmer, 2009).

Many existing books stress self-reflection and the importance of understanding one's own socialization and biases (Kezar & Posselt, 2020). These books call for a thoughtful approach to social justice and equity work, but crucial questions are still left unanswered:

1. How do I ground myself in a practice of individual self-reflection?
2. How do I shore myself up against the neoliberal psyche that insists on productivity and quick responses, when this work requires space for deep understanding and ongoing change?
3. How do I prepare myself to have sustained engagement in work that can be dehumanizing, resisted, and constantly evolving?

4. How can I resist the tendency to dismiss the experiences and opinions of others that do not fit into simplistic and rigid ideas of social justice speech, ideologies, or identities?

Our book provides explorations with these questions in mind and offers a structure that individuals and communities can use to establish *ways of Being* in social justice work that are *humanizing* to oneself and others. It presents process-oriented strategies for developing the internal fortitude that nurtures stamina to engage in difficult dialogues.

I (Sherry) often orient learners to a collaborative educational setting (e.g., a workshop, course, or consultation) with this phrase "I know exactly where we are going, and I have no idea where we will end up." I invite students along with me to board "a magic bus" analogous to the stories of Ms. Frizzle (Cole & Degen, 1990). In other words, as a teacher–facilitator, I design a roadmap for exploring and applying the content. As we collaborate together to understand the idea(s), our bus will go off the map into beautiful, unexpected, and unexplored pastures. As we ride together, the journey might lead us to a different destination than I envisioned. As a magic bus rider, you have the opportunity to impact how the journey evolves. As the instructor, I commit to incorporating your understandings. Together, we immerse ourselves in the ideas and explore. The journey evolves the destination or the meaning. In the spirit of the magic bus, I invite you, the reader, to embrace this open-ended ethos as you read this book. Join the journey, we welcome you. While our intention is to explain and apply the theory, the book is meant to be embraced as an educational process. Therefore, we invite you to engage with the book as a dynamic, not static idea, and as *a third thing*. It is our hope that you will inhabit Being and allow it to evolve in you and go where it takes you on the journey.

The theory of Being provides an anchor to a ship. In other words, this approach provides firm grounding that allows for waves of new ideas and approaches as well as storms of sudden controversies to move your ship without sinking it or sending it adrift. From this grounding, readers will be better prepared to explore strategies and ideas that most often result in their abandoning ship.

—The Editors,
Sherry, Duhita, Milad, and Charles

References

Brown, A. M. (2017). *Emergent strategy: Shaping change, changing worlds*. AK Press.
Brown, B. (2018). *Dare to lead: Brave work. Tough conversations. Whole hearts*. Random House.

Center for Courage & Renewal & Francis, S. L. (2018). *The courage way: Leading and living with integrity.* Berrett-Koehler Publishers.

Cole, J., & Degen, B. (1990). *The magic school bus inside the human body.* Scholastic Press.

DiAngelo, R. (2018). *White fragility: Why it's so hard for white people to talk about racism.* Beacon Press.

Freire, P. (1970). *Pedagogy of the oppressed.* Seabury Press.

Jana, T., & Freeman, M. (2016). *Overcoming bias: Building authentic relationships across differences.* Berrett-Koehler Publishers.

Kendi, I. X. (2019). *How to be an antiracist.* One World.

Kezar, A., & Eckel, P. (2002). Examining the institutional transformation process: The importance of sensemaking, interrelated strategies, and balance. *Research in Higher Education, 43*(3), 295–328. https://doi.org/10.1023/A:1014889001242

Kezar, A., & Posselt, J. R. (2020). *Higher education administration for social justice and equity: Critical perspectives for leadership.* Routledge.

McClintock, C. (2004). The scholar-practitioner model. In A. DiStefano, K. Rudestam, & R. Silverman (Eds.), *Encyclopedia of disturbed learning* (pp. 393–405). SAGE.

Oluo, I. (2019). *So you want to talk about race.* Seal Press.

Palmer, P. J. (2009). *A hidden wholeness: The journey toward an undivided life.* Wiley.

Patel, L. (2015). *Decolonizing educational research: From ownership to answerability.* Routledge.

Shaffer, T. J., & Longo, N. V. (Eds.). (2019). *Creating space for democracy: A primer on dialogue and deliberation in higher education.* Stylus.

Singh, A. A. (2019). *The racial healing handbook: Practical activities to help you challenge privilege, confront systemic racism, and engage in collective healing.* New Harbinger Publications.

Watt, S. K. (2007). Difficult dialogues, privilege and social justice: Uses of the privileged identity exploration (PIE) model in student affairs practice. *College Student Affairs Journal, 26*(2), 114–126. https://eric.ed.gov/?id=EJ899385

Watt, S. K. (2013). Designing and implementing multicultural initiatives: Guiding principles. In S. K. Watt & J. Linley (Eds.), *Creating Successful Multicultural Initiatives in Higher Education and Student Affairs* (New Directions for Student Services, no. 144, pp. 5–15). Jossey-Bass. https://doi.org/10.1002/ss.20064

Watt, S. K. (Ed.) (2015). *Designing transformative multicultural initiatives: Theoretical foundations, practical applications, and facilitator considerations.* Stylus.

ACKNOWLEDGMENTS

We give thanks to the many people in our circles who labored with us to birth the theory of Being. In the words of Marianne Houston's poem, The Paradoxes that Cradle Me, "*Friends . . . / help me carry the burdens and the gifts/help me hold and even cherish the two-horned mysteries.*" There were days words easily filled our conversations and pages about the theory of Being; and other days it was hard to see a path forward. We are grateful to be in relationship with individuals and groups who lifted us when we needed the extra push and carried the spirit of the work all these years.

The Multicultural Initiatives (MCI) Research Team members, past and present, have been so generous in sharing ideation and with their humanity. Thank you for trusting the process and believing in the theory of Being before it even had a name. Thank you for welcoming the silences and swirling. The theory and chapters bear the fruit of our conversations. While many of those conversations evolved into chapters in this book, there were others that fed the spirit of the work more formatively who are not authors, and that includes Brittany Conner, Nayoung Jang, Becca Neel, Milica Oliver, Alyssa Rae Plano, Tabitha Wiggins, and Raquel Wood. We are thankful for all those conversations inside and outside a classroom setting, in text messages, in hallway pass-byes, and in those serendipitous and especially during our signature "meetings-after-the meeting" moments.

The University of Iowa College of Education (COE) and Division of Student Life (DSL) were early adopters of the theory of Being. We thank Dean Dan Clay and Vice President Sarah Hansen for the funding and opportunity to share Being practices with the campus community. We extend gratitude to our COE and DSL colleagues who participated in the Being Circles pilot, the COE Anti-Racism Collaborative (ARC) steering committee, and our immersive partnership collaborators, with special thanks to Rusty Barcelo, Will Coghill-Behrends, Maria Bruno, and Teri Schnelle. In your articulation of your experiences with and sometimes in resistance to this work, you helped us settle into the language and practices that best embody the theory.

Thank you to the students in the Multiculturalism in Higher Education, Multicultural Initiatives, and Facilitating Controversial Dialogue courses who took the invitation for Being with each other and with Difference as well as those who freely shared with us their resistance and doubts. Special thank you to those students who took the lessons into their lives, professional practice, and later came to sing Being back to us.

Thank you to Ellen Fairchild, Bria Marcelo, and Ashley Cheyemi McNeil who helped us imagine possibilities for Being Circles and The Being Institute. The Center for Courage & Renewal has continued to be a wellspring of inspiration and support. Those fountains include Donna Bivens, Terry Chadsey, Beverly Coleman, John Fenner, Veta Goler, Gloria Gostnell, Sally Hare, Marcy Jackson, Rick Jackson, Kathryn McElveen, and Parker J. Palmer.

We are very grateful for John von Knorring for his support of this research over years, for his kind regard for our humanity, and especially for his generative questions.

A special thank you to Chris DeGuzman for not only lending his photography skills, but also for so generously and enthusiastically taking the invitation. And to Shelly Francis, whose questions and edits were always so timely and reminded us how to let our stories speak wholeheartedly throughout this book.

PART ONE

INTRODUCING THE
THEORY OF BEING

PART ONE INTRODUCTION

Sherry K. Watt

You are not a troubled guest on this earth,
you are not an accident amidst other accidents
you were invited from another and greater night
than the one from which you have just emerged

—David Whyte, *What to Remember When Waking*

This "Part One Introduction" introduces the theory of Being and describes the approach using dilemmas told through story. In Part One, chapter 1, "Being With Paradox and Possibility: The Origins of the theory of Being," my journey through the evolution of the theory is told. Chapter 2, "Living Into the theory of Being: A Process-Oriented Research Approach," by Chris R. Patterson, Duhita Mahatmya, and Multicultural Initiatives Consortium, describes the conceptual and empirical processes that established the theory. There are four sections in the "Part One Introduction." The first section discusses "Why the theory of Being?" This section provides the rationale for Being (process-orientation) versus doing (an outcome orientation), defining key terms, briefly reviewing the theoretical influences, and sharing the assumptions. The second section asks, "What are the four crosscutting tools for Being?" It includes a description of the key tools that create the container (environmental conditions) for Being with a conflict, namely, the use of Being *touchstones*, the utility of the *third thing* and the privileged identity exploration (PIE) model, and the *practice of open and honest questions* (see Appendices B–E). To demonstrate the utility of Being, I tell a story of how I use these crosscutting tools when Being with a conflict as introduced to me by one of my nieces. The third section explains "What are the components of the theory of Being?" The final section describes "What are the values of Being?" including its principles and the possibilities it presents for transforming how communities (or perhaps a family) deal with and act to address conflict.

2

Why The Theory of Being?

In my classrooms and community conversations, I often heard people rushing to solve problems because they did not know how to engage in a productive dialogue that might produce a more equitable and humane outcome. My fellow learners could identify the problem, but they feared and did not know how to participate productively in difficult dialogues, particularly surrounding social problems that are with no clear solution. The theory of Being describes a process-oriented approach to dialogue within community. It teaches the practice of (or a process for) aligning thoughts, feelings, and actions that support the conditions for building personal, relational, and community stamina. The theory of Being is a transformative learning theory (Mezirow, 1991). It offers life-giving *ways of Being* that support dialogue in the community when facing an impenetrable social conflict. The theory asserts that *ways of Being* practices create the possibility of transformational change in individuals and communities while Being with a conflict.

Key Terms

Three terms are central to the theory, namely, *conflict*, *Difference*, and *difficult dialogue*. The terms provide some context for what the theory addresses. In other words, this theory applies *ways of Being* to conflicts about controversial differences and guides communities on how to sustain and build the stamina for difficult dialogues.

For the purposes of the theory, a *conflict* could be an enduring social problem, a controversial decision, a disorienting dilemma (as described by Mezirow, 1991), a new, unknown, unfamiliar, or even a fundamentally disagreed upon difference, belief, value, idea, or experience. While the descriptions of the theory in this book focus on applications of the theory as it relates to social oppression, the theory could be applied to any disorienting interaction.

Difference is "having dissimilar opinions, experiences, ideologies, epistemologies and/or constructions of reality about self, society, and/or identity" (Watt, 2013, p. 6). This definition attempts to only acknowledge that differences exist and not to weight it as negative and threatening.

A *difficult dialogue* is "a verbal or written exchange of ideas or opinions between citizens within a community that centers on an awakening of potentially conflicting views of beliefs or values about social justice issues, such as racism, sexism, heterosexism/homophobia" (Watt, 2007, p. 112). It is vital to note that this definition acknowledges that there is an awakening or a newly realized conflict. It recognizes that in verbal or written exchanges a difficult dialogue often centers around a fresh conflict or a new awareness. The emergent nature of the conflict can throw a person into a disorienting spin and disconnect them from their thoughts and feelings, misaligning them with an intended action. The theory of Being views the onset and recognition of a difficult dialogue, Difference, and conflict as normal, and its practices are intended to help people be with or to create the space to intentionally align their thoughts and feelings with their actions.

The theory of Being provides practices for how (the process) to be in a dialogue with others about matters on which a community disagrees. A process-orientation does not exclude the importance of what the community decides to act on or the value of an outcome. The theory, however, highlights the positive yields for Being (process-oriented) versus doing (outcome-focused). Each of these key terms—conflict, Difference, difficult dialogue—shifts away from an adversarial position that focuses on pitting one person's identity, values, or beliefs against another or *an us-versus-them* mentality and instead invites *an us-and-them-exploring-it* mindset. It is important to identify the various productive ways in which a conflict might be situated in a community. Notice that a thread in each key term normalizes that disagreement as a natural and necessary part of being in the community where Difference is valued.

Being Versus Doing

Because process-oriented approaches support being in a long-term relationship for both individuals and communities, they may result in more just and equitable solutions for communities. The theory of Being proposes practices that abandon a singular focus on outcomes. It pushes away from an elusive and static definition of the problem. Instead, the theory suggests that prioritizing process creates an ongoing way of Being in a community relationship around shared problems. It assumes that prioritizing process is a more realistic and perhaps a nimbler way of addressing a complex social conflict. The theory acknowledges that no single outcome will fix structural inequities once and for all time. Structural inequities exist and evolve as society grows. With a focus on the "how" we engage and discuss the problem and evolve solutions to enable a community to address the constant change inherent in structural inequities.

The chart in Table S1.1 summarizes the contrasts and points of focus when people approach conflict through the lens of Being versus doing.

In part, there is a flawed assumption that underlies most outcome-focused approaches. Outcome-focused approaches prioritize what product or solution will address the problem. Such approaches often ignore the complexity of challenges faced by society and assume that there are simple fixes to structural inequities. Outcome-focused approaches sometimes view humans and their problems as stable and reductive and ignore the evolving nature of society and power within it. The focus on outcome means that a problem can be managed and that the goal is to focus on finding that single, measurable solution. Problem-solving approaches in this culture assume that our social and legal system have neutralized the systemic aspects of racism, sexism, and so on. From this perspective, society should then operate as if any collective marginalization is imaginary and all systemic barriers can be neutralized by individual hard work.

The theory of Being practices shift a community's focus away from prioritizing solutions as the driver toward being together with ongoing difficult problems. Being, or prioritizing process, shifts away from external focusing and directing work for others and moves toward situating the self and one's personal responsibility for outcomes within the community. In other words, a group is no longer facing a social problem by devising strategy for others

TABLE S1.1
A Comparison of Doing and Being Approaches to Conflict

DOING Outcome-Focused	BEING Process-Oriented
• The primary focus on an end goal, responsibility of others, external control, and the future • The goal is to first solve or fix current problems • Centers on needing to take action, direct activity, and demonstrate progress toward an outcome • Measurable or decisive end point to activity and engagement • Often named a task force to indicate power and control and dictate work to others; implies a broad and not always job/role-relevant translation	• The primary focus on preparation, personal responsibility, internal control, and the present moment • The goal is to first understand and explore an issue or idea • Centers on the self in relation to the idea, considering how and why you relate to the idea in certain ways • Ongoing process • Named a collaborative or collective to indicate the effort is inclusive, ongoing, with a job/role-relevant strategy

to carry out. Rather, each individual expects to reflect, make meaning of, and apply—in a personal and/or job relevant way—what they learned from a complex community discussion that explored various aspects of the social problem or issue.

This theory asserts that reinforcing the value of process and resisting sole dependence on outcome-focused approaches can be a generative way to deal with problems and transform communities. *Ways of Being* include learning practices that sustain people over time. A process-oriented focus allows for a private or professional community to be in an ongoing dialogue to incorporate the inevitable societal change and respond in ways that are nimble and adaptive when addressing complex social problems. Then, we as a community can prepare ourselves for being in a long-term relationship with evolving solutions, which persists as society changes, rather than buying into simple answers and quick fixes to enduring problems happening in our personal and/or professional lives.

Next, I describe the primary theoretical influences. I also touch on the relevant other influential conceptual ideas that inform the theory of Being.

Theoretical Influences

This section overviews the relevant theoretical influences on the theory of Being.

Paulo Freire

Guiding the theory of Being is Freire's idea of transformation. Paulo Freire's (1970) *Pedagogy of the Oppressed* suggests the need for and value of process in transforming persisting problems inherent in oppressive systems. He states, "men and women [people] develop their power to perceive critically the way they exist in the world with which and in which they find themselves; they come to see the world not as a static reality but as a reality in the process of transformation" (Freire, 1970, p. 12). A focus on process recenters humanity. Process-oriented practices reposition how people relate to each other and how the complex and polarizing differences are perpetuated in the oppressor-and-the-oppressed dynamic. Remember, the process-oriented approach, for the purposes of this theory, means that there is a priority placed on how we engage, not just what outcome we want. Freire believed that to transform our society, we must reimagine it together—oppressed and oppressor—and participate actively in the work of change. Freire (1970) stated,

> True generosity consists precisely in fighting to destroy the causes which nourish false charity. False charity constrains the fearful and subdued, the "rejects of life," to extend their trembling hands. True generosity lies in

striving so that these hands—whether of individuals or entire peoples—need be extended less and less in supplication, so that more and more they become human hands which work and, working, transform the world. (p. 45)

Carl Rogers

The theory of Being's focus on process is informed by both the concept of transformation as described by Freire (1970) and the person-oriented counseling process as described by Carl Rogers (1951, 1961). Rogers et al. stated (1967), "The good life is a process, not a state of being. It is a direction, not a destination" (p. 187). Inherent in the idea of how we engage around conflicts is that a good quality process will result in a more efficacious and enduring outcome that can transform a community from just surviving to thriving.

bell hooks

Paulo Freire (1970) and bell hooks (1994) describe a process whereby individuals and communities learn new methods for inclusion and deconstruct social problems by using learning strategies to question traditional ways of knowing (Watt, 2016). The theory of Being is highly influenced by the spirit of hooks's ideas presented in *Teaching to Transgress* (hooks, 1994). hooks (1994) discusses shaping a learning community whereby the learner (a person, a student, and a citizen) is situated along with the teacher/leader in a communal context where "education is the practice of freedom" (p. 13). hooks elaborates on this idea introduced by Freire and defines the practice of freedom as the way in which community members deconstruct systems of domination (hooks, 1994). hooks challenges the uses of power in communities and most particularly in academic settings and suggests that through an engaged pedagogy an environment can be transformed and become liberating. An engaged pedagogy means to teach and to relearn together in ways that go against the grain or tradition, that create free expression, that acknowledge that differences exists, and actualize a vision for a society liberated from systemic domination. She denounces distorting education as control and rarifies the idea that learning spaces can be radical places for transforming learners and society (hooks, 1994). The theory of Being assumes that all spaces within a community are for transformative learning (Mezirow, 1994). The theory reaffirms this view on how a community might live into a practice of freedom, particularly by teaching *ways of Being* that can be used to face conflict and move forward with dialogue that allows for intentionally deconstructing systemic domination.

Parker J. Palmer

Along with Freire and hooks, the principles and the practices of the Center for Courage & Renewal, a nonprofit founded by Parker J. Palmer, are also at the foundation of the theory of Being. As a facilitator prepared by the Center, I learned about the trust-building practices within the Center's Circle of Trust approach known as Touchstones, and I learned how to deal with my discomfort by using dissonance-provoking questions to reflect on my personal and inner life. As I lived into these principles and practices of the Center, I started to apply and extend them to frame my classroom teaching and then to my research. I wanted to create learning spaces that invited my students to bring their whole selves and to learn along with me. When introduced to the work of Palmer and hooks, I was also seeking guidance on how to live as a whole person in academic life. Palmer's thoughts on the courage to teach as an expression of who you are spoke directly to me, along with the work of hooks (1994) on engaged pedagogy.

I started to consider how I (we, the MCI Research Team) might shape our research line to include the theoretical foundations rooted in liberating pedagogy as envisioned by Freire, hooks, and Palmer. In other words, we, too, believe that communities that view the social change process as a practice of freedom are embracing a countercultural process that normalizes conflict, values authenticity, acknowledges the humanity in all, and prioritizes creative and critical perspective-taking.

Jack Mezirow, James Baldwin, Audre Lorde, and Toni Morrison

The MCI Research Team was likewise inspired by Mezirow's transformative learning theory, which introduces an aspirational goal for educational settings. His work describes conditions that support transformative learning experiences. Transformative learning is "the social process of construing and appropriating a new or revised interpretation of the meaning of one's experience as a guide to action" (Mezirow, 1994, pp. 222–223). Transformative learning reveals that participants are able to take action when they learn "to identify, explore, validate, and express affect" (Sveinunggaard, 1993, p. 292). Mezirow emphasizes that transformational experiences must involve reflecting on assumptions, underlying intentions, values, beliefs, and feelings (Mezirow, 1991). In terms of foundations, the structure of the theory of Being is informed by the assumptions of developmental aspects and tenets of the psychosocial identity theory (Erikson, 1963), psychoanalytic theory (Freud, 1979), cognitive-structural theory (Perry, 1970), counseling theory (Rogers, 1951, 1961, 1980), and ecological theory (Bronfenbrenner, 1979). The theory of Being also stands on the visions of resisting racist ideology expressed by James Baldwin on racism in *Notes of a Native Son* (1955) and *I Am Not Your Negro* (Peck, 2017); Audre Lorde on survival in *Sister Outsider* (1984); and Toni Morrison on being raced in her collection of essays, *The Source of Self-Regard* (2019), and interviews given on television, *The Charlie Rose Show* (Rose, 2015), and in the documentary film, *The Pieces I Am* (Greenfield-Sanders, 2019).

Assumptions

Four assumptions underlie the theory of Being. These foundational ideas of the theory explain, in part, why we shifted from a focus on outcomes to prioritizing process (also, see chapter 1, this volume). These assumptions draw from the primary influences of the previously mentioned theorists (Freire, 1970; Freud, 1979; hooks, 1994; Mezirow, 1991; Palmer, 1998; Rogers et al., 1967) and the results of our empirical and conceptual research (see chapter 2, this volume). The assumptions are as follows:

1. *Societal conditions* (racism, sexism, heterosexism, genderism, classism, and their intersections) are deeply rooted in culture, history, tradition, and practices of supremacy and domination. Societal conditions are ever-changing and nebulous.
2. *Controversy* is inevitable when facing inequities in societal conditions. Collective exploration of controversy has a greater potential to lead to more just and equitable outcomes for all. Communities need to be continually in a process of dialogue that deconstructs and reconstructs environments for inclusion across Difference. Actions to change societal conditions are disruptive for community members, institutions, and society. States of dissonance, discomfort, and defensiveness are inherently part of the learning process of organizing a community and taking action to change a societal condition.
3. *Transformation* of societal conditions occurs through working at the personal, institutional, community, and societal levels. All spaces within a community are for learning, especially transformative learning. Transforming societal conditions involves people in the community engaging together in dialogues that align their head (intellect and thought), heart (feeling, emotion, and spirit), and hands (practical and real world applications). Change in societal conditions needs to occur rather than retrofitting individuals to fit within a pathological social system that pledges compliance with an ideal and domination as a problem-solving

strategy. Change happens when people in the community embrace a learning ethos and face the problem, understand that they have agency, and actively engage in a dialogue about transforming the conditions in which they live.

4. *Process-oriented* practices have a greater potential to lead to transformational change. Process-oriented approaches create sustainable practices that guide ways of interacting around enduring problems whereby communities can continue to employ strategies that address conflict in ways that are nimble and responsive. Ultimately, quality processes while in dialogue strengthen communities as they work together to create environments and ways of sustainable interaction that have the potential to result in more just and equitable societal change.

The assumptions of this theory shift the focus toward prioritizing the process because communities are facing impenetrable social problems. Working in a community to address these types of problems requires accepting that there is structural inequity, that controversy is inevitable, and that transforming society requires an engagement on the personal, relational, and community levels and application of practices that engage head, heart, and hands. Finally, the theory of Being assumes that shifting focus from the outcomes to the process changes how we deal with a problem, and how the community works to resolve it. The focus on the process also shifts away from surviving the problem to the possibility of thriving as individuals and as a community.

This introduction has overviewed the relevant terms, the yields of Being versus doing, the theoretical influences, and the assumptions. The next section reviews the crosscutting tools of the theory of Being.

What Are the Four Crosscutting Tools for Being?

It is helpful if communities understand and personalize the use of Being *touchstones*, the utility of the *third thing* and the privileged identity exploration (PIE) model, and the practice of *open and honest questions* (see Appendices B–E). These crosscutting tools contain the tenets that help guide *ways of Being* practices. Each tool helps embody Being and supports dispositions that help sustain the practice of Being. I will briefly describe each tool and how together they help create the container or the environment for Being in a productive difficult dialogue. The appendices provide details about each tool. Again, Being is the *personal, relational,* and *community* work of aligning thoughts and feelings with actions. These four crosscutting tools help create the conditions for the environment where the work of Being can be done. The tools are instrumental in helping individuals and communities embody *ways of Being*.

Being Touchstones

The concept of Being *touchstones* (see Appendix B) is inspired by the Circle of Trust approach, a collection of principles and practices developed by Palmer and the Center for Courage & Renewal. The notion of *touchstones* suggests a way of interacting in solo and group reflection to help people more readily embrace their identity and integrity. The *touchstones* represent what Palmer (2009) calls "the kinds of boundaries that help create safe space for the soul" (p. 215). The *touchstones* support an environment where an authentic source of personal and societal healing can emerge with a focus on communal and positive social change.

The idea of Being *touchstones*, which is an adaptation of the Circle of Trust Touchstones, refers to intentional *ways of Being* together in a dialogue across difference within a community. The original *touchstones* help create optimal conditions for an individual to be with their own internal dissonance while in retreat with others, but not necessarily while in a dialogue about a common problem. The role of the others in the retreat is to be present with you while you reflect on your life and while each person in retreat reflects on their own circumstance. For example, the original *touchstones* are not intended to guide a cross-group dialogue. In other words, *the touchstones* provide parameters for a person who is dealing with a problem while being with others. There is no expectation to share the burden of an individual's problem with the others. The community is there to help the person by *listening deeply* to his/her/their reflections, but the intention of the original *touchstones* is to encourage one's own voice as the sole guide. These original *touchstones* dissuade input from others on the pondering shared by the individual. And yet, they offer framing for being with others in a compassionate way while exploring and learning about oneself. In contrast, the concept of Being *touchstones* extends the spirit of the original version to groups learning together with the intention of collaborating and Being in a dialogue together about complex problems. The Being *touchstones* provide parameters for having a dialogue in groups. The Being *touchstones* intend to honor the power of both individuals and a community together creating and holding a sacred space to explore and act on a complex social problem.

This description highlights the utility of Being *touchstones* that cuts across *personal, relational,* and *community ways of Being*. The Being *touchstones* provide guidance on how to be with each other and create a space where individuals can share ideas together as a community in a relationship with others.

Third Thinging

The theory of Being considers *third thinging* as both a verb and a noun. *A third thing or third thinging* is a process-oriented concept (Rogers et al., 1967; Saussy, 2011; Smith, 2005). As a noun, a *third thing* takes the form of text (poems, quotes, articles, etc.) or another visual means (music, art, storytelling, film, etc.) as a focal point in a dialogue. It allows one person (i.e., the first thing) and another person (i.e., the second thing) to share their experiences about *the third thing*. For example, the first person and the second person are in a dialogue about *the third thing*, which is a tree (see Appendix C). The first person and the second person can share their experiences about trees. They might have had good experiences building tree houses or negative experiences such as a tree falling on their house during a storm. As a verb, *third thinging* is the process whereby they can share about their upbringing and their observations about others interacting with trees. In other words, *third thinging* centers on the idea rather than just on a person's position in relation to the idea. This view of ideas holds each community member accountable to and beyond just their individual positionalities or identities. By focusing on the issue (and not solely on positionalities and identities), the community can reconsider how it relates to the conflict or idea by centering on it as the focal point of the dialogue.

Parker J. Palmer (1998) describes *a third thing* by situating it in the community interaction:

> If we want a community of truth in the classroom, a community that can keep us honest, we must put *a third thing*, a great thing, at the center of the pedagogical circle. When students and teacher are the only active agents, community easily slips into narcissism, where either the teacher reigns supreme or the students can do no wrong. A learning community that embodies both rigor and involvement will elude us until we establish a plumb line that measures teacher and student alike—as great things can do.
>
> True community in any context requires a transcendent third thing that holds both me and thee accountable to something beyond ourselves, a fact well known outside of education. (p. 119)

Palmer (1998) goes on to say that in a subject-focused discussion, the *third thing* is "so real, so vivid, so vocal" that it holds everyone in the dialogue accountable for what they say and do (p. 119). As you'll see in the stories throughout this book, our tool of *third thinging* focuses on exploring a conflicting social problem in ways that contribute to a wider view of the issue. *Third thinging* treats the issue as an opportunity for an exploration of contradictory ideas that exist simultaneously and in concert with each other.

Inviting a both/and perspective, *third thinging* allows for an examination of a controversial idea from many different angles while not disassociating the individuals in the community from their own experience of the phenomenon. In other words, *third thinging* invites individuals to place a complex social problem at the center of a dialogue to situate it in the community context and yet encourages them to consider how to embrace and value different individual positionalities and identities. A *third thing* can help evolve a community's understanding of a complex and impenetrable problem and the actions they choose to take to address it. With a *third thing*, we can reframe the conversation and share in the deconstruction of the problem with a focus on *the us-and-them-together-exploring-it* frame (the idea, the issue, or the system), away from *the us-versus-them* mentality.

When a community engages in *third thinging* about a conflict, its dialogue is centering on a complex social problem, such as racism, genderism, sexism, and heterosexism. It abandons the notion that the social problem is a personal burden and rather shifts the focus to examine the issues as a shared experience of a whole problem. *Third thinging* supports a way of Being in a dialogue that is not adversarial. In other words, *third thinging* shifts the exploration of complex social problems from the *us-versus-them* angle to sharing in the exploration together through the *us-and-them-exploring-it* lens.

This description highlights the idea that *third thinging* crosscuts *personal, relational,* and *community ways of Being*. For example, when I view racism as the central shared issue and not solely as my personal problem, I can explore it with others and examine the aspects that illuminate the dehumanizing of People of Color or racism while also unearthing the hyperhumanizing of White people or Whiteness. In the dialogue, my community is freer to name the whole of the problem and examine it more critically when we center on the issues rather than on the defense of our own identities.

Third thinging enhances an understanding of how to situate the truths that are close to heart while in dialogue with others in the community who may share a vastly different point of view on the same idea or experience. *Third thinging* "increases the possibility that communities will examine social problems in a way that those with dominant and marginalized experiences will share the burden of creating solutions" (Watt, 2015, p. 34).

Open and Honest Questions

One of my favorite *open and honest questions* came during a meeting from Milica Oliver, an MCI research team member. We do a regular check-in at the beginning of our meetings. We share how we are doing, and what has dampened or elated our spirits. We sometimes respond to what a team member has shared with *an open and honest question* (see more detail in Appendix D). An *open and honest question* helps to illuminate a person's inner life terrain more clearly for that person. It is the type of question that invites a person to be with or to explore his/her/their thoughts, feelings, and actions about an emerging issue. Posing these types of questions for another is meant to be in service of helping that person to reflect more deeply. It is a question for which the asker cannot know the answer. These types of questions are not meant to gather information about the person or the situation (e.g., how well do you know this person? Or how many times have you experienced this situation?); nor are they used to sneakily offer advice (e.g., have you taken this issue to a therapist?). *Open and honest questions* intend to help a person more deeply reflect. They are generally indirect questions that may inspire looking at the issue from a different angle.

In that semester, I was teaching a group of students that was especially difficult for me to handle in my Multiculturalism in Higher Education course. I did not share details about the students or the situation. Though I shared my despair with the team about how the stench of racism covers me like a coat regardless of wherever I go. During my class the week before, the students aggressively questioned me about assignments. It was not so much that they had questions, but how they asked. I could hear that I was being racialized in the way they questioned me and responded to my clarifications on the assignments—with a condescending and patronizing tone. I described to the team that there are times when I feel forced into this coat, and it is put on me without my permission. I elaborated on how this coat waits for me in the chair at the front of the any room I enter. I said that I do not bring the coat with me, nor do I voluntarily put the coat on. It is already in the room. This coat just sits near me and waits for someone to pick it up and force it on me. I said to my team that everywhere I turn there is a forced relationship that I have with this coat of racism.

After I shared and a time of silence, Milica asked me, "What type of coat is it?" I remember smiling at the delight of how her question helped me to feel heard. An image immediately formed in my mind. I said, "It is a jean jacket because racism is sadly casual and ever-present in my life." The question is *open and honest* because my fellow team member could not anticipate my response. It elaborated on my own phrasing. It invited me to see this problem from a different angle. It also offered me a chance to turn and face this problem—to be with the coat. By inviting me to add detail to the visual image, it offered an opportunity for me to deal with it and start to align my thoughts and feelings about how I was experiencing racism in that moment. While the question was posed to help me explore my inner turmoil, it also helped the group more vividly explore the despair of racism as a *third thing*. Our team reflected on how racism can deform any interaction. The idea that racism is mundane, involuntary, and omnipresent illuminated an aspect of how I experienced racism not previously explored by me or our team before Milica posed this *open and honest question*.

An *open and honest question* gifts a person with a chance to deepen their inner exploration and meaning-making. The process of *open and honest questioning* can help a group share the burden of exploring a societal problem beyond its personal consequences. *Open and honest questions* are a crosscutting tool that can help a person or a group embody the *personal, relational,* and *community ways of Being*. These types of questions can be posed to serve a person's reflection or to support a group's exploration around an issue. *Open and honest questions* can help expand the way individuals and communities explore personal, professional, and/or societal problems.

The Privileged Identity Exploration Model

The PIE model emerged from a research project that initially aimed to only focus on the ways people resisted learning about multiculturalism (Watt, 2007; Watt et al., 2009). The research process expanded our understanding of resistance. I began to see defensive reactions as a normal way to respond to dissonance-provoking information. Initially, I used the findings of eight defensive reactions (see Appendix E) as a diagnostic tool. In other words, I named the defenses only. I soon realized that only identifying them in myself and others was not the most productive use of the PIE model. In fact, identifying and diagnosing was counterproductive and added to the distress of the moment. I reimagined the use of defensive reactions. I asked instead, "How do I work through defensive reactions that derail productive communication about heated topics?"

In asking this question, I started to notice what happens internally when I am defensive and realized that I deal with the dissonance that I am experiencing in a different way. Hearing disorienting information makes me feel like I am being pushed off of a cliff. I desperately want to grab onto a rope to slow my descent into this discomfort. The defensive reactions act like knots in the rope that help me slow down the spiraling descent as I make sense of this cliff of information. As a facilitator, I empathize with participants in this same spiral, and I slow down to allow time for exploration. I try to support them in the process of incorporating this dissonance-provoking information into their understanding. I resist exacerbating their descent by just pointing out that they are defensive. I instead allow my awareness of defensive reactions to signal to me that a participant and possibly the discussion is in distress. Seeing the defensive reactions alerts me that this may be a teachable moment, and that I need to allow some time for individuals and/or the group to reflect. I allow the group to be with or work through aligning their thoughts, feelings, and actions in the face of this dissonance-provoking information. I learned that the PIE model defenses are best used as a signal that exploration of the issue has hit a vulnerable point in the dialogue where transformative learning might occur. As a useful tool for embodying Being, the PIE model crosscuts *personal, relational,* and *community ways of Being.* In other words, understanding defensive reactions helps me practice Being with my own defenses and Being with others as they feel defensive. The PIE model helps my understanding that defensiveness will arise in all community dialogues.

Over time, it has become a habit to orient myself to Being by scaffolding the four crosscutting tools (*touchstones, open and honest questions, third thing and third thinging, and PIE defensive reactions*) into my reflections and embodying them within my disposition whenever I work to align my thoughts, feelings, and actions, as the theory of Being prescribes. These four crosscutting tools help to create the conditions for Being with complex social problems as an individual in a community. These tools support *ways of Being* as posited by the theory of Being and cut across personal, relational, and community interactions. As you can see, I demonstrated how the crosscutting tools of Being *touchstones, third thinging, open and honest questions,* and the PIE model hold process-oriented tenets and work together to orient individuals and communities to Being. Next, I show how using these tools helped shape my actions as I grappled with a story about how I wrestled with a conflict introduced by my niece.

Applying Four Crosscutting Tools

My family started a new tradition during the pandemic. Every other week, we would get on a Zoom call and have wide-ranging discussions about the state of the world and the condition of our own souls. On the calls, there were all types of family connections among siblings, cousins, children, and their parents. Sometimes we would bring up pesky topics about unresolved personal or family issues. Pesky topics are things that unsettle us. Bringing a topic to the family Zoom call usually meant that we wanted to hear opinions from the people that we love and trust the most. My niece, India, put one of those pesky topics on the table for discussion. She had recently viewed a documentary on spanking and wanted to discuss it with the family. Specifically, she wanted to discuss how spanking can be traumatizing for children, and that it should not be used as discipline. India works in social services and attends many professional development activities. She is a resilient and intelligent young woman. She is enthusiastic and passionate about her work and her calling that involves helping people.

I am the parent to India and her three siblings, Brandy, Clyde, and Guy. My sister birthed my/our children before she passed away 21 years ago. When my sister passed, our children ranged in age from 10 months to 19 years old. They are all adults now ranging in age from 21 to 40 years old. My parents passed away soon after my sister. Therefore, I am the matriarch of the family. I became the matriarch way sooner than I had envisioned. I did not even have time to think about what it would mean for me. As the matriarch, I usually feel confident and proud that I made it through raising four children as a single mother while laying my parents and sister to rest and keeping afloat a career. And yet there are times when I question every decision and blame all the bad ones on the fact that I felt unprepared to parent and to unexpectedly become the leader of the family. Some of those bad decisions often fell under miscalculations. In other words, I regret when my parenting choices were not accurately calibrated to the needs of that child.

I have been "parenting" an 18-week-old chocolate labrador retriever since October 2021. His name is Baldwin Blaze, aka BB. I see many similarities between raising puppies and rearing children. You have to get to know their disposition. They have to learn to read you. You have to be consistent. You also have to provide them with security and stability by firmly letting them know that you are in charge, and that they do not have to worry. You have to also be forward with your love. Baldwin Blaze is like all lab puppies (or children)—he is unique. Both of my previous labs, Ankor and Padre, passed away at 13 and 14 years of age, respectively—with each I had a deep bond. I am grateful that I got to enjoy such a long life with them both. They each had very different temperaments. Ankor was dignified, gentle, and direct. He came into my life when he was 7 weeks and understood his mission to anchor me and help me to finish my dissertation. He kept me on track by nudging me—without fail—about every 3 hours to get up from the computer and go for a walk. I say he was direct because he was relentless about his mission. He would nudge my arm, he would verbalize, and he would motion by walking from my computer room and toward the front door. He would repeat that circle until I got up to walk.

Padre was wild, ornery, attentive, and funny. He came into my family's life when he was 6 months old while Ankor was in his last 2 years of life. We adopted Padre. He was found running wildly from farm to farm. He had some irritating yet humorous habits. My favorite was that he liked to greet you or thank you by nipping the smallest piece of skin on your behind! Padre and Ankor were partners in my healing from cancer, racism, and many other paradoxical challenges that shape my life (on which I go further into in chapter 1). Padre learned from Ankor how to help me heal. Since Padre was adopted later at the start of his life, he often seemed to work harder to get my attention: he felt he was a "troubled guest," especially while Ankor was living. Padre fully lived into his personality after Ankor passed, and he was the only dog in the house. He developed his own sense of care for me. For instance, he would appear by my side, pop my hand atop his head anytime he heard my voice raise or sensed stress. He reminded me to calm down.

Baldwin Blaze is calm, precocious, and affable. He came to me at 9 weeks old. He seems to embody some of the characteristics of both Ankor and Padre. He is dignified and direct like Ankor. Like Padre, he is funny and attentive to me. He looks directly into my eyes and awaits the next command. He learns commands very quickly. He is so easy to correct that I rarely need to discipline him. Ironically, I find myself questioning how to discipline Baldwin Blaze after being dizzied by questions from my niece about spanking. Baldwin Blaze is likely going to be over 100 pounds when he is fully grown. I find it imperative for him to follow my commands; this includes that he adheres to both my physical and psychological dominance while he is younger and smaller.

In Being with this dissonance about spanking and while disciplining BB, I noticed that I paused more often than I had in training my other dogs to watch for his responses. I doubted myself, for instance, when I yelled at him with a tone of disapproval. I even hesitated over being physical with him to get his attention. Now, being realistic, I know that raising dogs is not exactly the same as rearing children. He's a dog. Disciplining a dog seems black and white, especially since I have been a successful dog parent. I am not as confident about my success as a parent of children.

Applying Third Thinging

I spanked only as a last resort, and each of my children, I would estimate, got spanked by me maybe two or three times in their lives. In the new tradition of our family Zoom calls, we each shared our varying viewpoints on spanking *(the third thing)*. Our viewpoints were all along the spectrum *(third thinging)*. Some of the family members never spanked their children or were never spanked, while others sparingly spanked their children although spankings were part of their upbringing. The general consensus seemed to be that spanking was a necessary albeit rarely used option for disciplining children as a parent. Some of the children on the call expressed that their discipline, when it included spanking, was appropriate and did not feel traumatic. Our discussion included recognizing that spanking could be seen as traumatizing or not, depending on how the child processed it. We centered on the idea of spanking in our discussion, and we each discussed how we related to it or not as a way to discipline children. *Third thinging* allowed me to wonder about my parenting mistakes. I waxed and waned between defending, affirming, excusing, and questioning myself. The family listened and reflected along with me about their own parenting choices.

I did not ignore my feelings, but I understood that to be in a relationship with my niece I needed to be present for her exploration. My nieces and nephews are adults. I no longer need to emphasize my authority. This helped me to shift my position with regard to this conflict and the problem of spanking.

As I observed and unpacked my feelings and that thoughts about spanking, I recalled mixed emotions about being spanked as a child *(third thinging)*. I can recall more vividly only one or two times that I was spanked. One incident occurred with my father and another with my mother. In each incident, I recall that I had definitely pushed the boundaries. In one, I defied a reasonable and direct request from my parents, and in the other situation—I lied. I could rationalize why my parents resorted to a physical correction. They wanted me to take their authority seriously, and they did not want me to grow up behaving fecklessly. They taught me that I had to be twice as good as a Black person to get half as much. However, it definitely made me fearful of them, but mostly, I did not want to disappoint them or ever commit the wrong act again. I made sense of being disciplined in this way and that it was a necessary lesson. I trusted, loved, and admired my parents. I did not want my acts of defiance to disrupt our relationship. I did not feel traumatized by being spanked. I did feel disturbed, and it definitely got my attention. My parents never appeared to enjoy this type of discipline. I did not like seeing them upset. Therefore, I worked to resolve my incongruent feelings by interpreting this aspect of my relationship with my parents as part of my development as a person. As I reflected on my personal experiences with spanking, the family and I considered spanking as *a third thing*. *Third thinging* allowed each of us to contemplate our differing opinions and the complexities of spanking as a cultural phenomenon.

Applying Being Touchstones

Though it annoyed me that my niece continued to present me with this pesky issue via texting long after the first Zoom call was over, I embraced the tool of Being *touchstone* (See Appendix B). For example, it meant *practicing living the questions,* Being *touchstone* 8: What did it have to do with me? Why was she persisting on discussing it with me? Did she feel harmed by me? What work did I need to do as a family member to listen well to her concerns? Philosophically, I wondered: What is the cultural, racial background and experiences of the researchers who created that documentary? These are among the many questions that emerged as I faced my disequilibrium each time she persisted in wanting to discuss her newly found point of view on spanking.

Applying Open and Honest Questions

The next day and over the course of a month, my niece sent me a series of text messages. These texts came at random times and included quotes denouncing spanking, links to articles, and so on. It seemed as if she wanted to convince me of her point of view—that spanking is traumatic which aligned with the documentary. As a parent, I started to wonder why she wanted me to know about this research on spanking.

Truthfully, I felt dizzied by the random appearance of her text messages. I thought my children are adults now, and it had been many years since I had spanked anyone. I wondered: Why is she so insistent on having this conversation with me? I have always wanted to be a good partner in the journey of life for my nieces and nephews. I embraced the responsibility to parent, so I want to do my best in that role. I felt/feel an overwhelming sense of responsibility to teach them about what it means to be themselves, first, and then to also deal with a situation by being a good person, friend, partner, citizen, and family member. As I discerned the various motivations and the ways I was dealing with this conflict, I wanted to shift my way of Being with her as she explored what spanking meant for her. I wanted to be a cleaner conduit. To be in a relationship with her, I needed to make sense of the feelings and thoughts swirling around that were about me so that I could listen to her and be with her in the conflict. While we may never agree on the interpretation of the role spanking played in her upbringing, I care for her and her well-being. Though I was having trouble managing my own dissonance, and I did not use all of the tools at hand to be with her and the questions she was posing about spanking. I mostly explained my position rather than helping her to explore her inner terrain.

I did not ask her *open and honest questions*. Looking back, I wish I had asked her, "If you could go backward in time, what would you say to 5-year-old India now?" I might also have asked her, "What do you love about working with children and families?" Or "What does spanking represent to you?" Or "What was your best day as a child? What made it so wonderful?" Any of these questions might have helped her process what spanking meant to her and might have allowed for an exploratory conversation that focused on caring for and *listening deeply* to her.

Applying the Privileged Identity Exploration Model

Instead, I began to feel defensive and clouded. I could not discern if we were having a philosophical discussion about spanking, or if she was trying to find a way to tell me that she felt traumatized by her upbringing. My niece was raised in four households. She began with her biological parents, then she lived with my parents. She also lived with me for a short time, and she spent some time living with her father's family. I wondered if she was indirectly letting me know that she felt traumatized. I thought maybe she is just trying to make sense of her upbringing. I mused that she was just unsettled as she explored the use of spanking and its role in trauma. More to the point though, why did her bringing it up to me bother me so much? I tried to make sense of what this conflict meant for me.

These text messages felt like an ocean liner squeezed into my day and appearing randomly. This ship carried an unexpected amount of freight. She said, "Here is a short documentary on spanking. It could have more statistics, but it is still pretty good." I felt inconvenienced. I did not want to think about this pesky issue, especially not in the middle of my workday. As I started to face the complexity of my feelings and thoughts around spanking, I got angry. I did not like being forced to explore these different feelings and thoughts. I transitioned into a line of defense.

I responded to the text with an unnecessarily long and curt reply. Part of my text reply said,

> I resist research that uses White people as the model and studies that are blind to the life-threatening effects of racism and the terror and seriousness that Black parents face . . . . So if that is the underlying message of this documentary . . . it will just make me mad. And I doubt that the research is void of White savior madness.

My academic lioness emerged (PIE model *intellectualization*). I suggested to my niece that spanking could not be divorced from the cultural context of racism (PIE model *deflection*). Black parents cannot depend on a partnership with society to lovingly, fairly, and supportively help discipline their children, which is a luxury White parents enjoy. Law enforcement, for instance, often reacts to White children by seeing their own children, whereas they often instantly see Black children as criminals. Black parents live in fear that the police, the school officials, or any vigilante might overcorrect, disproportionately and harshly punish, and/or kill their child. This perspective and the inclusion of spanking as a tool to get a child's attention, given that racism exists, are not often considered by researchers. I wanted my niece to reconsider the source of this documentary. I told myself that I wanted to teach her to be a critical consumer of research. I wanted her to understand the utility of spanking given the cultural context of Black parents fearing society's retribution for the perceived bad behavior of their Black children.

My niece responded to my unnecessarily long and curt text with, "I love you! It says you can't talk about physical abuse without the 3 Rs: Race, Religion, Region. It does include studies in the black community as well." And I responded as an academic lioness defending her territory (herself) with (PIE model *minimization*),

> Still bet it was based on White framing so not watching it. If the conclusion is spanking is bad . . . don't want to hear it. You can tell me about it. I know this because I do research. I am still not watching that documentary.

I have to admit—I never intentionally considered to spank or not as a parent. Without much thought, I just applied my upbringing to my own parenting. I also had to question what made me link her challenge to racism. I convinced myself that the real source of my angst was hearing about White people's experiences as the role model again and now on spanking. While I think that this is a valid point, I had to wonder what made me use it in that moment. I was disturbed by her confidence in that research without questioning it. But I think what really disturbed me was her use of these researchers' authority as a weapon to question my authority as a parent.

I can embrace that we hold two different realities about the role of spanking in our relationship. There are many ways my niece and I interact (e.g., at family events or over other topics) while we hold this conflict. The whole of my relationship with her is not consumed by this one conflict. After the family Zoom call and our many text exchanges, my niece still insisted on reinforcing the message she gleaned from the documentary which was that spanking is traumatic. I apologized to her. I said I'm sorry if you felt harmed by being spanked. She responded, "You did not harm me. I am on a journey, and I am so grateful you are part of it." Ironically, I am still not completely clear about why my niece insisted on talking to me about spanking at this stage in our lives and relationship. Perhaps her thoughts, feelings, and actions are scattered. I wonder if I had sat with her and offered a set of *open and honest questions*, how it might have helped her explore the questions she was posing about spanking and trauma. While I am still curious about her motivation, my main concern is why talking with her about spanking disoriented me. In Being with it, I am intentionally trying to unearth why this is a dissonance-provoking dilemma for me. As is my habit, I will continue to be with this dilemma as it unfolds in my life and in my relationship with my niece and her siblings (and BB!).

The four crosscutting tools inform my disposition as I face the dissonance introduced to me by my niece's questioning the role of spanking in disciplining children. I shift now from story and applying the crosscutting tools to describing the theory. The next section reviews the components of the theory of Being.

What Are the Components of The Theory of Being?

The theory of Being offers life-giving ways to face impenetrable social problems so that we might create the possibility of transformational change in communities. It teaches the practice of Being, which is aligning thoughts, feelings, and actions that support the conditions for building stamina necessary to be present with conflict. Following are descriptions of these process-oriented practices. In chapter 1, I demonstrate how to apply the practices through story.

This book is divided into three parts that highlight *personal, relational,* and *community ways of Being.* Each of these areas of practice work together— not necessarily sequentially—but in concert with each other. These *ways of Being* together help individuals and communities to focus on the process of Being rather than on solely prioritizing outcome (see Appendix A for a theory in brief handout). The following is a description of each *ways of Being* practice.

Personal Ways of Being:

- Practices that focus on self-awareness and authentic personal connections to the conflict.
- These practices include *focusing on you, humanizing otherness in self, recognizing defenses, and discerning motivations.*
  - *Focusing on you:* Situating the self in relation to the conflict.
  - *Humanizing otherness in self:* Embracing that difference exists and exploring feelings around incongruities within the self and in relation to the conflict.
  - *Recognizing defenses* (PIE model): Noticing defensive and dissonant reactions as they arise in the self and in relation to the conflict.
  - *Discerning motivations:* Facing the sources of desire or motives from within the self as it relates to the conflict.

Relational Ways of Being:

- Practices that sustain being in an active authentic relationship with self and others with an intention, when dissonant during a conflict.
- These practices include *listening deeply, humanizing otherness in relationship and idea exploration, exploring defenses, and dissenting wisely and well.*
  - *Listening deeply:* Being present with expressions of self and others as you listen carefully to what is being spoken (verbally and nonverbally) as you deal with a conflict.

- *Humanizing otherness in relationship and idea exploration*: Embracing that difference exists in relationships and in views on ideas while also exploring feelings around incongruities across relationships and in relation to the conflict.
- *Exploring defenses* (PIE model): Supporting another person while expressing defensive and dissonant reactions in relation to the conflict.
- *Dissenting wisely and well*: Disagreeing and also embracing the whole humanity of the self and the other person while in a conflict with each other.

Community Ways of Being:

- Practices that face the conflict by shifting a group away from centering on individual survival toward expecting individual and community thriving.
- These practices include understanding *the third thing and third thinging, balancing dialogue and action, normalizing defenses, embracing trouble as a learning opportunity, and viewing missteps as developmental.*
  - *Understanding the third thing and third thinging*: Centering on an in-depth examination of the issue as a focal point for the community while exploring the conflict.
  - *Balancing dialogue and action*: Preparing intentionally for a dialogue that leads to community action in addressing the conflict.
  - *Normalizing defenses* (PIE model): Acknowledging defensive and dissonant reactions as natural parts of community deliberations when addressing the conflict.
  - *Embracing trouble as a learning opportunity*: Welcoming trouble as an opportunity to learn and grow as a community surrounding the conflict.
  - *Viewing missteps as developmental*: Embracing mistakes and/or missteps as a normal, necessary, and facilitative aspect of learning together as a community about the conflict.

The theory teaches practices that strengthen a community's capacity to have the stamina to be with complex social problems and transform the conditions in which it lives. Next, I highlight the values of Being.

What Are the Values of Being?

Being is a nuanced concept. It has the ability to shift what we traditionally value which is outcome. The practices of the theory allow for an emergence of *personal, relational,* and *community ways of Being* with a conflict. The theory of Being practices are companions to outcome-focused strategies and can also be a stand-alone resource that offers practical guidance on how to facilitate meaningful and productive dialogue across Difference (Watt, 2015). It is essential to focus on strategies for the "how," or the *ways of Being* together. Doing so can increase the quality of interaction between individuals and within groups, which strengthens the likelihood of traversing problems associated with controversial social difference in ways have the potential to result in more sustainable outcomes.

Human beings are multifaceted, and the inherent problems communities deal with are ever-changing. To address this type of uncertain complexity, leaders need approaches that are flexible and adaptive rather than linear and reductive. The focus on Being as a practice allows for an evolving exploration of what it means to be human and live in a community while Being with complex social problems that foment divisiveness.

The following list includes values of Being:

- *Reframes Difference*: Reframes Difference as central and additive, not as necessary and marginalized.
- *Humanizes otherness*: Embraces the view that the human condition brings new arrivals (information, experiences, illness, uncertainty, etc.) and invites one to embrace otherness as a constant and welcome it as a state of Being.
- *Normalizes fear, defensiveness, discomfort, and dissonance*: Understands that fear, defensiveness, and discomfort are normal responses to conflict; sees the conflict as an opportunity; and believes that conflict is inherent and beautifully difficult.
- *Repositions otherness*: Situates Difference as an object of collective exploration and wonderment, shifts away from team mentality that protects individual interests, and focuses on the societal condition that deforms all.
- *Embraces uncertainty*: Understands that human beings are multifaceted, and that communities deal with ever-changing problems; to address this type of complex uncertainty uses approaches that are flexible and adaptive rather than linear and reductive.
- *Invites, assumes, values, knows wholeness*: Expects to nurture health and thriving; intentionally veers away from viewing life as segmented or divided; resists facing conflict as problem-fixing only to survive and solely as curing illness; and rejects a focus on deficit and rather shifts toward a foundation that is focused on promoting health and wholeness.
- *Welcomes paradox*: Embraces conflict with curiosity; expects contradiction, complexity, and disagreement; and values exploration and consideration of varying perspectives.

- *Centers on the community*: Values coalition-building across Difference that is in the interest of the collective; situates individual needs in context of the larger community's interest; and recognizes the benefit of dialogue about inclusion of polarizing viewpoints in order to create better solutions for a community to thrive.
- *Cultivates liberation*: Aspires to be together as a community upholding central values such as truth, love, kindness, generosity, integrity, and shared power and responsibility; prioritizes collective action and reflection; questions and suppresses traditional uses of patriarchal power such as coercion, extortion, intimidation, shame, retaliation, and patronization; boldly pursues life and thriving even in the face of death and extermination; respects that there is a need to simultaneously consider accountability, responsibility, justice, and defense of life; pursues an offensive strategy rather than a reactionary response that produces primarily a defensive action.

This section "What are the Values of Being?" highlights the possibilities that might arise from individuals and communities prioritizing Being with the complexities of social conflict. In short, the value of Being is that it orients people to a liberating way of existing under socially oppressive conditions. The Being practices can also provide a way to navigate other disorienting dilemmas—such as a personal challenge interjected by a family member—to support staying in a relationship.

Conclusion

In this introduction, I described the theory of Being and illustrated the utility of the *ways of Being* as I wrestled with conflicting views on spanking presented as a pesky problem by my niece. I reviewed the rationale for the theory of Being, its key tools and components, and the values of Being. It is our hope (mine and the MCI Research Team's) that the theory of Being teaches how individuals and communities can build the stamina to face impenetrable problems and engage in productive dialogue about solutions. We hope that individuals and communities find the courage to engage productively in difficult conversations using these practices as a guide.

References

Baldwin, J. (1955). *Notes of a native son.* Beacon Press.

Bronfenbrenner, U. (1979). *The ecology of human development: Experiments by nature and design.* Harvard University Press.

Erikson, E. H. (1963). *Youth: Change and challenge*. Basic Books.

Freire, P. (1970). *Pedagogy of the oppressed*. Continuum.

Freud, A. (1979). *The ego and the mechanisms of defense*. International Universities Press.

Greenfield-Sanders, T. (Director). (2019). *Toni Morrison: The pieces I am* [Film]. Magnolia Home Entertainment.

hooks, b. (1994). *Teaching to transgress: Education as the practice of freedom*. Routledge.

Lorde, A. (1984). *Sister outsider: Essays and speeches*. Crossing Press.

Mezirow, J. (1994). Understanding transformation theory. *Adult Education Quarterly, 44*(4), 222–232. https://doi.org/10.1177/074171369404400403

Morrison, T. (2019). *The source of self-regard: Selected essays, speeches, and meditations*. Vintage.

Palmer, P. (1998). *The courage to teach: Exploring the inner landscape of a teacher's life*. Jossey-Bass.

Palmer, P. (2009). *A hidden wholeness: The journey toward an undivided life*. Jossey-Bass.

Peck, R. (Director). (2017). *I am not your Negro* [Film]. Magnolia Pictures.

Perry, W. G., Jr. (1970). *Forms of intellectual and ethical development in the college years: A scheme*. Holt, Rinehart, and Winston.

Rogers, C. (1951). *Client-centered therapy: Its current practice, implications and theory*. Constable.

Rogers, C. (1961). *On becoming a person: A therapist's view of psychotherapy*. Constable.

Rogers, C. (1980). *A way of being*. Houghton Mifflin.

Rogers, C. R., Stevens, B., Gendlin, E. T., Shlien, J. M., & Van Dusen, W. (1967). *Person to person: The problem of being human: A new trend in psychology*. Real People Press.

Rose, C. [The Charlie Rose Show]. (2015, September 4). *Toni Morrison beautifully answers an "illegitimate" question on race (Jan. 19, 1998)* [Video]. YouTube. https://www.youtube.com/watch?app=desktop&v=-Kgq3F8wbYA

Saussy, H. (2011). Comparison, world literature, and the common denominator. In A. Behad & D. Thomas (Eds.), *A companion to comparative literature* (pp. 60–64). Wiley-Blackwell. https://doi.org/10.1002/9781444342789

Smith, M. K. (2005). Parker J. Palmer: Community, knowing and spirituality in education. In *The encyclopedia of informal education*. http://infed.org/mobi/parker-j-palmer-community-knowing-and-spirituality-in-education/

Sveinunggaard, K. (1993). Transformative learning in adulthood: A socio-contextual perspective. In D. Flannery (Ed.), *34th Annual Adult Education Research Conference Proceedings* (pp. 275–280). Pennsylvania State University.

Watt, S. K. (2007). Difficult dialogues, privilege and social justice: Uses of the privileged identity exploration (PIE) model in student affairs practice. *College Student Affairs Journal, 26*(2), 114–126. https://eric.ed.gov/?id=EJ899385

Watt, S. K. (2013). Designing and implementing multicultural initiatives: Guiding principles. In S. K. Watt & J. Linley (Eds.), *Creating Successful Multicultural Initiatives in Higher Education and Student Affairs* (New Directions for Student Services, no. 144, pp. 5–15). Jossey-Bass.

Watt, S. K. (Ed.). (2015). *Designing transformative multicultural initiatives: Theoretical foundations, practical applications, and facilitator considerations.* Stylus.

Watt, S. K., Curtis, G. C., Drummond, J., Kellogg, A. H., Lozano, A., Nicoli, G. T., & Rosas, M. (2009). Privileged identity exploration: Examining counselor trainees' reactions to difficult dialogues. *Counselor Education and Supervision, 49*(2), 86–105. https://eric.ed.gov/?id=EJ868066

Watt, S. K. (2016). The practice of freedom: Leading through controversy. In K. L. Guthrie, T. B. Jones, & L. Osteen (Eds.), *Developing Culturally Relevant Leadership Learning* (New Directions for Students Leadership, no. 152, pp., 35–46). Jossey-Bass. https://doi.org/10.1002/yd.20207

BEING WITH PARADOX
AND POSSIBILITY

The Origins of The Theory of Being

Sherry K. Watt

> *So I will try to let my guard down*
> *and be present to the butterfly*
> *as it flutters.*

—Danna Faulds, "Possibility Is the Word of the Day"

My personal and professional journey is inextricably linked to the ebbs and flows of my life, career, and our society. The theory of Being evolved, in part, from a process I used to make sense of a life full of paradox. This book summarizes how the threads of my research line evolved into the theory of Being. The theory describes *ways of Being* (practices and process) and explains how they help have difficult dialogues within the social and political contexts of institutions that emerged with a specific focus on controversies related to racism. In this chapter, I will share the paradoxes that shape my life and show how the theory of Being provides a pathway for me to hold out the possibility of hope amid despair. Being teaches me how to be with impenetrable problems in ways that are life-giving and transformative. Actively doing the inner work of aligning my thoughts, feelings, and actions helps me build the stamina to deal with conflict. As defined earlier, a *conflict* could be an enduring social problem, a controversial decision, a disorienting dilemma (as Mezirow, 1991, describes), a new/unknown/unfamiliar or even a fundamentally disagreed upon difference, belief, value, idea, or experience. When I face a conflict, I often ask myself: "What does this conflict invite me to do? What opportunity for growth does this conflict present for me? What work do I need to do on myself around this conflict? What work is there for me to do in my relationships? What part of this work do I need to do in my community?"

As follows, I reflect on being a person, a researcher, and a community member. As the theory guides me, I deal with the fluidity of my *personal, relational,* and *community* connections, experiences, and identity. I share how the process of intentionally aligning my thoughts, feelings, and actions with the practice of Being shapes my relationship to conflict (as described in the "Part One Introduction"), which then guides my personal and professional practice.

Being a Person

As a person, I ponder the question, "Who am I?" The question helps me make sense of my constantly changing surroundings and a myriad of contradictions that shape my personal life. I am an upper-middle-class, cisgender, heterosexual, breast cancer thriver, African American woman who was raised in a two-parent home with one sibling. I grew up as an army brat. Both of my parents were college educated. My father retired as a lieutenant colonel from the United States Army. He was an engineer and transportation specialist. My mother was a nurse and a homemaker. Our family lived and traveled in the United States and abroad. We lived in army officer housing, which was predominantly White on each base. Most, but not all, People of Color on the army base lived in enlisted officer housing, which was located away from the officer sections. Generally, army officers are college educated, whereas enlisted officers join the service with at least a high school diploma. As a child, I went to public school with officers and enlisted children of all races whose families were from many different countries, and we all lived at varying socioeconomic levels. On every military base, my education in the public school systems embodied and valued White-dominant and socioeconomically affluent cultural ways. My life is shaped by a mix of privilege and marginalization that creates tension leading me to search for resolve and seek balance.

I became an instantaneous single parent to four children that my sister left behind after being murdered by her husband. My sister was a teacher, a loyal friend, and a supreme storyteller. She had an exuberant sense of humor. Her husband was a Black man raised in a middle-class family, a drug addict. I theorize that as a child he might have been like my nieces and nephews—smart, curious, expressive—the kind of Black child that the U.S. educational system is unsure of where they fit and how to work with him/her/them. I offer this not as an excuse for his crime, not even as an expression of compassion, but as another example of the paradoxes and how racism—my constant companion—encases my life and work.

I am part of the African American community. While my racialized experiences are common to most other highly educated African Americans, I did not grow up socioeconomically disadvantaged. In this way, I do not fit neatly into the stereotypical view of African Americans. The stereotypical image that is reinforced by media and poorly designed research studies is that most Black people are not highly educated, grew up in poverty or live in very low-socioeconomic status households. I grew up in settings where I was usually the only Person of Color. In my experiences, the combination of my socioeconomic and educational background can be seen as a betrayal of the Black community if you are limited in your view by the stereotype. This image is held not only by some White people and our systems but even by some Black people who have difficulty resisting the stereotype. Therefore, I am often asked to prove that I am Black enough. I am constantly dancing between being human, being Black, and being Black and human. And because I live with the threat of death by cancer amid the constant constraints of racism and have experienced the tragedy of losing my sister, I have discovered that *ways of Being* with paradox and conflict that help me manage the overwhelming contradictions I face in my life.

Being With Fundamental Disagreement

During the pandemic and racial reckoning of 2020, I entered into a conversation with a friend whose political point of view is conservative while mine leans liberal. My friend is a White woman, kind, and is highly educated in the medical sciences. She called to talk one day during pandemic times to share her discontent with the behavior of people as she walked through Target on the first weekend when the quarantine restrictions were lifted. She was very sympathetic to the message that we have to open the economy but was especially unnerved by the number of people in the store at one time and the fact that many were not wearing masks and disregarded the sacrifice she was making working in the hospital. I was actually surprised when she called. I suspect we were both avoiding calling each other because there was nothing that we could discuss that was not laced with political tensions.

We both seemed baffled by the state of our country. We both watched different media outlets. I perceived that she identified with the media outlet aligned with the rhetoric of Fox News. I believe she also listens to public radio. I, rather, frequented all liberal media outlets including MSNBC. I also listen to Fox News and public radio during intense news cycles to try to decipher what truth is, which in my view lies somewhere in between the messages sent by these various news outlets. However, I am, without a doubt, drawn to political points of view that reject what I perceive as Trump-like perpetuation of racism, xenophobia, and selective valuing of the privileged over those who are marginalized in this society. I am baffled by the principle of valuing the economy without consideration for humanity. I reject the Darwinian logic of survival of the fittest. In this conversation, she appeared torn over these sets of contradictions too. She was frustrated with the disregard for healthcare workers, and yet she values individual freedoms and is suspicious of big government. She also seems to want to continue to believe in the American Dream, which is that anyone can achieve with just hard work. We both seemed to be questioning that ideal, given that our country could no longer deny its flaws after witnessing the racially motivated death of George Floyd.

We are friends. We both made intentional decisions to stay in a relationship. I believe we remain open to hearing each other because we share one common thread—we both value humanity and wholeness. I am heartened by our stamina to remain friends when we each buy into different points of view. However, I believe, if we were honest, we would admit that we both have had moments when we questioned whether or not our friendship would survive this particular moment in time. I wondered if I can stay in a relationship with someone who believes in values that are so antithetical to my existence and my experience as an African American in this country. I accept that we will likely never agree or see the social problems the same way. I wondered whether or not it is possible to be with her around issues that amplify our very opposing points of view such as the pandemic and racism. The conflict is that we fundamentally disagree, and yet we are friends.

Applying *Personal Ways of Being*

In the long days of the pandemic, I pondered how applications of the theory of Being can help sustain our engagement in difficult dialogues on matters where there is fundamental disagreement. I wondered: How can we sustain engagement in difficult dialogues? What are the unspoken assumptions and beliefs that are at the root of those discussions? If we improve our process, will our outcomes result in deep, pervasive, and meaningful social change or perhaps personal or relational transformation? This conflict with my friend presented me with an opportunity to practice the theory's idea of Being. I applied the principles and practices of Being in our discussions surrounding this fundamental disagreement. My friend and I discussed the theory only in casual conversation. Therefore, she was familiar with the idea of Being in an informal way because some of the theory's principles and practices are embodied in the spirit of relating to each other as friends.

During a tense moment in one of our pandemic conversations, my friend was articulating a version of the American Dream. The American Dream sentiment that I heard from my friend boils down to the view that life is not fair, but if you work hard, then you have access to the dream. Essentially, I heard from her that there is equal access to opportunities. I heard that there are no systemic barriers—and if there are systemic barriers, they are surmountable. I view this as a typical conservative political position. In other words, it is antiseptic. It is scrubbed clean of any acknowledgment of the history of racism in this country and dismisses the thought about how it still shapes our social and economic systems today. This position ignores the fact that there are systemic disadvantages for People of Color and systemic advantages for White people. I fixated on this point in our conversation.

In this tense moment, I paused and decided to be with her ideas. I stopped trying to convince her to see me and my point of view. I practiced in this conversation the *personal way of Being,* that is, *discerning motivation* and *humanizing otherness in self.*

As a Being practice, I started to reflect on my motive in the conversation. I admitted to myself that my hope was to open her eyes to seeing me and my perspective. I wanted to convince her that racism existed. I wanted her to understand racism and I wanted to convince her by helping her see how her experiences as a woman in the sciences related to systemic oppression. Once I realized my motivations, I was able to consciously ask myself: "Did my motives align with what I wanted? Did I really want to center her seeing me?" Getting in touch with my motivations allowed time for me to align my thoughts and feelings and ponder how to take action in this conversation. I realized that once I shifted my focus to the fundamental disagreement, I released my wanting to be right or win her over. I was able to listen with a different type of investment. We named the roots of our beliefs. I had to acknowledge that I had not thoroughly explored how I had arrived at my sociopolitical perspective. Together we explored how we arrived at our beliefs. We *humanized otherness in the self* by questioning where and when we departed from the beliefs of our family. We examined the impact of the current times (the Trump presidency, COVID-19, and racism) on our beliefs. We discussed what changed and what remains the same about our beliefs. Once I shifted my way of Being with this fundamental disagreement, it opened up the possibility for me to explore my own upbringing and to deal with the flaws inherent in each of our political positions, not just her position.

My engagement with her shifted something else in me. I started to notice a habit developed from internalized racism, of which I had not been previously fully conscious. In *discerning my motivations* and shifting my focus away from her, I paused on convincing her to acknowledge my existence and experiences with racism. Then I could see that I was centering her, her Whiteness, and making her into a proxy for all White people whom I could convince to see me and hear me. Perhaps my flawed thinking was: "If I can only convince her to see me, then I can move on to the next White person and the next, and so on." This realization helped me to see how focusing on this outcome was not only exhausting and unsatisfying, but also a strategy that was not in sync with my intention to focus on process-oriented ways to deconstruct systems that reinforce oppression.

I believe that when we align our thoughts and feelings with our actions, then we are likely to make conscious decisions that reinforce the actions we want to see in our communities. "Being with" or reflecting on these two *personal ways of Being* invited me into a process of alignment that strengthened my stamina to stay in this difficult dialogue with my friend surrounding this fundamental disagreement. Shifting my approach to being with this fundamental disagreement put me into a learning posture which enlightened my practice of teaching and facilitating surrounding racism that is intentional about not centering Whiteness.

Being as a Researcher

In some form, I pose the *Who am I?* question to every student I teach to ponder, in all of the research projects I supervise, to my faculty colleagues in meetings, and on all types of committees in which I sit. I love that question. This question guided me to initially investigate constructs such as racial identity, womanist identity, faith development, and privileged identity (Constantine & Watt, 2002; Watt, 2003; Watt, 2006). Studying identity evolved my way of understanding ideas, experiences, and the research process. The question "who am I?" pushes me to move beyond focusing on reductionist ways of viewing human beings in research. I resist seeing people and ideas as objects or problems for me to either fix or manipulate. I prioritize process. In other words, by exploring the question "who am I?" in an expansive way I am invited to situate myself, the other, constructs, and problems within contexts as each evolves over time. Asking myself that question in relation to my research and to my personal life shifted my orientation to process and changed the way I teach, conduct research, and explore ideas. I began to focus on knowing as a process, not as a destination or an outcome.

My research findings on social identity led me to become frustrated with the limits of studying constructs. I shifted away from interpreting the results of any research about the human condition as finite and portable notions. Specifically, I began to do research on how one engages in difficult dialogues given his/her/their social identity (i.e., who you are and how you experience the world) within classroom settings. I discarded the notion that I can know a construct (identity) outside its social context (racism) without considering the fluidity of human experience (living), particularly within learning environments. I began to question the value of reducing the human experience to an aggregated summary of many individuals and as a step to address discrimination. I found that type of summary research misses the mark and potentially reinforces structural inequity. This type of research generally focuses on individuals as the problem and minimizes the importance of context. It felt unsatisfying and futile to tediously describe, document, and name racism as the end goal of a research project and then to only be able to speculate on what that means for addressing discrimination.

I arrived at this perspective on that type of scholarly inquiry as I researched racialized experiences of both Black and White learners (Watt, 2006, 2007; Watt et al., 2009). I am in my 35th year working in higher education institutional settings. I have worked as a student affairs practitioner, educator, and researcher across four different institutions (University of North Carolina at Greensboro, Shaw University, Radford University, and the University of Iowa). I have spent close to 22 years as a faculty member at University of Iowa. I have participated in many efforts on college campuses aimed at improving the conditions for minoritized students, faculty, and staff. I have concluded that the outcomes of my research and my work in the field can lead to minoritized students, faculty, and staff becoming ornamental. In other words, I am often reduced to a product or a representation of diversity, equity, and inclusion. The institution points to my employment as an achievement while being devoid of actually including my identity, experiences, and culture in the essential and valued functions of the institution.

I began to question the aims of outcome-focused research as well as practices and began interrogating not just *what* but *how* to explore holistic human experiences with integrity and with consideration for the fluidity of a constantly changing environment. This process-oriented approach evolved over time and these revelations came to me in part because my survival as a whole human required 'being with' racism in both my personal and professional life. The process of managing racism both as a teacher and a researcher shapes my understanding of what the scholarly inquiry is and how I approach it. Resultantly, I shifted my way of Being with ideas to make sense of my experience and to be authentic within my pursuits as a scholar. I began the work of aligning my thoughts, feelings, and actions as a way of finding meaning and evolving as a knower and as a social scientist.

As you might conclude, I am disenchanted with academic life and its singular focus on outcomes. I reject the way social science researchers, as presented in traditional academic publishing, look away from the powerful influence of White dominant, westernized, capitalist, neoliberal culture and the ways it shapes designing of research studies, the reporting of results, and structuring of learning environments. I question the lack of criticality that leads to devaluing non-dominant cultural ways of knowing and that decontextualizing factors that perpetuate racism. It disturbs me that our traditions in higher education research and teaching often commodify students and ideas, glorify researchers, and perpetuate dehumanizing structures. I lament that these ways of existing in academic setting interfere with generative learning and authentic engagement with students and among colleagues which limits our ability to address the world's big problems through educational systems. Prioritizing a simple focus on outcomes in this way prevents an expansive thought process that informs and applies research in ways that can change society.

Paradoxically, I value the opportunities afforded to me as an academic. In this profession, I am able to actively resist these structures that limit my life. I apply my research in ways that contribute to the transformation of learning environments into spaces that are humanizing. The practices and processes provided by the theory of Being help me create pathways in an academic setting where I can exist more authentically as a whole person.

Being an Outsider

In 2012, I started the Multicultural Initiatives (MCI) Research Team 5 years after I became a tenured associate professor, because I reached a point of tension. My courses were elective and not required on the doctoral level. Although doctoral students were sometimes advised on taking courses with me, my research was considered peripheral to the learning of students and to the work of the department. I felt like an ornament.

During campus visit days and other recruiting events, I would teach a sample course to the prospective master's degree students. This way of featuring me as a part of the faculty sent a convenient, unspoken, and not entirely truthful message: "Our only African American faculty member is valued, and this means that this is a safe place for you. We are not racist, and since we feature her, we are benevolent." It is a paradox. While there may be a commitment to having a socially just higher education program, just my person and my lasting presence are often pointed out as proof that "we" are not racist. The fact that I endured the racism to get tenured and become a full professor is lifted as an accomplishment for the program, department, and institution.

This type of ornamenting action is a performative antiracism strategy that cloaks an inclusion effort. On the one hand, I am featured because I am a good teacher. My engaging teaching style invigorates the interest in our program for prospective students. On the other hand, I am also being used, intentionally or not, as an ornament. *Ornamenting* is when I am pointed to as a representative and/or an accomplishment that legitimizes an organization's view that it is not systemically racist. I am a decoration, and my presence is used to enhance the perception that the organization is inclusive. As a decoration, I am not considered a whole person. I am a one-dimensional object that serves as an accent to the central and traditional research. The program, department, and institution point to me as their representation of racial diversity meanwhile treating my work and my contributions as peripheral. I do not think this paradox at my institution is unique in that regard.

As I reached this latest, particular point of tension, I passed in the hall Eugene T. Parker III, a doctoral student at the time and now an associate professor at the University of Kansas. He was one of the students advised against taking my courses because they were not required. We had greeted each other in the halls and socially chatted but had never had a conversation. Gene earned his BA at the University of Iowa and returned to work on his PhD. Interestingly, he was often described to me as a "good guy." This usually meant that a student did not have strong research skills. Since he was African American, I understood this to also mean that the institution was doing him a favor by letting him in the program. We arranged to meet.

In our conversation, we discussed how we were surviving academia. I was honest about my struggles. As I listened to him, I started to realize that we were both being used as ornaments. He is a brilliant scholar. He has very strong research skills. He was more than an appendage of the program. In fact, he made significant contributions to the research projects he participated in. We both pondered the culture of the program that isolated us from each other and from applying our research interests in meaningful ways. We decided to work together to create a space where we could talk about these existential dilemmas of academic life and conduct research together. We invited students—all students—to join, and these meetings and collaborations evolved into the work and the community that is now called the MCI Research Team.

At this time in my career, my exhaustion with being made ornamental reached a pressure point. I wanted to create a life-giving space for myself and others to reflect on and to strategize how to survive academia's traditions. Traditions that did not include me living as a whole person. I had to figure out a way to be with this conflict (not just survive it but thrive in it) and shift my position in the institution. The conflict that exhausted me was that I was being treated as ornamental by my institution.

Applying *Relational Ways of Being*

As I dealt with paradoxes in my life as an academic, I practiced using the *ways of Being* to sort through the conflict and sustain my engagement. In starting the MCI Research Team, I employed *relational ways of Being* practices of *dissenting wisely and well* and *humanizing otherness in a relationship and idea exploration.*

I thought about leaving academia at numerous points in my career. In 2012, I reached another one of those inflection points. I wanted to leave the university and I was angry. I did not like that the institution, the department, and the program intentionally relied on having a sole Black faculty member as its one good strategy, albeit superficial and passive. And I could not easily leave. As a cancer thriver and a parent, I needed the security of the job and its benefits. I also needed a space that was generative for my soul and my work life. We began the MCI Research Team to create space for dialogue that might help us survive academia. Our initial invitation was to all students. The MCI Research Team evolved over time and began to include students, faculty, alumni, and staff.

I wanted to create a space that was not completely reactionary to my discontent. As a facilitator of the team, I needed to be a clean conduit in order to generate a healthy environment for dialogue and idea generation. I embraced *dissenting well and wisely* as it related to my relationship with colleagues and my hopes for racial equity and inclusion in our program and at our institution. I tapped into the energy I was putting toward creating a transformative program with regard to racial equity and inclusion that felt futile at the program and institutional levels. I shifted my focus to doing this work within the smaller community of the MCI Research Team. I pointed out, although did not fixate on, the inconsistency between the action and the message and the superficiality of the unsubstantiated performances and expressions of how inclusive we are as a program and as an institution. In my dissenting moments, I did my best to hold the humanity of my colleagues with care.

By *humanizing otherness in a relationship and in my exploration of ideas*, I guided our open discussion as a research team toward examining our current practices regarding racial equity and inclusion efforts. I also tried to acknowledge that my lens was not the only way to view our program and institution.

I accepted that it is possible that my way of viewing our inclusion efforts as a program is not the only route. I tried to consider this view while simultaneously remembering that what I was feeling was true as the only Black faculty member. I managed the paradox. I also considered the possibility that my colleagues are taking different routes to racial equity and inclusion that may have value. I questioned whether my vision for moving toward racial equity and inclusion was the only way. While I was open to collaborations that supported various approaches, I also explored being with the dissonance inherent and reflected on the question: Is there any value in the other ways of doing equity and justice work that I typically think are superficial?

I believe that these *relational ways of Being* transformed my view of my relationship with my colleagues and helped me nurture the capacity to facilitate healthy ways of Being for the MCI Research Team. The reflections on these two ways of Being allowed me to shift my energy from prioritizing my frustration with being othered by my colleagues and our institution toward addressing how to deconstruct and reconstruct communities that are racially equitable and inclusive. I began exploring my discontent in the community and through research. These frustrations informed my view, and yet I situated them in a way that it helped our research team to be able to consider the various routes to racial equity and inclusion.

The MCI Research Team confronts through dialogue various ways a community can sustain the motivation to face difficult questions such as: How is our community complicit with traditional academia? In what ways is traditional academia reinforcing inequity and structural racism? How does the intersection of traditional academia and structural racism collide and how is it being reinforced in our community? We resist traditional academic commodification and owning ideas. We share in the creation and the credit for our research projects. The MCI Research Team embraced a process-oriented approach to exploring ideas to a *way of Being* together in the community that allowed me to express both my love of academia and my frustrations.

Being a Community Member

I make sense of my life through my relationships with others in a community. I am in a relationship with people from different upbringings. I maintain relationships with people whose values or experiences I do not share. Higher education settings provide me with exposure to constant change and opportunities to interact across different cultures, races, and ideas. It is likely that I chose to work on a college campus because academic life mimics what I experienced growing up moving from army base to base. I value the constant striving to learn and evolve that is ever-present in an academic environment. There are contradictions. I live and work in predominantly White settings. My connections support my belief that community reaches beyond race and extends into other realms of culture, interest, and commonalities.

However, I am often reminded that deep and sustainable community connections cannot transcend the conflicts rooted in historical and social history of racism. For instance, I am part of a community that shares a love of the sport of wrestling in Iowa. My nephew-son, Guy, has wrestled from grade school through college. I have relationships in those circles I cherish. And I love the sport! Simultaneously, I know that many members of that community buy into a political ideology that leans into and denies racism's roots and influence in our country. I am generally on guard at wrestling tournaments. I (or my child) fear and have been treated with hostility due to race. Though, the paradox is that the love of the sport distracts from expression of racism in many of our interactions. I have learned a great deal about navigating fundamental and conflicting differences while in relationship around a commonality such as a sport.

My community also includes connections with other African Americans and People of Color. I need a space with people who have a common experience to express rage over being hit from so many angles all rooted in racism (such as threats to health, life, financial security, etc.). I need to share the burden by talking/crying it out as such atrocities are happening in our lives, to our families and in our communities. I fear daily for my own life and the lives of my children constantly, and especially every single time I see a reported murder of a Black person by the police or some vigilante. At this moment in history, it is difficult to socialize in my community without discussing the two pandemics of racial reckoning and worldwide disease. I feel despair. I am discouraged at the lack of progress on deconstructing racist systems. It helps me to be with other People of Color and to make sense of the constant barrage of systemic barriers.

Contradictorily, I feel a constant pressure to be Black one way when in community. I do not fit the stereotypical one way to be Black. I am an African American woman who benefited from the Civil Rights Act of 1964. I did not grow up under the poverty line. I have many interests that do not fit a Black stereotype. I grew up living a version of Martin Luther King's dream. I went to integrated schools and participated in a mixed-race setting throughout all of my schooling. As a result, I am socialized to predominantly White settings and with those who shared the same socioeconomic position—and while it is a racially diverse group—much of my daily work and social interactions are with White people and in settings where White social norms shape interactions. There is reasonable suspicion about being in community this way among African Americans. Therefore, my commitment to Blackness and Black community is constantly under question due to (and among other things) my intersectional identity of being an upper middle class African American.

I get fooled into thinking that I must be a representative or an instrument for change for other People of Color in the higher education system. I misconstrue and sometimes believe that I need to represent the struggles of the stereotypical version of "all Black people" and this will help move forward the race. I feel the pressure to be Black one way. I struggle with the best way to make contributions to the Black community to disrupt the limits of racism. Though I remind myself that each time I give in to being Black one way, I am reinforcing the system that is reductive. It uses one version of what it means to be Black as a tool that simplifies the experience. When I comply with being Black one way, I am lending myself to be a tool that keeps the White supremacist system operating.

Being With Betrayal

Finding the other so senseless and unknown,
we go to war to feel free of the fear
of our own minds, and so come
to ruin in our hearts of ordinary days.

—Rebecca Seiferle, "Love My Enemies, Enemy My Love"

In our college, we began an antiracism collaborative (Watt et al., 2021) in response to George Floyd's murder. I lead the effort along with the dean, the human resources director, the associate deans, the director of The Baker Teacher Leader Center, and an alumnus who has a long career working in equity issues. This collaboration centers on cross-racial, action-oriented dialogue and is informed by the theory of Being. ARC is described as:

> The Antiracism Collaborative (ARC) intends to inspire and normalize conversations that deconstruct how racism operates in our organization, our community, and our society. These conversations will critically examine how racism operates within the functional aspects of the College (such as curriculum and teaching, admissions and recruitment, policy and practices). As important, the ARC structures will invite all in the College of Education community to think and act together boldly and creatively to implement practices that are intentionally antiracist. (Iowa College of Education, 2022, paras. 1–2)

Racism is a social disease that has psychological and health consequences. Racism is dehumanizing. It severely diminishes the quality of life, and its biases are intrusive factors in the majority of my social interactions. Racism depletes what nourishes us. My encounters with other African Americans and People of Color set us against each other. We sometimes feel that we are in a vicious competition in predominantly White academic settings. We are often pitted against each other. There is a "favored one" at any given moment in these academic organizations. We are all under attack, and as we hover in our corners and when someone approaches, we sometimes lash out at whomever we feel is betraying us.

More than one of my college Colleagues of Color felt that this new ARC initiative was encroaching on their territory of expertise. In the competitive academic environment, my colleagues likely feared that there could be only one expert getting attention at a time. Many resisted the effort because they thought it was too kind to White people. The ARC initiative does not condone nor debate the existence of racism but rather normalizes dialogue that builds from the reality that racism exist. ARC does not focus on intentionally making people uncomfortable as a primary focus to teach about racism. The approach depends on the truth of racism being discomforting in and of itself. I understand that the historic evolution of antiracism efforts emphasizes discomfort as a strategy for social change by proving racism exists through naming ordinary and horrific accounts of senseless racist acts. This classic approach reflects a propensity to center and hyperhumanize Whiteness and is driven by the desire for People of Color to be seen and validated by White people. The Being approach intends to decenter that desire to center Whiteness (by centering structural racism) and avoids reinforcing that socialization by making White people's comfort or discomfort a primary objective of the effort. Therefore, I can see how the approach can be misconstrued as being too comfortable for White people since the action of purposefully inducing discomfort is not placed at the center of the initiative.

And to be fair, those of us who study racism, social justice, and equity issues were all in uncharted territory—now the entire world was listening. George Floyd's death disrupted us all, and there was a lot of uncertainty and many potential pathways to take to address this racial awakening. As researchers and educators, we had been sounding the alarm about what needed to be done to fight discrimination through scholarship in education, history, humanities, sociology, and so forth. It was in this moment that all of our work over the years was now sought after and desperately needed.

In the initial stages, the collaborative made an attempt to coordinate efforts across scholars who study race and racism in the college. A few refused to share information or be a part of coordinating efforts. One Colleague of Color said directly to me that she would only speak directly to the dean and never to me. Her refusal to talk to me felt like a betrayal. I did not know that I was her enemy. While I felt betrayed in this situation, I realized that she might see me as a betrayer. As an upper-middle-class African American, I am constantly being asked in some cloaked way whether I am Black enough and why I trust White people. I felt like this was an undertone of her refusal to cooperate with me. I felt like she was not only questioning and dismissing the ARC effort, but more so, she was establishing that she saw this effort and me as competition. It caught me off guard. I did not see our academic work as a competition, but as a complementary strategy for facing down racism in real time. She perhaps viewed an effort focused on racism as skirting a chance to hold White people accountable for racism. Her research names racism and various places it exists, with naming seen as the outcome.

Whereas I view efforts that just focus on naming racism as the outcome as only one helpful step forward but rather insufficient. I believe that prioritizing naming where racism exists centralizes on Whiteness and White people as the targets of the message. I do think this research is an important part of the larger efforts to deconstruct racism and racist systems. And, also, George Floyd's death permits our society to move beyond naming to a more obvious place of knowing that racism exists and toward strategizing to deconstruct racist systems. Focusing on racism as the problem in a process that deconstructs and reconstructs environments is an important strategy to defeating structural racism. One of its values is that it shifts the strategy away from centering Whiteness and White people as the sole and primary audience. This shift allows an entire community across racial identity to share responsibility in disrupting the practices that uphold racism.

Viewing racism as the target of my concern is disorienting for many. I align with Freire's (1970) view that racism is a systemic oppression that has consequences both for the oppressed and the oppressor. I believe we must address this systemic barrier by working across racial lines. Many of us who do this work can easily lose sight and think that antiracism efforts are about a fight to be seen by White people and it is *us-versus-them*. This desire to be seen by White people may have some use; it does demand and resist the denial of the historic legacy of racism in this country. And yet, by viewing structural racism as the problem and not seeing it as an *us-versus-them* individual problem, I am practicing an alternate strategy. I want to stop centering White people and Whiteness and work toward systemic disruption of racism. From my perspective, this requires humans of all races deconstruct and reconstruct a new reality. It is not *us-versus-them*, but *us-versus-them-exploring-it*. I understand that this approach is experienced by People of Color as letting White people off the hook. I believe this fundamental tension was at the core of the conflict with my colleague. The conflict is is the inherent betrayals that happen in relationships when approaches to racism are pitted as *us-versus-them*.

Applying *Community Ways of Being*

I am one of the leaders of the ARC effort. ARC aims to deconstruct and reconstruct our college's environment to be a more racially equitable and inclusive place to work. As one of the leaders, I practiced at least two of the *community ways of Being: embracing trouble as a learning opportunity* and *normalizing defenses* (PIE model). Practicing these *community ways of being* helped me to manage conflict in relationships at work when there are feelings of betrayal.

I embraced this conflict as an opportunity to learn and grow by exploring the disagreements. Personally, it disturbed me that I felt betrayed and that I was being viewed as a betrayer of my race. I could see both sides of this conflict and why we disagreed on how to address racism. We, as the leaders viewed ARC as an opportunity to address racism as a community concern and practice multiple strategies for changing racist policy and practice. Some of my Colleagues of Color did not want to get their hopes up for this type of collaborative because they had been disappoint by past attempts to address racism in the college. They did not want discussions regarding racism to offer any comfort for White people. Understanding their concern, I questioned this approach to addressing racism. In the ARC community meetings, we invited the possibility that this approach may or may not work. We admitted that we do not know exactly what will work to disrupt a racist system. We admitted that the approach might feel like it comforts White people. I wanted to learn from my colleague's dissent. I was open to questioning this approach. I embraced this conflict as an opportunity to learn about myself, my community, and/or about antiracism strategy. By *embracing trouble as a learning opportunity*, I hoped that by openly facing the feelings of betrayal in an effort such as the ARC might help us to deal with the conflict in a community way. It was also our vision that this *community way of Being* would invite more authentic and expansive dialogue within our college and through ARC to normalize disagreement. As leaders, we hoped that this *way of being* might help to create space in dialogue that would allow for conflicting ideas to live in concert with each other, which could reveal various points of view and lead to different solutions to community problems.

As for my feelings of betrayal, I feared that maybe I pushed too far beyond the traditional boundaries of antiracism work by inviting collaboration and that moving beyond the naming of racism might not be the right strategy. I felt defensive about my work. My Colleagues of Color were perhaps displaying defensive reactions as well. *Normalizing defenses* as a *way of Being* helps to acknowledge that defensiveness is a normal and natural part of community deliberations. Understanding this way of Being directs me not to harbor ill will and to not be surprised by defensive reactions. These *community ways of Being* support sustained engagement with people while they disagree and are also working toward deconstructing and reconstructing practices and policies to be a racially equitable and inclusive community space.

Conclusion

This chapter captures the ways I apply the theory of Being to various aspects of my life. My survival as a whole human depends on my active participation in the community efforts of change. I need to be active in preventing the harm done to me and others by racism. The theory of Being provides me with *personal, relational,* and *community* practices that help me think and act on injustices.

Applying Being practices allows me to address injustices in a way that is life-giving and that embodies thoughtful action while working with others in community. Cultivating and applying liberating practices described in the theory of Being allows communities to be with a problem, to transform destructive social conditions that limit our expression of humanity, and to resist acts that restrict our ability to generate possibility for fundamental social change within learning environments.

References

Constantine, M. G., & Watt, S. K. (2002). Cultural congruity, womanist identity attitudes, and life satisfaction among African American college women attending historically Black and predominantly White institutions. *Journal of College Student Development, 43*(2), 184–194. https://psycnet.apa.org/record/2002-02165-003

Freire, P. (1970). *Pedagogy of the oppressed.* Seabury Press.

Iowa College of Education. (2022). *Anti-racism collaborative.* https://education.uiowa.edu/about/anti-racism-initiatives/anti-racism-collaborative

Mezirow, J. (1991). *Transformative dimensions of adult learning.* Jossey-Bass.

Watt, S. K. (2003). Come to the river: Using spirituality to cope, resist, and develop identity. In M. F. Howard-Hamilton (Ed.), *Meeting the Needs of African American Women* (New Directions for Student Services, no. 104, pp. 29–40). Jossey-Bass. https://doi.org/10.1002/ss.105

Watt, S. K. (2006). Racial identity attitudes, womanist identity attitudes, and self-esteem in African American college women attending historically Black single-sex and coeducational institutions. *Journal of College Student Development, 47*(3), 319–334. https://doi.org/10.1353/csd.2006.0038

Watt, S. K. (2007). Difficult dialogues, privilege and social justice: Uses of the privileged identity exploration (PIE) model in student affairs practice. *College Student Affairs Journal, 26*(2), 114–126. https://files.eric.ed.gov/fulltext/EJ899385.pdf

Watt, S. K., Curtis, G. C., Drummond, J., Kellogg, A. H., Lozano, A., Nicoli, G. T., & Rosas, M. (2009). Privileged identity exploration: Examining counselor trainees' reactions to difficult dialogues. *Counselor Education and Supervision, 49*(2), 86–105. https://doi.org/10.1002/j.1556-6978.2009.tb00090.x

Watt, S. K., Mahatmya, D., Coghill-Behrends, W., Clay, D. L., Thein, A. H., & Annicella, C. (2021). Being with anti-racism organizational change efforts: Using a process-oriented approach to facilitate transformation. *Journal of College Student Development, 62*(1), 130–133. https://doi.org/10.1353/csd.2021.0011

2

LIVING INTO
THE THEORY OF BEING

A Process-Oriented Research Approach

Chris R. Patterson, Duhita Mahatmya, and
Multicultural Initiatives Consortium

Each design and method should be taken on its merits as a means of facilitating (or obscuring)
the understanding of particular research problems, and that a fetishistic espousal of favoured
designs or methods and an excessive preoccupation with their epistemological underpinnings
can only stand in the way of developing such an understanding.

—Bryman, *Research Methods and Organization Studies*

What exists outside the boundaries of what we know? In traditional social science research methods, researchers and practitioners often favor a specific methodological orientation for how to investigate the social world—quantitative, qualitative, or mixed methods. More broadly, across the sciences (formal, natural, social), research methods are informed by our assumptions about the world (ontology) and how to study that world (epistemology), with different orientations often drawing firm boundaries around what subsequently constitutes research (Henn et al., 2009). And yet, it is within and outside of the boundaries that the theory of Being emerged. We open with the Bryman quote to situate our research in a larger idea of understanding phenomena around us. To understand research phenomena we must notice how we engage with the idea and with others during our explorations and be open to the potential for the phenomena and ourselves to transform in the process.

A process-oriented research approach encouraged us, as individual conscious scholar–practitioners (Watt, 2015) and a research team, to apply and transcend our individual research paradigms to be in a relationship with each other and our ideas via *ways of Being*. For example, in placing ourselves

46

and our stories in the center of our conversations, we were key inform-ants. In measuring constructs rooted in student outcomes, we were aca-demic assessment coordinators. In using the results to inform larger research questions, we were research scientists. As results were put under discussion and new ideas formed, our measures changed, and we became psychometri-cians. As the measures changed, new data emerged that both supported and challenged previously formulated ideas. Each person on the team navigated these shifting roles using individual skillsets to inform conversation and form new ideas.

The theory of Being and *ways of Being* developed out of our process-oriented research approach. Through our process, we realized that the the-ory of Being is a living theory denoting and depending upon an individual's openness to transformational change; it is an orientation toward scholar-ship and facilitation that prepares people for transformative learning. In this way, our research praxis became part of the theory development. Our praxis provided a *third thing* (see Appendix C) that we (and other researchers and practitioners) used to guide our thoughts, feelings, and actions around cre-ating the theory. This chapter describes the process of how the theory of Being came to be as we answered three important and guiding questions:

1. How do the underlying assumptions of the privileged identity explora-tion (PIE) model and the authentic, action-oriented framing for envi-ronmental shifts (AAFES) method allow for the emergence of the theory of Being?
2. How do people develop the stamina to manage the cognitive dissonance and emotions that arise when interacting across Difference? (Watt, 2013)
3. What tensions emerge between developing and teaching the theory of Being?

In this chapter, we describe our process-oriented approach and then offer specific examples of how we applied the approach in our research team meet-ings to reveal the theory of Being. The end of this chapter shows the results of our process-oriented approach that establish the tenets of the theory of Being described in Part One and chapter 1.

Developing Our Process-Oriented Methods

In our search for the theory of Being, our research process drew on literature and inspiration from multiple disciplines and methodologies to identify best practices in Being with research and our lived experiences. Our process was a natural result of the interdisciplinary makeup of the research team—team members were graduate students (like the chapter coauthor, Chris Patterson), staff, and affiliated faculty at the University of Iowa (like the chapter coauthor, Duhita Mahatmya), as well as alumni of the research group who are now at other institutions of higher education. Ultimately, we were motivated by an exploration of the phenomena of Being, using the *third thing* ideology (Palmer, 2003; Saussy, 2011; Smith, 2005). Figure 2.1 shows our iterative process of arriving at the theory of Being.

Our iterative process involves multiple cycles, and sometimes entrances and exits, around the diagram. In some ways, our diagram mirrors the inductive and deductive reasoning process many of us learned in our introductory science or research methods courses. We were taught that inductive and deductive reasoning were aspects of the scientific method and inform data gathering and inference testing (Haig, 2005). Where inductive reasoning draws first from our observations to form generalizations and a theory, deductive reasoning seeks to test theory-driven hypotheses. The human desire to explain the world around us has broader connections to human cognition and philosophy (Anderson, 1986; Lombrozo, 2012). While deeper exploration is beyond the scope of this chapter, we acknowledge these ontological roots to describe the ways in which we applied and interrogated scholarly ways of reasoning in creating the theory of Being and *ways of Being*.

For the Multicultural Initiatives (MCI) Research Team and its different formations over the past decade, there has been a consistent cycle of questioning, conversing, data gathering, calibrating, and (re)conceptualization to uncover the theory of Being (Figure 2.1). Instead of posing one research question and analyzing one set of data to test hypotheses, the research group identifies "wild and juicy" questions or observes tensions based on recent teaching experiences, current events, or literature. The first step of the iterative approach uses the question/tension as a catalyst for conversations among research team members. As a team, we explore what the question/tension makes us think about, feel, wonder, and how we connect as a group over these associations. We often began our thinking and conversations inductively by bringing our stories into the research space: What brought us to this research team and Being? Why? What keeps us here?

As conversations converge, a partial theory is formed, or enough of an idea of what the theory is, to test through teaching and facilitation. We invite external thought partners to learn about the theory in classes, workshops, or trainings facilitated by Sherry K. Watt and the research team. Then we collect their narratives about the ideas that stuck. We also share ideas and dialogue with others to get feedback on the theory. Answers gained from narratives, observations, or experts may present tensions with the theory.

Figure 2.1. Illustration of MCI Research Team's iterative process.

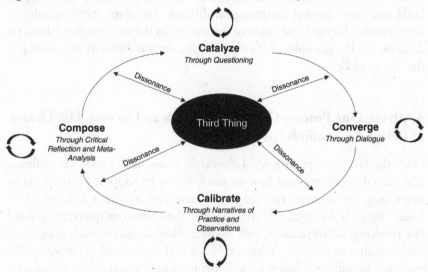

The research team must calibrate and make sense of this tension to move forward. When tension exists, the team investigates the source of the dissonance and composes the next set of questions to explore. Because the team's approach is process-based rather than outcome-focused, the idea evolves through the process; therefore, exploration of new questions and tensions will lead to unexpected directions. This starts another iteration of the approach, where conversation forms around a new *third thing*—the new tension between theory and lived experience. The research team used this iterative process approach to name and define the theory of Being.

Historically, our iterative process also intersected with the COVID-19 pandemic and a critical inflection point in America's reckoning with racial injustice. There was fervent energy around implementing antiracism efforts to transform individuals, relationships, and communities. Internal and external partners eagerly sought Watt's expertise in learning how to navigate these waters. Watt and the MCI Research Team focused on embodying the theory of Being and its process-oriented approach to change how we do antiracism work. We no longer felt that diversity, equity, and inclusion (DEI) action plans, task forces, or lists of demands were sufficient (Watt et al., 2021). And true to our process, the research team refined the theory of Being content and pedagogy not only through discussion and analysis, but also by honoring the very human emotions and lived experience of being together in this moment. In making space for our relationships with dissonance-provoking stimuli, data, and each other, we drew upon the *touchstones* (Appendix B) and practiced how to be with a *third thing* (i.e., the theory of Being) to build our own stamina in staying in difficult dialogues, while simultaneously moving forward our vision of the theory. In the sections that follow, we describe specific examples of the iterative process and different ways it shaped the theory of Being.

Applying Our Process-Oriented Methods to Uncover The Theory of Being: An Example

Over the last 5 years, the MCI Research Team has focused on defining and describing Being and how to teach Being to support participants in developing the stamina to engage in conversations about charged social issues. In early iterations of the process, the following questions guided our thinking, conversations, and analysis: How do individuals experience (dis)engaging in difficult dialogues? What is the relationship between (dis)engaging in difficult dialogues and Being? These questions emerged at a time when Watt and the team were asked to present workshops around DEI issues to academic departments and community organizations. As a team, we spent time discussing how best to scaffold the curriculum to facilitate learning of the theory, how we (as facilitators and researchers) practice the theory ourselves and developed conjectures around the core components of the theory as a result. So, from the beginning, teaching and researching Being happened concurrently. As a team we simultaneously studied (head), experienced (heart), and taught (hands) the theory of Being while developing the theory's foundational principles and practices. In the following we describe a specific example of the observations and tensions that emerged as we taught and studied the stamina to stay in difficult dialogues that ultimately informed the theory of Being.

Catalyst: Questioning PIE and AAFES

The process of uncovering and naming the theory of Being drew heavily on the research and practice of the PIE model (Watt, 2007; Watt, 2015) and the AAFES method (Watt, 2015). Table 2.1 describes the main assumptions of the PIE model and AAFES method (see Watt, 2015, for more in-depth descriptions of both). Generally, while the PIE model focuses on the individual Being skills and explains the concept of how privileged social identities manifest in dialogue, the AAFES method describes a framework for creating the environmental conditions under which to conduct dialogue. Both the model and the method are commonly referenced in the process

TABLE 2.1

The Assumptions of the *PIE Model and *AAFES Method (Watt, 2015)

Assumptions of the PIE Model	Assumptions of the AAFES Method
1. The exploration of privileged identity (i.e., White, heterosexual, and male) is an ongoing socialization process.	1. There is a pathology manifested in our society.
2. People must engage in dialogue about difference to unravel how their socialization shapes their worldview and ultimately their actions.	2. Transformation occurs when individuals in the environment are participants in the deconstruction and reconstruction process.
3. Defense modes are innate and normal human reactions.	3. Transformation requires engagement that balances intellect (head), emotion (heart), and action (hands).
4. There is an intersection of privileged and marginalized identities within each person.	4. The act of inclusion is a riveting process for community members and the institution.
	5. A shift in the environment and its inhabitants needs to occur rather than retrofitting individuals with non-centralized identities to fit within a pathological system.
	6. Increasing the capacity of community members/citizens to engage skillfully with difference equips people with the skills to face a culture that is ever-changing and nebulous.

*The Privileged Identity Exploration (PIE) Model and Action-Oriented, Framing for Environmental Shifts (AAFES) Method.

of multicultural transformation (Watt, 2015). As our research team discovered in our search for the theory of Being, unpacking the assumptions underlying the model and the method PIE and AAFES was essential to our understanding of how the theory of Being becomes a unifying framework for transformative learning.

PIE Assumptions

The PIE model (Watt, 2015) describes the range of defensive reactions someone forms when they experience dissonance due to Difference. Difference is defined as "having dissimilar opinions, experiences, ideologies, epistemologies, and/or constructions of reality about self, society, and/or identity" (Watt, 2013, p. 6). Difference is broadly defined to cover a person's ontology and epistemology while addressing the parts of the self that are informed by systems of power and oppression. *A dissonance-provoking stimulus* (DPS) occurs when someone encounters a stimulus that challenges their current stance on the world. The dissonance is animated by fear (afraid to go deeper) or entitlement (should not have to go deeper), which creates disequilibrium.

The original PIE study (Watt, 2007) revealed a pattern of eight defensive reactions associated with behaviors that individuals display when engaging in difficult dialogues about social justice issues and/or circumstances. Understanding one's own privileged identities brings about an awareness of individual patterns. The eight defenses identified in the PIE model are divided into three groups: recognizing (denial and deflection), contemplating (minimization, rationalization, and intellectualization), and addressing (false envy, principium, and benevolence) privileged identity. When individuals confront the dissonance, the PIE model serves as a guide that helps define the range of unconscious and preconscious defenses a person adopts.

A key assumption of the PIE model is that defenses are normal and learning about them helps reposition our motivations around the dynamics that happen within and between individuals when dissonance occurs to sustain engagement in difficult dialogues. Part of the PIE research included developing an instrument to measure the different PIE defenses (Watt et al., 2021). Based on feedback from peer reviewers as well as feedback from MCI team alumni who were teaching the PIE framework in their coursework, we kept circling around a tension of how to use the PIE model as an instrument in a way that did not weaponize the information. We had to ask ourselves whether we were using PIE to categorize people or as a formative assessment and learning tool.

AAFES Assumptions

Along with PIE, the AAFES method (Watt, 2015) is a foundational piece of the theory of Being. The AAFES method provides an approach for facilitating dialogue for social change and transformation. The method teaches skills to help individuals understand how to sustain their engagement in difficult dialogues. The approach includes supporting individuals and groups in the practice of noticing, nurturing, and naming dissonance that comes up because of an individual's relationship to and critical reflection about Difference. In gaining the skill of authenticity, people may change the way in which they relate to Difference to move toward transformation of self and communities. Because the transformation of self and communities is an eternal process, the AAFES method also focuses on developing stamina (Watt, 2015). Stamina is needed to stay immersed in the different elements of difficult dialogues, such as dealing with discomfort and practicing reflexivity to work toward critical consciousness.

Finally, the AAFES method focuses on the action of deconstructing and reconstructing the environment for inclusion, rejecting the idea of surviving through dehumanization (Watt, 2015). During this process, *third things* (Palmer, 2003; Saussy, 2011; Smith, 2005) are created and become the center of dialogue and action. *Third things* are complex constructs like race, gender, and sexual identity that are placed at the center of dialogue (Palmer, 2003; Saussy, 2011; Smith, 2005). By having a *third thing* in a dialogue, participants focus on and talk about their own experiences rather than focusing on the differences between one another. Such a countercultural approach takes practice, yet by using a *third thing*, the group develops the skills of being flexible, healthily skeptical, reflective of missteps seen as learning opportunities, and managing and dissecting paradoxes (Watt, 2015). In research team meetings, a common tension we reflected upon was whether the AAFES was a concept to teach learners explicitly or was it more of a guiding framework that future facilitators and leaders could apply to structure their learning environments.

The *catalyst phase* of the cycle usually starts with tension or questions that come with relating new information to the original *third thing* and ends when conversation moves from questioning to convergence. Questions can come from any relationship in conversation; examples could be questioning the way our disciplinary background relates to the *third thing*, how identities relate to the *third thing*, how we relate to the team via the *third thing*, and/or how we react to the conversation(s) happening around them. The end of the catalyst phase of the cycle comes when the team feels comfortable with each other and exploring the tension or question(s) together. For our team, the catalyst phase started when we placed the notions of PIE and AAFES as our *third thing* and explored the gaps between their assumptions. We transitioned to convergence when we felt comfortable enough as a team to explore this tension together to uncover something larger. As we explored the tension between both concepts, we moved toward convergence when we realized that they were two separate pieces of a larger puzzle.

Convergence: Conversations About Foundational Principles and Practices of The Theory of Being

Over the years, through presentations and workshops facilitated by Watt and the MCI Research Team, we observed that PIE seemed like a "sticky" concept. Privileged identity was the idea most salient and memorable to learners as they engaged with the topics of difficult dialogues and Difference (Watt, 2013). Our team also debriefed moments of derailment—or when applications of PIE and/or AAFES went awry. (Some of the subsequent chapters in this book reveal more about these derailments and reconsiderations.) Such subtleties and nuances led us to question how we could observe and measure PIE and AAFES to understand the learning processes and outcomes associated with engaging in difficult dialogue.

Our research group realized that the processes and assumptions of the PIE model and AAFES method may be part of a larger idea of Being with Difference during difficult dialogues. For example, when engaged in difficult dialogues, individuals, especially those with dominant and privileged identities, encounter a dissonance-provoking stimulus rooted in experiencing Difference (Watt, 2013). As the dissonance is processed, individuals will not only defend their knowledge but may engage in critical self-reflection about both why and how they defended themselves. At the same time, those in self-reflection must also stay in tune with the conversation to be present in the space. The hardship in this process is that during a difficult dialogue, there is not usually just one stimulus where you take time to self-reflect and can casually reenter the conversation; dissonance-provoking stimuli are constantly being presented, and those affected must navigate critical self-reflection while staying in dialogue with others. People must have an openness for continuous engagement with the dissonance. For many, confronting a dissonance in conversation can be physically, mentally, and emotionally taxing, so immersing in this process of self-reflection multiple times, while remaining in dialogue, requires us to have a large amount of stamina. Stamina is not usually something that we are born with—as with any skill, we must train and immerse in experiences that help build stamina.

In considering the ways in which individuals practice Being in difficult dialogues, the underlying question that the group kept returning to was: How are people able to navigate all the moving and taxing parts of dialogue in order to open the heart to enact change? Through dialogue within the research group, supported by a meta-analysis of literature, we realized that the theory of Being did not directly connect the tenets of PIE and AAFES but was instead the foundation on which they stood. To fully understand and engage with both PIE and AAFES, individuals need the skills to build the stamina to interact with the dissonance that arises when experiencing PIE and AAFES. The theory of Being offered the unifying framework that outlined how stamina could be built to exist in difficult dialogues.

As conversations converged, we sensed that as we talked more about PIE and AAFES, and the gaps between the two, we recognized deeper commonalities between them. Those commonalities became our assumptions of the theory of Being, which were as follows:

1. To fully realize the theory of Being, you must be open to difficult dialogues.
2. The ability to have a difficult dialogue requires cognitive stamina (head), emotional stamina (heart), and physical stamina (hands).
3. The theory of Being requires you to focus on how you exist in relation to a *third thing* rather than on how you can solve a problem (process-oriented versus goal-oriented).

In reaching these assumptions, the team reached convergence. Because we had reached a point of conversational saturation and agreement, we had to find a way to see if our hypotheses about the theory of Being rang true in a practical setting. Here, we transitioned into calibration.

Calibration: Teaching The Theory of Being

After reaching a saturation point with conceptualization and conversations within the team, we needed a way to share our ideas with people outside of our group. We also needed to bring new stimuli into the research group to disrupt and catalyze our thinking about the ideas we had. As the next part of the iterative process highlights, we positioned our ideas in relation with others' lived experiences in navigating difficult dialogue and learning the skills to help navigate dissonance. To do so, we collected anonymous narratives of practice from students and alumni of a graduate program where the ideas of PIE and AAFES were utilized to teach about multi-culturalism in higher education. Those who responded to this call shared many experiences around disengaging during a difficult dialogue, reengaging during a difficult dialogue, and developing the stamina to stay engaged in a difficult dialogue.

Disengagement

In the call for students and alumni to share their experiences, we asked the following questions: "How do you know when you have checked out of a difficult dialogue? What factors contribute to that?" The research team categorized the responses into three themes: perceptions of the dialogue, perceptions of others' engagement during a dialogue, and intrapersonal characteristics during a dialogue. At times, the dialogue felt stagnant or the conversation was not perceived to be productive in helping the individual or the group explore their relationship with the controversial social issue. While participating in the dialogue, some people checked out of the conversation because they perceived others lacked engagement or were actively antagonistic. Noticing silence from others discouraged participants to continue their own engagement. At the same time, noticing defensiveness drew participants back into the *us-versus-them* mindset rather than into the mode of *me/us-and-you/them-exploring it*. During a difficult dialogue, when participants felt antagonized by another person in the group, especially when they felt vulnerable, they disengaged due to fear of or frustration toward the antagonist. Elements of intrapersonal characteristics, like discomfort, lack of stamina, and/or lack of self-efficacy to participate were also noted as characteristics of the difficult dialogue, making a participant more likely to refrain from engaging.

Reengagement

After being asked about checking out of a conversation, students and alumni were prompted by the question: "When you have realized you checked out but still need to be present within difficult dialogue, how did you check back in to reengage?" Practicing self-reflection and self-regulation and strategizing were recognized as main themes across the narratives collected by the research team. If someone checked out because of discomfort, they used critical self-reflection to find the root of the discomfort. When the root was found and someone wanted to reengage in the conversation, they would do so either silently through holding onto their new knowledge as they navigated the conversation or by explicitly stating their discomfort and using that opportunity to outwardly explore their relationship with the *third thing*. Some responses mentioned that emotional self-regulation was important when they checked out. Others said that feeling frustration or having an emotional reaction during the dialogue required that they simply notice the emotion and reflect on it later. Many people noted using specific strategies to reengage in the dialogue. Some mentioned that it was easier to physically separate from the community and return when they were ready to reengage. Other strategies included asking questions, perspective-taking, and reflecting on ground rules set for the dialogue. It is important to note here that some people actively chose not to reengage in the dialogue, stating exhaustion and/ or not wanting to confront others as reasons for not checking back in.

Developing Stamina

Finally, we asked the same students and alumni, "What specific skills and/ or practices do you draw upon to stay engaged during times of difficult dialogue?" Some of the skills included simultaneous self- and environmental assessment and practicing empathy and perspective-taking. Individuals who described themselves as being able to stay in sustained dialogue noted how they were able to bring their own feelings into awareness while also "reading the room." Employing a mix of relational trust and *personal ways of Being*, along with observing their environment, some individuals were able to navigate and regulate emotions while still reflecting on their experiences with *a third thing*. Others explicitly mentioned practicing empathy and general perspective-taking on how they stayed in the dialogue. Some said they were able to better understand other learners' relationships to a *third thing* through perspective-taking or empathizing with others, which helped them reflect on their own relationship with the *third thing*. Finally, some elements of being allowed for people to ensure their own physical or emotional safety during the dialogue. For instance, they would physically move to another spot in the room or explain to the aggressor or antagonist about how the aggression or antagonism was not welcomed in the space. Some mentioned they would assist the aggressor/antagonist in exploring the underlying reasons of the aggression and/or antagonism to stay in dialogue with one another.

Now that we had stories from those who practiced our teachings, new information was introduced into the theory generation process. Some of the previous stories were consistent with what the team thought would happen, and other stories were contrary to what we predicted. Using this information, we moved to the next phase of the cycle.

Composing The Theory of Being: Meaning-Making of Tension Within the Context of the Research Question

From these initial narratives, paired with observations that the team made during workshops and trainings, we revisited the content and structure of the theory of Being. We used the tensions that arose between defining the foundational principles and practices versus teaching them. For instance, while we can list and describe what the *personal, relational,* and *community ways of Being* are, we constantly thought about and adjusted the teaching of the *ways of Being*. As we discussed during team meetings, it was not enough for participants in workshops or students in class to know what the theory of Being is: learners needed time to practice the *ways of Being* and embody the theory of Being as an orientation toward Difference (Watt, 2013). Traditional ways of assessing learning (through surveys or focus groups) were insufficient to name the ways in which people were absorbing the theory and shifting toward embodying the principles during the workshop, presentation, or teaching about the theory. Likewise, the data points and the team's position around and interpretation of the data were not fixed and evolved from week to week in each team meeting and workshop. The experience of building and teaching the theory lived as a process-oriented approach.

At this point, we used our weekly team meetings to discuss and make sense of the dissonance between our assumptions and narratives of practice. As we realized the source of the tension between defining and teaching the theory, more questions started to form about that source. At the same time, we started questioning how this tension lived within the theory of Being and whether it was supposed to occur at all. For us, the composing phase started when we were presented with new information and ended when we were able to smoothly place the tension as a *third thing*, and the team started thinking of questions to explore.

Thus began the next iteration of theory development. We collected additional narratives and focus group responses from undergraduate students, graduate students, and higher education faculty and staff who participated in additional trainings provided by Watt and the MCI Research Team. While we mostly used similar questions across the groups, we also adapted them to align their content with the evolution of the theory of Being. As the data were interpreted and introduced into the discussion surrounding the theory of Being, the research group was able to see where participants' experiences aligned or misaligned with the foundational principles and practices of the theory of Being.

Table 2.2 summarizes the analytical and experiential parts of our process-oriented methods that led to the theory of Being.

TABLE 2.2
Summary of Inductive and Deductive Processes of The Theory of Being

Analysis of The Theory of Being	Experiences With The Theory of Being
1. The theory of Being involves building stamina for sustained dialogue. 2. Because difficult dialogues involve the head, heart, and hands, stamina must also be cognitive, emotional, and physical. 3. The theory of Being acknowledges derailment, but also invites coming back to the third thing. 4. The theory of Being is the foundation for the PIE model and AAFES method.	1. It takes a lot of physical and mental energy to exist in sustained difficult dialogue. 2. Derailment happens easily when we forget the goal of the process, when exhaustion is reached, or when someone wishes to derail. 3. *Third thinging* is a countercultural process that takes time getting used to. 4. The theory of Being helped people understand the use of PIE and AAFES in dialogue.

While this book intends to summarize the theory of Being and the process that allowed us to uncover it, the research team acknowledges that this theory is not finite. Just as the theory of Being took form over time through an iterative process, we expect the theory to change over time. This does not mean that the theory of Being is incomplete—rather, the theory of Being places itself as its own *third thing* that can be explored by our and other research teams in the future. As our team continues to use the theory of Being to guide our research, we will find that the theory may manifest differently in different spaces. Looking to the future, we encourage other teams of researchers, practitioners, and mixed teams to use both the theory of Being and the iterative process approach to explore both theoretical and practical issues in higher education and beyond.

Conclusion

The group's integrative and iterative research process is important to note as the process required us to place the theory, and research associated with the theory, into the center of conversation as a *third thing* (see Appendix C). In viewing and navigating our research as a *third thing*, our process-oriented approach encouraged us to inductively and deductively live into the theory of Being. In this way, we studied Being foremost in recognizing and inviting our whole selves into the process. For Chris, within the first half hour of his first research team meeting, he realized that his perspective on research was vastly different, but as the team started the process of uncovering the theory of Being, he saw (along with Watt) the potential for statistics and assessment to complement theory generation and storytelling. The cycle of thought generation, measuring constructs, storytelling, and the return to conceptualization to create a theory was new and challenged his way of thinking about research and theory generation. Likewise, Duhita was invited to a team meeting to provide quantitative support for the Privileged Identity Exploration scale development project but stayed with the team long after the analysis was completed to join in conversation about the theory of Being. In many previous research teams and projects, her role and identity were defined by her quantitative skills; on the MCI Research Team, she discovered her multiple identities and skills allowing her to experience a more humanizing research practice. For both authors, these newly found insights helped them explore Being and how *ways of Being* can be studied.

As the theory development remained at the center of the process, different research methods were used to advance it. While putting the emerging theory and research approaches into conversation with one another, the research group itself had to engage in sustained dialogue and utilize the yet-to-be-named theory of Being to stay present in the dialogue. As a result of this process-oriented research praxis, we were able to explore the foundational ideas of PIE and AAFES that allowed for more research to take place. The authors of this chapter, as well as the rest of the research team who were immersed in this research process, implore readers to take this chapter into consideration as a *third thing* when being in dialogue about research methods, theory generation, and/or research on difficult dialogues and transformational change.

References

Anderson, D. R. (1986). The evolution of Peirce's concept of abduction. *Transactions of the Charles S. Peirce Society, 22*(2), 145–164. https://www.jstor.org/stable/40320131

Bryman, A. (1989). *Research methods and organization studies* (1st ed.). Routledge.

Haig, B. D. (2005). Exploratory factor analysis, theory generation, and scientific method. *Multivariate Behavioral Research, 40*(3), 303–329. https://doi.org/10.1207/s15327906mbr4003_2

Henn, M., Weinstein, M., & Foard, N. (2009). *A critical introduction to social research* (2nd ed.). SAGE.

Lombrozo, T. (2012). Explanation and abductive inference. In K. J. Holyoak & R. G. Morrison (Eds.), *Oxford library of psychology. The Oxford handbook of thinking and reasoning* (pp. 260–276). Oxford University Press.

Palmer, P. J. (2003). Teaching with heart and soul: Reflections on spirituality in teacher education. *Journal of Teacher Education, 54*(5), 376–385. https:// doi.org/10.1177/0022487103257359

Saussy, H. (2011). Comparison, world literature, and the common denominator. In A. Behad & D. Thomas (Eds.), *A companion to comparative literature* (pp. 60–64). Wiley-Blackwell. https://doi.org/10.1002/9781444342789

Smith, M. K. (2005). Parker J. Palmer: Community, knowing and spirituality in education. In *The encyclopedia of informal education.* http://infed.org/mobi/parker-j-palmer-community-knowing-and-spirituality-in-education/

Watt, S. K. (2007). Difficult dialogues, privilege and social justice: Uses of the privileged identity exploration (PIE) model in student affairs practice. *College Student Affairs Journal, 26*(2), 114–126. https://files.eric.ed.gov/fulltext/EJ899385.pdf

Watt, S. K. (2013). Designing and implementing multicultural initiatives: Guiding principles. In S. K. Watt & J. L. Linley (Eds.), *Creating Successful Multicultural Initiatives in Higher Education and Student Affairs* (New Directions for Student Services, no. 144, pp. 5–15). Jossey-Bass. https://doi.org/10.1002/ss.20064

Watt, S. K. (Ed.) (2015). *Designing transformative multicultural initiatives: Theoretical foundations, practical applications, and facilitator considerations.* Stylus.

Watt, S. K., Mahatmya, D., Coghill-Behrends, W., Clay, D. L., Thein, A. H., & Annicella, C. (2021). Being with anti-racism organizational change efforts: Using a process-oriented approach to facilitate transformation. *Journal of College Student Development, 62*(1), 130–133. https://doi.org/10.1353/csd.2021.0011

PART TWO

INTRODUCTION TO
PERSONAL WAYS OF BEING

PART TWO INTRODUCTION

Sherry K. Watt

This part focuses on *personal ways of Being* practices that center on self-awareness and explore authentic personal connections to conflict. Each chapter, "Empathy" by Chris R. Peterson, "Shame" by Audrey Scranton, and "Silence" by Charles R. Martin-Stanley II, uses storytelling to apply *personal ways of Being*. The authors describe how they brought awareness of personal connections by way of noticing (thoughts, information), nurturing (emotion, personal connections), and naming (meaning-making) Difference and conflict. Empathy, shame, and silence are three windows into each author's dilemma as they explore what it means to be with conflict. They explore such dilemmas by bringing their personal stories into conversation within various areas of scholarship, meanwhile highlighting the *personal ways of Being* practices.

These practices include *focusing on you, humanizing otherness in self, recognizing defenses,* and *discerning motivations.* As you engage with these chapters, we invite you to review the following questions to reflect on how the authors employ Being practices in exploring their dilemmas. Moreover, it will be helpful to apply these questions to your own story of confronting Difference and conflict to further reflect upon and personalize these *personal ways of Being* practices.

- *Focusing on you*: Who am I? How do I relate or not to this conflict? What changes or does not change about me now as I encounter this conflict? How am I situated with the particular conflict being explored? What feelings arise in me as I contemplate my relationship to this conflict? How then shall I live?
- *Humanizing otherness in self*: How does this conflict shift depending on who I know myself to be? When have I experienced this type of conflict in my past? How did I arrive at this being a conflict? Who (what) taught me about this conflict? What feelings do I associate with this conflict?

What information do I need to gather to learn more about this conflict? How will I go about gathering information about this conflict? How might I act to resolve this conflict from within? What might I do next to explore this conflict?

- *Recognizing defenses* (PIE model): What am I conflicted about in this moment? What sensations (physical) do I have when I am conflicted? What do I notice about my reactions in those moments of conflict? When did I have this reaction before in my life? What information is associated with my resistance?
- *Discerning motivations*: What do I really want from my adversary? Why do I want it? What is the central issue underlying the conflict? What will I gain or lose if I win? What values, beliefs and ideas drive my relationship to this conflict? How deeply do I believe what I believe about this conflict? What is my desire as it relates to this conflict? What expectations surround my desires? What experiences inform my position on this conflict?

Supplementary materials for the application of Being practices are provided by the authors in Appendix F.

EMPATHY

Chris R. Patterson

> *If you really want to understand slaves, slave masters, poor black kids, poor white kids, rich people of colors, whoever, it is essential that you first come to grips with the disturbing facts of your own mediocrity. The first rule is this—You are not extraordinary. It's all fine and good to declare that you would have freed your slaves. But it's much more interesting to assume that you wouldn't have and then ask, "Why?"*

—Coates, "A Muscular Empathy"

M any people claim to be good empathizers, yet there seem to be renewed and growing calls today to practice empathy (Clark, 1980; Lanzoni, 2019; NorthwesternU, 2008; Trout, 2009). Through the tension that arises from this contradiction, two questions come to my mind: Who are the ones claiming to practice empathy, and who do they practice empathy for? By placing empathy as a *third thing*,[1] anyone can share their experiences as practitioners and receivers of empathy. At the same time, using a process-oriented method like *third thinging* may bring about internal dissonance—we may not be ready or expect to hear stories that counter our own experiences and opinions. "Living into" the theory of Being can help explore such dissonances productively, examining our own existence in and our relationship with conflicts where we employ empathy. This chapter begins with some history of empathy in the United States. Next, I share and dissect my own experiences with empathy through the lens of the theory of Being. I then use the literature on empathy and *personal ways of Being* to introduce intellectual empathy, and end this chapter with activities provided for the readers to explore their intellectual empathy.

A Brief History of Empathy

Empathy became an interest to United States psychologists through a research collaboration with German psychologists in the early 1900s (Lanzoni, 2018). The word "empathy" came as a translation from the German word *Einfühlung* (translation: "feeling-in") and was initially understood as the projection of feelings onto both inanimate and living objects, more specifically onto other humans. Gordon Allport (1954), an early empathy researcher, noted that empathy is a learned skill paired with an innate trait of neuroplasticity. Using this two-part definition and his positionality as a White man in academia, Allport advocated for empathy to become a tool for White people to understand the experiences of African American men. Around the time Allport rose as a face for civil rights in academia, Kenneth Clark rose to prominence as an African American researcher in the psychology of race and empathy. Clark (1980) viewed empathy as a key element in racial equality and reinforced Allport's (1954) conceptualization that empathy can be learned and is also an innate skill. He also called upon the field to conduct more research on empathy.

The call was answered, as empathy became studied as a popular therapy technique (e.g., Bohart et al., 2002). For therapists, empathy was redefined as a tool to understand another person's thought processes, emotions, and experiences. As therapists learned and mastered the skill of empathy, it became widely assumed that empathy was too complex as a skillset to be born with, challenging Allport's and Clark's positions on empathy as an innate trait. Generalizing the idea of empathy from academic research and therapy practices, Frank (1985) claimed empathy was an ability anyone can gain through education, whether formal or informal. Frank also connected the dots between empathy and social systems, noting that empathy most often becomes a way people connect with a victim or someone in a "lesser" position than them in society. Frank's idea of empathy, seen through the lens of social class, provided insight into how empathy across all social identities was possible. Clark (1980) made that same call to action, with his specific example being about how White people should be practicing empathy toward African American people.

Today's popular definition of empathy is authored by Lanzoni (2018): it is "our capacity to grasp and understand the mental and emotional lives of others" (p. 3). As the definition of empathy has become more concrete over time, society sees that empathy is an employable skill used to learn about others' experiences. At the same time, the questions I pose at the beginning of this chapter remain unanswered. For this chapter, I invite the reader to keep the following questions in mind:

1. When I practice empathy, who or what do I pay attention to?
2. What do I learn from the process of empathizing?

Turning to Wonder With Empathy

Placing empathy at the center of conversation may help answer the two questions I posed; but it is important that I first situate myself in the conversation between us (author and reader). The theory of Being invites us to explore our own relationship with a conflict by first calling on us to discern our motivations for existing with conflict and those involved in it. Here, I hope to apply *personal ways of Being* by reflecting on the ways I have practiced empathy as well as my exploration of the dissonance that resulted from this reflection.

I was raised in a small, Midwestern farming community in Wisconsin. I could count the number of People of Color on one hand, and "diversity" was not a topic of discussion. Being a White man, I saw myself represented in all parts of the community—my family, friends, local role models, and authority figures were all White and predominantly male. As a result, it was easy to exist as myself, seeing that almost everyone I encountered looked like me. At the same time, being raised in a homogenous environment resulted in being sheltered from discussions on racism, sexism, or any other system of oppression. It was not until I came out as queer and autistic that I started to internalize the power and role of empathy in conflict, but, as my reflection later in the chapter will reveal, my marginalization did not mean that I knew how to empathize with those who were marginalized in identities where I held privilege.

Now that I have briefly talked about how I appear in spaces, let me discuss how I came to embody the theory of Being. In graduate school, I was in a course where the discussion topic was about our experience with race and racism. Given my own identities and background, this was my first real experience explicitly talking about race and doing so alongside People of Color who spanned different races and ethnicities. In listening to my fellow classmates, particularly those who were not White, talk about their experiences with racism, I employed empathy to try and listen and understand their experiences. In their stories, I imagined myself navigating the events they described and dissected their emotional state as best I could. By the end of each of their stories, I thought I had an idea of how to respond to keep the conversation going. When I responded, I immediately felt tension in the room. Hearing my classmates, specifically those who were People of Color, talk through some of their feelings about my response, I became angry and even more tense, but I did not know where it was coming from. I decided to practice living the questions by "turning to wonder" (Rauppius, 2016, para. 2) to start a conversation with myself to reflect on my internal dissonance while navigating dissonance in the larger dialogue.

In the process of *turning to wonder*, or starting a process of questioning the source of my internal dissonance, many questions ran through my mind: "I wonder why tension now exists when I meant no harm? Did others in this conversation misunderstand me? Why did my classmates, some of whom I consider friends, not respond to me in a positive way? Why am I getting angry at them, when they are simply listening to what I am saying? So, is it my fault for this tension? How did I cause this tension within our conversation about race? What was it about what I did that caused tension? Did I not empathize well enough?"

The privileged identity exploration model (PIE; Watt, 2015b) describes different defenses someone employs when a dissonance-provoking stimulus is introduced during a conflict (also see Appendix E). If someone has privilege in relation to the stimulus, the PIE model explains how their immediate defensive reaction is often an attempt to protect themselves from confronting that privilege. Applied to this moment, I realized that the ways I acknowledged racism were different in certain spaces. I could talk about racism through theories I was learning in my graduate education with other White people. I wanted to show off my knowledge in how much I knew about race and racism through intellectualization (i.e., excessive reasoning). In spaces where I was with People of Color, I used denial or deflection to show that racism exists, but that I was not a part of the problem. In my example, my defenses showed up when I practiced empathy in conversation and conflict. I realized that I grew up practicing empathy on those who were like me, in ways that did not allow for personal reflection. Gone unchecked, I internalized that practice as the only way to practice empathy, and so I often practiced empathy toward People of Color or women in the same way that I used empathy to relate to other White men. There was no acknowledgement of racism and sexism when I used empathy in conversation, which led to more conflict.

So, was I even practicing empathy? How was I positioning myself within the conversation? Does the way I practice empathy have to differ depending on whom I am empathizing with? I turned to prosocial and empathy development research to help me reflect on the experience.

Dissecting Empathy

Empathy comprises two emotional and cognitive components (McDonald & Messinger, 2011). Emotional empathy is the ability to recognize and imagine another's emotional state (Knafo et al., 2008; McDonald & Messinger, 2011; Zahn-Waxler et al., 1992). Cognitive empathy is the ability to accurately describe another's imagined experience and the feelings that come with it (McDonald & Messinger, 2011). As a result, anyone is capable of empathizing (McDonand & Messinger, 2011), but the way we empathize or whom we empathize with differs from person to person.

Empathy development is claimed to start as soon as we are born and gradually progresses as we develop both emotional and cognitive awareness. More specifically, children develop the ability to empathize quickly. For children, emotional connections to others manifest almost at birth (McDonald & Messinger, 2011), while language development and social skills, as well as factors of cognitive empathy (Lobb, 2017; McDonald & Messinger, 2011) develop in early childhood. Part of the reason for rapid empathy development is that children are very mentally malleable—they can easily (and subconsciously) learn and articulate patterns exposed to them and carry them into adulthood (Eisenberg et al., 1999; McDonald & Messinger, 2011). The internalization of patterns also applies to empathy, as we are prone to practicing empathy in the ways we are exposed to it (Nook et al., 2016). Given differences in how people of different social identities practice empathy (Eisenberg et al., 2010; Lobb, 2017) and that we live in an interlocked system of privilege and oppression, empathy may actually be used to knowingly (or not) uphold these systems rather than learning how to dismantle them.

Research shows that adults can more easily practice empathy toward members of their own cultural identity than toward others of different identities (Bruneau et al., 2012) and are more likely to allocate group-based resources toward helping an ingroup member, even at the cost of the greater good for the group (Batson et al., 1995). Applied on a societal scale, we are more likely to use our full capacity for empathy toward people who look and act like us than for people who look different or act differently from us. We are also willing to drain resources from others at the cost of "helping our own." In other words, to subconsciously uphold our privilege, we must become unwavering in our faith to others who hold privilege and to social norms (Clark, 1980).

Assuming that everyone holds a combination of privileged and marginalized identities (Watt, 2015b), it seems like everyone, in some way, contributes to upholding at least one system of oppression. Studies in prosocial behaviors (e.g., Kraus et al., 2010) and neuroscience (e.g., Bruneau et al., 2012) seem to support this idea. In the latter study, researchers found that participants used less of the brain's empathetic pathways when attempting to understand experiences of those in different cultural groups than when empathizing within the same cultural group. As a result, we can claim that empathy is something that is often used, yet used inequitably, which reinforces oppressive systems.

Naming Intellectual Empathy

The misunderstandings and missed applications of empathy by people with a privileged identity come from the lack of knowledge and internalization of systems of power and oppression. As currently practiced in dialogue, empathy is often a tool, or commodity, to maintain power structures by imposing inaccurate judgments about others' experiences (Lobb, 2017), rather than being an experience to learn more about our own relationship with privilege. I call this kind of unacknowledging empathy—intellectual empathy. Intellectual empathy is the empathy practiced when someone holds a privileged identity and fails to understand or recognize the systemic factors that affect the story of the person with whom they are empathizing.

Intellectual empathy does not signify a lack of empathy. Rather, intellectual empathy signifies a lack of contextual knowledge when using empathy to understand someone different than the empathizer. We link empathy to head (thoughts), heart (feelings), and hands (action). Using cognitive empathy to imagine experiences would be the head, emotional empathy to feel the physical and mental disposition of another would be the heart, and communicating what you are feeling would be the hands. In the context of intellectual empathy, all three components are still used, but the head is communicating incomplete information to the heart and the hands, which in turn misinforms how the heart and hands manifest in feeling and explaining others' experiences. Consistent practice of intellectual empathy can lead one to commodify empathy to solve problems. Empathizing becomes an outcomes-based experience, where the primary goal is to be as accurate in empathizing as possible. In other words, someone's *discernment of motivation* within the theory of Being is misplaced.

When someone practices intellectual empathy to assume or imagine similar lived experiences across Difference (Watt, 2013), they do not have to listen deeply to feel like they understand another's experience or really focus on the dissonance of their thoughts, feelings, and actions. Intellectual empathy threatens the Being process because it can derail a conversation so that the empathizer focuses on self-protection, resulting in distancing from the conversation. In turn, the one being empathized with cannot focus on their relationship with the conflict; instead, they must redirect their energy toward their relationship with the empathizer, preventing them from practicing Being. The goal of empathy should not be to "win" at empathizing; rather, practicing empathy should be a vehicle to understand our own relationship with the conflict (e.g., *focusing on you* and *humanizing otherness in the self*).

Intellectual empathy can manifest in many ways, and therefore I present it as an umbrella term for any form of empathy that lacks awareness of one's privilege via systems of power and oppression. Chauvinistic empathy (Clark, 1980), role-playing empathy (Allport, 1954), projection empathy (Lanzoni, 2018), and doxic empathy (Lobb, 2017) are all examples of intellectual empathy. Chauvinistic empathy describes how people cannot empathize across social groups, especially if the empathizer(s) hold privilege and power in society. Role-playing allows people to gain an immersion-based experience in empathy by acting as a person in a different social group. Although it may have been effective for previous generations (Axline, 1948), we know today that role-playing allows the actors to "return" to their original positions in society, which lets them distance themselves more easily from the lessons of the exercise. Projection empathy is an early, more artistic form of empathy, where people place feelings of strife and movement into objects. Projection empathy prevents emotional empathy from playing a role, only focusing on the physical nature of a person. Finally, doxic empathy is the most similar to intellectual empathy as it describes empathy through the lack of acknowledgment of systems of power and oppression. This leads into intellectual empathy, as without that acknowledgment, one cannot practice the theory of Being to be able to exist in conflict and dialogue.

In summary, intellectual empathy lives in three ways:

1. It lacks acknowledgment or recognition of systems of power, oppression, and one's privilege (lack of *focusing on one's self*).
2. It uses empathy without the end goal of internal reflection on one's relationship with conflict (lack of *discerning motivation*).
3. It falsely internalizes the stories of those who are marginalized where one holds privilege (lack of *humanizing otherness in self*).

Assumptions of Intellectual Empathy

Three assumptions inform the idea of intellectual empathy. The first assumption is that experiencing empathy is a learned skill, as previously mentioned. The second assumption is that in learning to empathize, intellectual empathy will be inevitably practiced by those with privileged identities (i.e., White, heterosexual, male). Privilege has proven to be a barrier in empathizing with others across cultural difference (Bruneau et al., 2012; Kraus et al., 2010), and therefore people must deconstruct their socialization into privilege to move past intellectual empathy. Individuals with privileged identities must learn more about their privilege and relationships with society before they can fully realize empathy as a process. The third assumption is that to build stamina for sustained dialogue, one must practice empathy and reflect on the experience. To build stamina, one must engage in dialogue with others and interact with Difference (Watt, 2013, 2015b) around a *third thing*. Using others to practice empathy for the sake of practicing may reinforce systems of oppression, and utilizes empathy as a weapon for one's gain, rather than experiencing empathy as a guide for self-reflection. Moving beyond intellectual empathy and into the theory of Being requires from us to consistently unlearn and relearn our own privileges and to use a fully realized empathy as a way to catalyze that unlearning and relearning.

Existing in and Working Through Intellectual Empathy

In the beginning of the chapter, I talked about how I *turned to wonder* to dissect why I was causing more conflict instead of advancing conversation. I used intellectual empathy to derail dialogue by placing my own thoughts and feelings at the center of the dialogue, rather than using others' stories to explore more of my relationship with the *third thing* of race.

Existing in intellectual empathy is difficult. Without interrogating how we empathize, we might think we are good empathizers, but we cannot see how we can derail conversation. More specifically, derailment happens because we, the empathizer, focus more on our ability to empathize correctly with someone different from us, rather than using those abilities to reflect on our own relationship with the *third thing*. Working through intellectual empathy required me to reflect on how I empathize. I placed the theory of Being, research on empathy development, and my own experiences in dialogue with one another, with empathy as a *third thing*.

I realized that intellectual empathy could be examined with the help of the PIE model. Specifically, I used the PIE model as a tool to dissect my relationship with empathy and conflict. In doing so, I realized I was practicing *personal ways of Being—focusing on myself, humanizing otherness in myself,* and *discerning motivations—*all while *recognizing my own defenses*. Table 3.1 shows the connections I found between intellectual empathy and the PIE model. Through the connections, I created questions to ask myself during a dialogue to keep myself accountable to using empathy as a tool for personal reflection.

TABLE 3.1

**Relating Intellectual Empathy (IE) and the Privileged Identity Exploration (PIE)
Model Within The Theory of Being (TOB)**

PIE Defense	Denial	Deflection	Minimization	Rationalization	Intellectualization	False Envy	Principium	Benevolence
Summary of Defense	Rejects/ Denies existence of the dissonance-provoking stimulus (DPS)	Shifts focus of DPS toward another source	Downplays emotional impact of DPS	Generates tolerable alternative explanations to justify DPS	Attempts to explain DPS with scientific evidence	Expresses affection toward a (feature of a) person that represents the DPS	Uses a personal value or principle to argue against DPS	Uses a large gesture to buffer one's relationship with the DPS
Quality of IE in relation to TOB	Lack of focusing on self		Lack of humanizing otherness in self			Lack of discerning motivation		
Questions to Engage Personal Ways of Being	If ism exists, how would that affect my interpretation of the story I am listening to? What identities do I have in relation to them or the conflict?	If I am responsible for upholding the ism, how do I imagine my role in the story I'm listening to?	What would I feel if I fully acknowledge their emotional and physical experiences with this conflict?	Why am I trying to generate new explanations if the story I'm listening to is the one I need to empathize with?	How am I imagining others' relationships with this conflict when they speak about their experiences? How can I disregard what I know from research in order to empathize with the person in front of me?	What does my want to compliment or express affection tell me about my goal of using empathy?	What would I learn if my value(s) didn't exist when I practiced empathy? How can I step outside of my beliefs to listen to their story?	How can empathy become my gesture in a dialogue, instead of talking about my life outside of this dialogue?

Note: Isms refer to a distinctive system, practice, behavior, and/or quality associated with social constructions that purveys dialogue such as racism, heterosexism, sexism.

Another way of working through intellectual empathy is by thinking about the relationship between one's marginalized and privileged identities. As this chapter emerged, I placed empathy as a *third thing* in dialogue with many others, including the editors of this book. In doing so, we arrived at a conversation about how one could use their marginalization in one identity to understand their privilege in another. For example, as a gay man, I experience marginalization in comparison to straight and straight-passing people. As a White person, I experience immense racial privilege.

Here, I can practice living into the theory of Being by placing my gay identity and my White identity in conversation with one another, placing empathy as a *third thing*. When I think about the process of empathy, I find that my gay identity wishes more people would listen to my story and internalize my emotional distress from marginalization, but my White identity does not feel that same strife. Since both identities exist within me, I have worked to center the thoughts on marginalization when in a dialogue on race. In turn, I practice *personal ways of Being* through *humanizing otherness within myself* and *practicing listening with authenticity and depth*. I use others' experiences, along with conversations between my own identities, to try and move past the barriers my privilege brings in dialogue to reflect on my relationship with conflict.

Again, given that each of us has a collection of marginalized and privileged identities (Watt, 2015b), I encourage the reader to host a conversation between their own marginalized and privileged identities about how you give and receive empathy. In doing so, my hope is that the reader gains an insight into the ways empathy is practiced in different spaces, and how one can listen with full authenticity in each dialogue. Readers can also feel free to use the questions in Table 3.1 to guide that internal conversation. In other words, ask yourself: "Do my privileged identities practice empathy in a way that would honor my marginalized identities?"

Unfortunately, I do not believe that there is a definitive or finite answer to the questions in Table 3.1, or to the questions an individual may pose in a dialogue with another person. As society changes and our relationship to our identities changes, we will also change in how we interact with others. My hope is that these questions can help readers observe their empathy patterns when interacting with others. These questions are not meant to be answered as a way for us to say that we are practicing (or not) intellectual empathy. Just as we can be unaware of our privilege, we can also be unaware of how we are using intellectual empathy in a dialogue. Therefore, practicing reflection on empathy does not mean we get to pat ourselves on the back for "learning to empathize correctly," but rather we can learn how to exist in a dialogue at the personal level.

Conclusion

The way we currently practice empathy may work in some circumstances, but not when we consider the complexity of identity. In empathizing with people of different identities about experiences that involve our privilege or marginalization, we must consider the ways in which our privilege and marginalization show up in dialogue. We must also account for the ways in which privilege or marginalization appears in our relationship with the experience being described. When we do not account for these, we practice intellectual empathy.

Intellectual empathy involves not knowing or ignoring Difference and the systems of power and oppression that constitute it (Watt, 2015b). This inhibits our ability to use empathy as a guide for reflection on how we relate to both others and the conflict within dialogue. By practicing intellectual empathy, we can make others in a dialogue feel othered or singled out, resulting in an us-versus-them derailment of dialogue. As a result, intellectual empathy may do more harm than good by reinforcing systems of power and oppression through othering those of marginalized identities.

Navigating intellectual empathy is difficult to do, but the theory of Being serves as a guide in this reflection. By asking ourselves questions and placing empathy as a *third thing* alongside our own identities, we can reflect on how intellectual empathy emerges at the personal level. Identifying when and how we use intellectual empathy in various dialogues will help us improve our ability to live into the theory of Being.

As a White, autistic, gay man, I am better able to empathize with those who are White, autistic, gay, and/or men. That is part of our socialization into this world—we naturally group with and empathize more authentically with those who are like us. It also meant I had a lot of work to do as I entered a field as diverse as higher education. In a single conversation about race, I noticed my own dissonance and had to confront it. In that moment, I started answering questions I posed for myself as a point of reflection and found that how I empathized with People of Color was not fully authentic; my lack of knowledge of my own privilege became a barrier in practicing something so commonly talked about today.

I hope my reflection on this moment will serve as a point of reflection for the readers. By naming intellectual empathy, I felt more empowered to examine how I exist in dialogue, living into the theory of Being through continuous reflection on my *personal ways of Being*. I hope this chapter also helps the reader to reflect on the ways we practice something that we take for granted, like empathy, in dialogue in the spirit of the theory of Being.

Note

1. A *third thing* is a process-oriented concept (Saussy, 2011; Smith, 2005) which places complex social constructs (e.g., race, gender) as subjects at the center of dialogue to examine them as shared experiences between those in dialogue together. Treating these social constructs as transcendent third things holds each community member accountable to the subject *including as well as beyond their particular positionality* (Watt, 2015a).

References

Allport, G. W. (1954). *The nature of prejudice*. Addison-Wesley.

Axline, V. M. (1948). Play therapy and race conflict in young children. *Journal of Abnormal and Social Psychology, 43*(3), 300–310. https://doi.org/10.1037/h0053655

Batson, C. D., Batson, J. G., Todd, R. M., Brummett, B. H., Shaw, L. L., & Aldeguer, C. M. R. (1995). Empathy and the collective good: Caring for one of the others in a social dilemma. *Journal of Personality and Social Psychology, 68*(4), 619–631. https://doi.org/10.1037/0022-3514.68.4.619

Bohart, A. C., Elliott, R., Greenberg, L. S., & Watson, J. C. (2002). Empathy. In J. C. Norcross (Ed.), *Psychotherapy relationships that work: Therapist contributions and responsiveness to patients* (89–108). Oxford University Press.

Bruneau, E. G., Dufour, N., & Saxe, R. (2012). Social cognition in members of conflict groups: Behavioural and neural responses in Arabs, Israelis and South Americans to each other's misfortunes. *Philosophical Transactions of the Royal Society B, 367*(1589), 717–730. https://doi.org/10.1098/rstb.2011.0293

Clark, K. B. (1980). Empathy: A neglected topic in psychological research. *American Psychologist, 35*(2), 187–190. https://doi.org/10.1037/0003-066X.35.2.187

Coates, T-N. (2011, December 14). A muscular empathy. *The Atlantic.* https://www.theatlantic.com/national/archive/2011/12/a-muscular-empathy/249984/

Eisenberg, N., Eggum, N. D., & Di Giunta, L. (2010). Empathy-related responding: Associations with prosocial behavior, aggression, and intergroup relations. *Social Issues and Policy Review, 4*(1), 143–180. https://doi.org/10.1111/j.1751-2409.2010.01020.x

Eisenberg, N., Guthrie, I. K., Murphy, B. C., Shepard, S. A., Cumberland, A., & Carlo, G. (1999). Consistency and development of prosocial dispositions: A longitudinal study. *Child Development, 70*(6), 1360–1372. https://doi.org/10.1111/1467-8624.00100

Frank, G. (1985). "Becoming the other": Empathy and biographical interpretation. *Biography, 8*(3), 189–210. https://doi.org/10.1353/bio.2010.0479

Knafo, A., Zahn-Waxler, C., Van Hulle, C., Robinson, J. L., & Rhee, S. H. (2008). The developmental origins of a disposition toward empathy: Genetic and environmental contributions. *Emotion, 8*(6), 737–752. https://doi.org/10.1037/a0014179

Kraus, M. W., Côté, S., & Keltner, D. (2010). Social class, contextualism, and empathic accuracy. *Psychological Science, 21*(11), 1716–1723. https://doi.org/10.1177/0956797610387613

Lanzoni, S. (2018). *Empathy: A history.* Yale University Press. https://doi.org/10.2307/j.ctv5cgb7s

Lanzoni, S. (2019, February 22). Why empathy is the key to dismantling white racism. *The Washington Post.* https://www.washingtonpost.com/outlook/2019/02/22/why-empathy-is-key-dismantling-white-racism/

Lobb, A. (2017). Critical empathy. *Constellations: An International Journal of Critical and Democratic Theory, 24*(4), 594–607. https://doi.org/10.1111/1467-8675.12292

McDonald, N. M., & Messinger, D. S. (2011). The development of empathy: How, when, and why. In J. J. Sanguineti, A. Acerbi, & J. A. Lombo (Eds.), *Moral behavior and free will: A neurobiological and philosophical approach* (pp. 333–359). IF-Press.

Nook, E. C., Ong, D. C., Morelli, S. A., Mitchell, J. P., & Zaki, J. (2016). Prosocial conformity: Prosocial norms generalize across behavior and empathy. *Personality and Social Psychology Bulletin, 42*(8), 1045–1062. https://doi.org/10.1177/0146167216649932

NorthwesternU. (2008, July 15). *2006 Northwestern commencement—Sen. Barack Obama* [Video]. YouTube. https://www.youtube.com/watch?v=2MhMRYQ9Ez8

Rauppius, K. (2016, July 7). *Turning to wonder: Hidden truths below the surface.* Center for Courage & Renewal. https://couragerenewal.org/wpccr/turning-to-wonder-hidden-truths/

Saussy, H. (2011). Comparison, world literature, and the common denominator. In A. Behad & D. Thomas (Eds.), *A companion to comparative literature* (1st ed., pp. 60–64). Wiley-Blackwell. https://doi.org/10.1002/9781444342789

Smith, M. K. (2005). Parker J. Palmer: Community, knowing and spirituality in education. In *The encyclopedia of informal education.* http://infed.org/mobi/parker-j-palmer-community-knowing-and-spirituality-in-education/

Trout, J. D. (2009). *The empathy gap: Building bridges to the good life and the good society.* Viking.

Watt, S. K. (2013). Designing and implementing multicultural initiatives: Guiding principles. In S. K. Watt & J. Linley (Eds.), *Creating Successful Multicultural Initiatives in Higher Education and Student Affairs* (New Directions for Student Services, no. 144, pp. 5–15). Jossey-Bass. https://doi.org/10.1002/ss.20064

Watt, S. K. (2015a). Authentic, action-oriented framing for environmental shifts (AAFES) method. In S. K. Watt (Ed.), *Designing multicultural transformational initiatives: Theoretical foundations, practical applications, and facilitator considerations* (pp. 23–39). Stylus.

Watt, S. K. (2015b). Privilege identity exploration (PIE) model revisited. In S. K. Watt (Ed.), *Designing multicultural transformational initiatives: Theoretical foundations, practical applications, and facilitator considerations* (pp. 40–57). Stylus.

Zahn-Waxler, C., Radke-Yarrow, M., Wagner, E., & Chapman, M. (1992). Development of concern for others. *Developmental Psychology, 28*(1), 126–136. https://doi.org/10.1037/0012-1649.28.1.126

4

SHAME

Audrey Scranton

It was during a conference presentation in graduate school that I first encountered shame in my efforts to be a part of social justice. I was presenting my first single-author paper, and I was nervous. I was afraid not just because it was my first presentation alone, or even because it was the first time a respondent would provide feedback (and a very high-profile scholar, at that); I was anxious about how my paper would be received because it was about experiences of Muslim women, and I am a nonreligious White person. While I had not seen anything wrong about it when I was writing the paper, it occurred to me as I was about to present to a room full of people that it might be an issue: I was representing a group to which I did not belong.

My trepidation escalated each time applause filled the room. When it was my turn to present, I explained that I wrote this paper as part of a class on how stories can be a form of resistance against oppression and that I studied Muslim American women's identity presentations in stories they posted online. I described how I analyzed the stories and argued that the women practiced resistance to dominant oppressive narratives about who they are by emphasizing their complexities. When I finished, the respondent stood and spoke. When she got to my paper, she voiced tough, but fair, critiques to the room full of people. The biggest were that I failed to describe my positionality and that I was remarginalizing these women by assuming in my paper that Muslim meant they all had Middle Eastern heritage. I had not been aware of that assumption while writing my paper, but when she spoke, I knew it to be true. In effect, I was implicitly imposing a simple and unilateral identity upon all these women, limiting the complexity of ways in which these women can represent themselves. I therefore directly contradicted the point I had been trying to make.

When these critiques fell upon my ears, my body reacted immediately. My cheeks grew hot as my hands began to shake. My throat burned. I bit my tongue to keep tears from rising in my eyes. I kept my head down to avoid meeting someone's eyes, afraid of what they would see if they peered into my mind. Shame had taken over me, coursing from my face to my feet and paralyzing my body and voice. I did my best to answer the questions the audience asked, but I felt disconnected from my body.

When a Muslim woman came to talk to me at the panel's conclusion, I felt myself shrinking as she made suggestions for how to talk about Muslim identities in the future. Even though she also had positive things to say about the paper, I could barely comprehend what she was saying, as I was so drawn into my internal experience. I could feel my mind swimming in shame, guilt, and even some defiance, as I was confused about how I could have done something wrong. I felt like I had failed in trying to think of every possible outcome that would prevent me from hurting someone, from misrepresenting, from making me feel this way. My mind was preoccupied all day with the respondent's comments, and I had never felt smaller.

As I struggled to make sense of what that encounter meant for my determined passion to be a part of social justice, I found myself in desperate need of guidance. I had made an egregious error; I had spoken for an oppressed community to which I did not belong without being in conversation with anyone who held those identities. Though I could state that my intentions were good, my biases, of which I had not been aware, caused harm and I was called out for it, as I should have been. But somehow this information was not influencing me to learn what I had done wrong and act differently in the future. The shame I experienced from making a mistake consumed me. It knocked me down so hard that I was not sure whether I deserved to get up again in this arena or had a place within it. I questioned whether I, with the privileges that I had, could ever speak or fight for oppressed communities without remarginalizing them.

For almost a year after that encounter, I avoided social justice topics or advocacy. To be "safe" and to prevent myself from ever feeling that way again, I withdrew from participating in causes for which I used to be passionate. I constantly questioned my ability to contribute because I was afraid of hurting people. The risk seemed too great that I might make another mistake.

Being With Shame

If social justice matters to you or you try to be an ally to marginalized groups, this situation might be familiar. If you advocate for justice or inclusion for a group to which you do not belong, at some point you will make a mistake.

When we are made aware of these mistakes, difficult and uncomfortable feelings can arise. We might feel confused, defensive, guilty, or a messy combination of all three. Out of all the tough emotions that can arise shame is the most damaging, both to ourselves and others. I tell this story because I think the experience of wrestling with shame in social justice is one to which many people can relate. More importantly, I want to illustrate that, in this instance, shame, related to my privileged identities, prevented me from productively engaging in the fight for equity. The fact that I started to withdraw into myself and found it difficult to hear other people supports this point. If we become skilled in processing these emotions by adopting *ways of Being*, they can transform into increased understanding so we can make better mistakes in the future. If we do not, we tend to offload our pain onto someone else or internalize feelings of unworthiness.

In this chapter, I will outline how the theory of Being can help us work through shame that emerges in response to reckoning with our privileged identities, or the shame of privilege. I speak specifically about it because I want to distinguish between this experience and shame that arises from holding marginalized identities. The theory of Being offers us a path to pause, intentionally be with messy feelings, and use them as fuel to move forward for social justice. I will explain what shame is, discuss how it is different from guilt, and explore why it can be so destructive. I will describe how the theory of Being helps us learn how to first be with this type of shame and transform it before acting, preventing us from falling into common pitfalls and harming ourselves and others. Finally, I will describe specific skills that we can practice to recognize and to transform shame in kind and productive ways.

Exploring the Shame of Privilege

To work through an emotion as dark and difficult as shame, we must first understand it. Experiencing shame in response to being made aware of one's privilege or mistakes is common. Becoming aware of our mental tendencies can help us effectively notice when difficult feelings arise so we can better know how to manage and transform them.

What Is Shame?

Shame is one of the most powerful and destructive emotions humans experience. Lewis (1995) illustrates how shame can feel: shame "encompasses the whole of ourselves; it generates a wish to hide, to disappear, or even to die" (p. 2). Shame is a universal emotion (Wong, 2019), and it often hides under secondary emotions like pain, embarrassment, grief, or anger

(Malik, 2019). Shame is a self-conscious experience and involves our beliefs about how other people view us (Gilbert, 2019). Most of our experiences of shame are related to social rejection, isolation, or devaluation, and shame may function as a motivator to uphold these relationships. Shame is also used as a form of social control (Gilbert, 2019). When unprocessed, it can lead to self-harm, social withdrawal, and depression (Wong, 2019). It can also be destructive externally, in the form of aggression toward other people (Brown, 2010; Elison, 2019). Even though shame is a ubiquitous experience, culture plays a large part in the construction of situations that we perceive as shameful (Wong, 2019). For instance, perceiving our body, job, or ability level as shameful is constructed through cultural narratives. Shame is pervasive and can wreak havoc on society and our relationships. As Brown (TED, 2012) says, "shame is an epidemic in our culture, and to get out from underneath it, to find our way back to each other, we have to understand how it affects us and how it affects the way we are parenting, the way we are working, and the way we look at each other" (18:13).

Guilt Versus Shame

The differences between shame and guilt are critical in informing how we engage in relationships (Gilbert, 2019; TED, 2012). Brown (2010) explains the difference between the two and how they function. In her research, Brown (2010) defines guilt as a psychological discomfort that comes from acting against our values. In other words, guilt says that you did something bad, whereas shame says that you are something bad. In contrast to shame, guilt holds who we want to be up against something we did and motivates us to act differently in the future. It is uncomfortable, but adaptive, whereas shame is destructive. Gilbert (2019) uses an evolutionary analysis to distinguish between shame and guilt. She says that shame is associated with social sanction, stigma, and being diminished in some way, whereas guilt focuses on the harm being done. Guilt can lead to attempts at restitution (Brown, 2010) such as White people developing favorable evaluations of affirmative action (Swim & Miller, 1999). However, guilt about one's privileges is not necessarily productive; guilt can still be a self-focused emotion, characterized by a preoccupation with one's internal state and the extent to which one is responsible for doing harm (Roseman et al., 1990). Furthermore, attempts to salve such guilt might not be useful for targets of oppression (Iyer et al., 2003). Nevertheless, guilt tends to be more productive than shame.

If guilt focuses on behaviors, shame focuses on the self. Shame crumbles a person's sense of self-worth and fuels disengagement (Brown, 2010).

Brown (2010) discusses shame's ability to paralyze. Shame, she says, is the intensely painful experience of believing that because we are flawed, we are unworthy of love and belonging. She explains its ability to destruct:

> Shame is the mother of all negative emotions. We may become angry, when we are humiliated or shamed; depressed and even suicidal, when we are ashamed of our own existence; rude and arrogant, when we want to cover up our inferior feelings; lonely and isolated, when we feel too ashamed of ourselves to reach out; addicted, when we are too ashamed to live with our failure and guilt. (Brown, 2010, p. 5)

Shame is highly correlated with violence, bullying, and aggression, while guilt is inversely correlated with these behaviors (Gilbert, 2019; TED, 2012). Brown warns that when we try to compartmentalize or avoid such pain, "it festers, grows, and leads to behaviors that are completely out of line with whom we want to be" (Brown, 2015, p. 59). Shame is perhaps the most powerful force that keeps people from moving forward, and it can prevent people from taking part in activism.

Understanding the Shame of Privilege

I will explain why shame might emerge when we are made aware of our privileges by explaining how this works with White privilege. I am using White privilege as an example because it is a context that I am familiar with both academically and personally. Although I am explaining one privileged identity in the context of the United States, I believe there are many parallels to other privileged identities.

White people think of racism in ways that absolve them of blame. Most White people in the United States grow up with the understanding that racism is an attitude, and therefore exists within individual people. With this conception, many people see "color-blindness," or ignoring people's races in efforts to treat everyone fairly, as the best way to promote equality (Bonilla-Silva, 2014). However, racism is also alive through structures. Structural racism refers to "a network of social relations at social, political, economic, and ideological levels that shapes the life chances of the various races" (Bonilla-Silva, 2014, p. 32). Structural racism describes how discrimination, unequal treatment, and exclusion of People of Color exist and persist through social, political, and legal mechanisms. Explanations of structural racism draw attention to the fact that White people have oppressed People of Color for centuries. Therefore, this knowledge can be a dissonance-provoking stimulus for White people (Watt, 2007), who might suddenly become aware that racism is all around them.

Learning about White privilege can also be distressing to White people. The term "privilege" shifts conversations about oppression, drawing attention to unacknowledged advantages of groups that are not marginalized in mainstream society. Discussions of White privilege shift thinking away from ideas that White people tend to internalize. McIntosh (1988) explains: "Whites are taught to think of their lives as morally neutral, normative, and average, and also ideal, so that when we work to benefit others, this is seen as work which will allow 'them' to be more like 'us'" (p. 166). McIntosh argues that using the term "White privilege" makes White people accountable in the fight for racial justice by asking White people to lessen, end, or give up their unearned power. This term confronts them with the fact that White people cannot escape the fact of their whiteness; their racial identities continue to benefit them in ways that they cannot control. Such a perspective directly contradicts the idea many White people grow up with, which is seeing oneself as "an individual whose moral state depend[s] on her individual moral will" (McIntosh, 1988, p. 166). This newfound awareness and distress are also common for awareness of other forms of oppression and privileges, such as ableism, sexism, or heterosexism. When someone becomes aware that they have benefited unknowingly from systems that discriminate against others, uncomfortable emotions can arise.

As difficult as these emotions can be to manage, they are necessary for people to experience to process their privileges. For example, White identity development models (e.g., Helms, 1995; Linder, 2015; Scott & Robinson, 2001) all incorporate dissonance, guilt, or shame as part of the process of emerging awareness of White racial identity. Because racial dissonance marks a moment when a previous schema for understanding race no longer makes sense (Helms, 1995, 2008), it is deemed necessary for White awareness and racial engagement; it is a decision point, or a time in which someone must make a decision about who they are going to be (Knefelkamp et al., 1978). This discomfort makes us reflect on the work we do, our audiences, and how our identities interact with the cultures within which we live (Mueller & Pickett, 2015).

The Destruction of Shame

Experiencing shame does not determine whether you will take positive actions to address your privileges. However, because of its focus on the self, shame can be destructive in a variety of ways. Gilbert (2019) and Elison (2019) distinguish between two common responses to feeling shame: external aggression toward others, or internal criticism and flagellation. These automatic responses are attempts to manage the intensity of shame's painful feelings. In social justice, shame can offload responsibility onto other people in two primary ways: defensiveness or internalization.

In an effort to protect one's sense of self, a common response of shame is to get defensive and push responsibility for one's privilege onto others. Watt's (2007) privileged identity exploration (PIE) model examines some of the defensive reactions people have to difficult dialogues about racism, sexism, homophobia, and ableism. The model assumes that people have primal responses to protect the ego—or sense of self—when cognitive dissonance (or an incompatible belief) occurs. Dissonance is brought about by new information or awareness that challenges how people think about themselves (Watt, 2007). Fear is the baseline response to new information, like telling people that they personally have advantages that other people do not and they individually might participate in racial oppression. Such a response might also occur due to the unconscious fear of having to give up power (Watt, 2007). Defensive barriers emerge to prevent such exploration of one's identities. The cognitive dissonance that arises from information that your history was built on institutional "isms" that enabled your privileges can trigger a sense of your own personal badness.

Because shame is highly correlated with violence, aggression, and other destructive behaviors (Gilbert, 2019; TED, 2012), the connection between the feeling of shame and the erection of these defenses makes sense. The defenses—which include *denial, deflection, rationalization, intellectualization, principium, false envy, benevolence, or minimization*—ultimately provide external explanations that absolve an individual from taking responsibility for their privilege. Watt (2007) provides an example of what denial of one's privilege looks like in conversation in her study of students' written responses to issues of privilege and oppression:

> I worked hard for where I am today and deep down I don't really want to recognize my White privilege because I don't want to have this White privilege and I'm not sure it exists. I just don't believe it exists, I mean look at how many Blacks are on television today. (p. 120)

In this example, the speaker is not able to reach a place where they wish to take some rectifying action to make up for the wrongs their privilege accumulates. In response to feeling bad—or perhaps to avoid feeling bad—the person directs the defenses at the expense of marginalized folks.

Besides triggering our defenses, shame can also cause self-flagellation that paralyzes us and causes us to retreat. Elison (2019) explains that there are four primary responses to shame—attacking others, attacking ourselves, withdrawal from others, and avoidance (or hiding from oneself). Attacking ourselves or avoiding any situation in which we might make a similar mistake in the future are common reactions to protect ourselves (Baumann & Handrock, 2019). When we turn on ourselves in shame, we feel unworthy and broken (TED, 2012). Rather than focusing on outward explanations to prevent us from feeling a personal sense of badness, internalization punishes ourselves, which can lead to unproductive responses. One could argue that internalization and retreat are also defensive reactions in social justice because it involves avoiding the possibility of confronting our internalized oppression toward others. It is an unproductive response because it involves retreating into our privilege. Shame is more likely to help us feel as if we are broken and lead to attacking or withdrawing from others or ourselves. Shame is ubiquitous but also tricky to work with and requires a conscious approach. So what do we do with it? We fight its tendency to shut us down and face it instead.

Facing the Shame of Privilege

Even though shame can be devastating to experience, embracing it is necessary to transform it for individual and collective growth (Wong, 2019). Working through shame is not only productive individually, but can also model to others how to stay engaged, thus having positive ripple effects into our communities. The theory of Being teaches us particular ways to work with ourselves and others effectively so that we can transform our relationships, communities, and society. Understanding how shame factors into our actions and decisions is important to understanding how to engage it productively. We want to get to a place where we are compassionate with ourselves while also taking accountability for our mistakes, identities, and experiences. This work is difficult, but entirely possible. Here are some places to start.

Personal Ways of Being

Learning how to relate to shame in productive ways often starts with ourselves. The theory of Being outlines *personal ways of Being* that help us focus on self-awareness and our authentic personal connections to conflict. Personal Being practices involve us noticing, nurturing, and naming what is going on inside us. Upon noticing shame, you can practice *focusing on you*. Focusing on self involves asking questions regarding how you relate to the conflict: How am I situated with the particular conflict being explored? What feelings arise in me as I contemplate my relationship to this conflict? When shame arises, it can be tempting to offload the discomfort onto someone else or spiral it in toward yourself. Asking introspective questions about what's going on in your mind, heart, and body can help you be intentional in working through it.

When we feel strong discomfort or unpleasant emotions, first pause with them. Watch your first reactions without judgment. Do feelings of anger, defiance, or embarrassment come up? Notice those emotions and speak to yourself in a compassionate way. Think about what you might say to soothe a friend who was feeling this way (without blaming or attacking another person; Neff, 2011). Remind yourself why these emotions emerge when doing this work; structurally, privilege feels very personal. Tell yourself that many other people feel or have felt this same way before. Remind yourself that failing is a normal part of this work, and reapproach the situation to understand what you can do better once you are ready. Be aware when feelings of inadequacy turn to the tendency to blame others, lash out, or prove yourself to others. Notice these propensities and do not judge yourself for them. These are normal reactions. Take a moment to understand why they emerge, but be very careful about expressing them. Tell yourself you will not act until you have time to cool off and think more clearly about the situation.

One of the tools that I have found most transformational for focusing on yourself is mindfulness. Mindfulness can be understood as being fully present and awake to our lives and experiences (Kabat-Zinn, 1990). It has roots in ancient spiritual traditions, most systematically articulated in Buddhism, which is over 2,500 years old (Vanderheiden, 2019). It is associated with several practices, including meditation, that help you observe your thoughts and emotions without getting caught up in them. The result of practicing mindfulness is that we become acquainted with our tendencies. This can provide us a deep familiarity with our natural defensiveness when shame is triggered. Mindfulness coupled with self-compassion can bring greater clarity to difficult emotional situations and help guide us forward after processing the emotions. Chödrön (2002) explains this relationship: "If this process of clear seeing isn't based on self-compassion, it will become a process of self-aggression. We need self-compassion to stabilize our minds. We need it to work with our emotions. We need it in order to stay" (p. 27).

Mindfulness was introduced into Western psychology and medicine in the 1970s with differences in conceptualization and implementation between cultures (Vanderheiden, 2019) as well as appropriation. Whereas the spiritual traditions of Eastern mindfulness focus on our interconnectedness and communal nature, Western mindfulness often divests itself of this perspective and sees mindfulness as a tool for individual stress management (Ishikawa, 2018). Although mindfulness practices can certainly be individually beneficial, such a perspective upholds capitalism by using mindfulness as a tool to create greater productivity (Ishikawa, 2018). If we carry individualism with us in practicing mindfulness, we not only perpetuate the misrepresentation and appropriation of its spiritual traditions, but we also miss opportunities for collective healing of shame (Wong, 2019). Collective healing recognizes that we are all part of broken systems that perpetuate shame. Having a communal perspective on mindfulness also recognizes how our privilege has a role within the systems and motivates us to change structures for social justice. Ishikawa (2018) explains, "although mindfulness is individually practiced, it serves a much larger purpose; our sense of interconnectedness allows us to *better serve others*" (p. 108). If we start with ourselves and model for others how to create deliberate and sustained engagement through difficult topics, we can heal our communities.

Relational Ways of Being

Shame emerges in relationship with others, and it can also be healed in relationship with others. *Relational ways of Being* reflect thoughts, feelings, and actions that focus on relational awareness about the self and others while in conflict. *Exploring defenses* is a relational strategy to help us understand what informs how we view things and how to be in the moment: What perspective or experiences inform how I and others relate to this conflict? How can I be good company while exploring conflict? I will explore what cultural beliefs exacerbate our tendencies to get defensive according to the PIE model.

The belief in individualism that permeates through Western societies sets us up to see mistakes as personal failures. Messages from every facet of culture including media, our caregivers, and relationships teach us to seek personal happiness through hard work and to pull ourselves up by our bootstraps (Weber, 1958). Although the value of hard work is not problematic within itself, a harmful side effect of this story is that when you experience discomfort or make mistakes, the fault is entirely on you as an individual. Without the right support, it is unfair for individuals to be held to such unrealistic standards. As Martin Luther King Jr. famously said, "it is cruel just to say to a bootless man that he ought to lift himself by his own bootstraps" (WLRN, 2014). This mentality coupled with capitalism's focus on quick fixes (Roberts, 2014) in response to feeling discomfort (such as being made aware of one's privileges) can lead us to respond to shame automatically by offloading responsibility onto others or attacking ourselves. Offloading responsibility can look like *benevolence* or *minimization* (Watt, 2007), which are defenses that occur when attempting to address privileged identity. Both *benevolence* and *minimization* focus on individual actions or attitudes in attempts to solve the uncomfortable feelings that emerge when we are confronted with our privileges. When we recognize that we experience such a defensive reaction, our challenge is to intentionally replace them with new ones that understand our interconnectedness, the forces that shape us, and the power and privileges we have. When you feel a sense of personal failure around your privileges, recall the historical forces that have positioned you to have such privilege. Envision yourself as one member of a larger community positioned there by forces out of your control, then recall that you do have control over your future actions and how you use your privilege.

Another harmful belief fostered by Western culture is that if we can do everything perfectly, we can avoid pain, discomfort, or causing harm to others. Brown (2010) describes perfectionism as one of the ways we try to protect ourselves from shame. Perfectionism can foster denial or deflection (Watt, 2007), or defensive reactions that argue against the presence of or avoid coming to terms with a dissonance-provoking stimulus. *Humanizing ourselves and others in idea exploration* is a crucial part of transforming shame. As Chödrön (2002), an American Buddhist nun, explains, "in . . . Buddhism it is said that wisdom is inherent in emotions. When we struggle against our energy, we reject the source of wisdom" (p. 29). When we deal with our experience long enough and get to know our immediate reactions intimately, we can grow compassion for other people and learn about what actions to take in the future. Learning to feel our discomfort keeps us from perpetuating harm and oppression.

Rigid thinking is the third belief that can get us into trouble. When our sense of self-worth is threatened, we want certainty and easy answers. In a conflict, we want to see one person as right and the other person as wrong. Rigid thinking is a foundational belief in the defensive reaction *principium*, in which a person avoids exploring their privileges based on a fundamental religious or personal principle (Watt, 2007). What will cause us to grow, however, is holding the tension of paradox. We can exist with multiple conflicting emotions (such as shame and resentment or confusion and defiance) if we consciously choose to believe that enigma and uncertainty are present in every situation. The first step is to become consciously aware of our beliefs, how they affect our actions, and consciously shift what we tell ourselves makes a difference. Exploring and naming our reactions in relationships as well as the beliefs that undergird our tendencies to shut down from shame allow us to go deeper in conversation and relationship instead of causing more harm.

Community Ways of Being

Because shame is socially constructed, untangling its darkness requires Being with a community. To engage in collective healing, we must help one another.

Shame festers and grows in secrecy, silence, and judgment, but it is shrunk by empathy (Brown, 2010). When we feel connection with others and can keep our mistakes in a broader perspective, we can bypass shame's destructive tendencies and instead take positive actions. *Community ways of Being* align thoughts, feelings, and actions that focus on community awareness as a group about a conflict. In community, we can practice *viewing missteps as developmental.*

Sharing our shame with trusted others can help. When we experience shame, it can be difficult to see ourselves worthy of love and care, but receiving empathy and understanding reminds us that we are not our failures. We can also deconstruct how we are socialized and keep our mistakes within a broader context when we practice Being in a community. *Community ways of Being* can help us to see our errors as part of our story rather than the whole of who we are. When reaching out to someone to discuss your shame, choose someone whom you trust will be loving and manage your story with care. Consider naming what you are struggling with, that is, shame, and that you are looking for support and advice on what to do in the future. You might even ask questions in your conversation about how you can view your mistake as a developmental one: How might we embrace our failings as lessons rather than seeing the other as fatally flawed? What if we focused on the possibilities that might come from this conflict rather than its limitations?

When choosing someone in whom to confide about our blunders, it is important to be mindful of the social identities of all involved. For example, there is a time and a place to talk about the shame and difficult emotions that accompany being White while engaging in racial justice. If you are in a setting that is devoted explicitly or implicitly to creating space for People of Color to talk about their experiences with racism, bringing up your emotions could ultimately be counterproductive. One solution is to talk with White people who are also working for racial justice. This gives you a space to work through these emotions without burdening People of Color, making them teach you about racism, or co-opting spaces for People of Color to speak about their experiences in a safe space that they so often have to fight for.

Even though shame is a deeply personal and individual feeling, the skills to address it are relational and communal, and they are learned from the theory of Being. Recognizing our emotional reactions can feel very individual, but we need close relationships with other people to help normalize our defenses and humanize ourselves. If we learn to relate to one another in ways that allow for the tension of paradoxes and sustained engagement despite difficult emotions, we rewrite culture's beliefs to provide more fertile ground for our communities and future generations to incorporate these practices more naturally.

Shame is uncomfortable, and our first response is often to internalize, push it away, or off-load it through blame. Doing social justice work, while holding privileged identities, makes it necessary to befriend shame. The consequences of not being willing to face the dissonance that comes with this work are too great for individuals and society as a whole.

References

Baumann, M., & Handrock, A. (2019). Shame and forgiveness in therapy and coaching. In C. H. Mayer & E. Vanderheiden (Eds.), *The bright side of shame: Transforming and growing through practical applications in cultural contexts* (pp. 471–488). Springer Nature. https://doi.org/10.1007/978-3-030-13409-9

Bonilla-Silva, E. (2014). *Racism without racists: Color-blind racism and the persistence of racial inequality in the United States* (4th ed.). Rowman & Littlefield.

Brown, B. (2010). *The gifts of imperfection: Let go of who you think you're supposed to be and embrace who you are.* Hazelden Publishing.

Brown, B. (2015). *Rising strong: The reckoning. The rumble. The revolution.* Spiegel & Grau.

Chödrön, P. (2002). *The places that scare you: A guide to fearlessness in difficult times.* Shambhala Publications.

Elison, J. (2019). Interpreting instances of shame from an evolutionary perspective: The pain analogy. In C. H. Mayer & E. Vanderheiden (Eds.), *The bright side of shame: Transforming and growing through practical applications in cultural contexts* (pp. 395–412). Springer Nature. https://doi.org/10.1007/978-3-030-13409-9

Gilbert, P. (2019). Distinguishing shame, humiliation, and guilt: An evolutionary functional analysis and compassion focused interventions. In C. H. Mayer & E. Vanderheiden (Eds.), *The bright side of shame: Transforming and growing through practical applications in cultural contexts* (pp. 413–432). Springer Nature. https://doi.org/10.1007/978-3-030-13409-9

Helms, J. E. (1995). An update of Helm's White and People of Color racial identity models. In J. G. Ponterotto, L. Casas, A. Suzuki, & C. M. Alexander (Eds.), *Handbook of multicultural counseling* (pp. 181–198). SAGE.

Helms, J. E. (2008). *A race is a nice thing to have: A guide to being a White person or understanding the White persons in your life* (2nd ed.). Microtraining Associates.

Ishikawa, M. (2018). Mindfulness in Western contexts perpetuates oppressive realities for minority cultures. *Simon Fraser University Educational Review, 11*(1), 106–115. https://doi.org/10.21810/sfuer.v11i1.757

Iyer, A., Leach, C. W., & Crosby, F. J. (2003). White guilt and racial compensation: The benefits and limits of self-focus. *Personality and Social Psychology Bulletin, 29*(1), 117–129. https://doi.org/10.1177/0146167202238377

Kabat-Zinn, J. (1990). *Full catastrophe living.* Doubleday.

Knefelkamp, L., Widick, C., & Parker, C. A. (Eds.). (1978). *Applying new developmental findings.* Jossey-Bass.

Lewis, M. (1995). *Shame: The exposed self.* Simon & Schuster.

Linder, C. (2015). Navigating guilt, shame, and fear of appearing racist: A conceptual model of antiracist White feminist identity development. *Journal of College Student Development, 56*(6), 535–550. https://doi.org/10.1353/csd.2015.0057

Malik, A. (2019). Working with shame in psychotherapy: An eclectic approach. In C. H. Mayer & E. Vanderheiden (Eds.), *The bright side of shame: Transforming and growing through practical applications in cultural contexts* (pp. 381–394). Springer Nature. https://doi.org/10.1007/978-3-030-13409-9

McIntosh, P. (1988). White privilege: Unpacking the invisible knapsack. In P. S. Rothenberg (Ed.), *Race, class, and gender in the United States: An integrated study* (6th ed.; pp. 165–169). Worth Publishing.

Mueller, J. A., & Pickett, C. S. (2015). Politics of intersecting identities. In S. K. Watt (Ed.), *Designing transformative multicultural initiatives: Theoretical foundations, practical applications, and facilitator considerations.* Stylus.

Neff, K. (2011). *Self-compassion: The proven power of being kind to yourself.* Harper-Collins.

Roberts, P. (2014). Instant gratification. *The American Scholar, 83*(4), 18–23. https://theamericanscholar.org/instant-gratification/

Roseman, I. J., Spindel, M. S., & Jose, P. E. (1990). Appraisals of emotion-eliciting events: Testing a theory of discrete emotions. *Journal of Personality and Social Psychology, 59*(5), 899–915. https://doi.org/10.1037/0022-3514.59.5.899

Scott, D. A., & Robinson, T. L. (2001). White male identity development: The key model. *Journal of Counseling & Development, 79*(4), 415–421. https://doi.org/10.1002/j.1556-6676.2001.tb01988.x

Swim, J. K., & Miller, D. L. (1999). White guilt: Its antecedents and consequences for attitudes toward affirmative action. *Personality and Social Psychology Bulletin, 25*(4), 500–514. https://doi.org/10.1177/0146167299025004008

TED. (2012, July 28). *Brené Brown: Listening to shame.* [Video]. YouTube. https://www.youtube.com/watch?v=psN1DORYYV0

Vanderheiden, E. (2019). "Nothing I accept about myself can be used against me to diminish me": Transforming shame through mindfulness. In C. H. Mayer & E. Vanderheiden (Eds.), *The bright side of shame: Transforming and growing through practical applications in cultural contexts* (pp. 505–520). Springer Nature. https://doi.org/10.1007/978-3-030-13409-9

Watt, S. K. (2007). Difficult dialogues, privilege and social justice: Uses of the privileged identity exploration (PIE) model in student affairs practice. *College Student Affairs Journal, 26*(2), 114–126. http://files.eric.ed.gov/fulltext/EJ899385.pdf

Weber, M. (1958). *The Protestant work ethic and the spirit of capitalism.* Scribner.

WLRN Public Radio. (2014, January 17). *MLK: A bootless man cannot lift himself by his bootstraps.* https://www.wlrn.org/news/2014-01-17/mlk-a-bootless-man-cannot-lift-himself-by-his-bootstraps

Wong, P. T. P. (2019). From shame to wholeness: An existential positive psychology perspective. In C. H. Mayer & E. Vanderheiden (Eds.), *The bright side of shame: Transforming and growing through practical applications in cultural contexts* (pp. v–ix). Springer Nature. https://doi.org/10.1007/978-3-030-13409-9

5

SILENCE

Charles R. Martin-Stanley II

If you are neutral in situations of injustice, you have chosen the side of the oppressor. If an elephant has its foot on the tail of a mouse and you say that you are neutral, the mouse will not appreciate your neutrality.

—Desmond Tutu

D esmond Tutu was a social justice activist who made a conscious effort not to remain silent when he felt passionate about something. Silence is nuanced and its purpose is controversial. That being said, according to the Merriam-Webster dictionary, silence is the complete absence of sound or noise. In this chapter, I refer to silence as a conscious decision not to speak up when faced with the realities of privilege or oppression. Most people would say that silence is a passive trait. However, when we choose not to verbalize our thoughts, silence still can reflect the beliefs and values of an individual.

This chapter explores how silence specifically connects to the theory of Being (for details see Watt's "Part One Introduction," this volume). In this chapter, I argue that silence is an example of inaction where conflict is inherent. In addition, the theory of Being is broken down depending on the *ways of Being*. *Ways of Being* are the practices or processes of aligning thoughts (head), feelings (heart), and actions (hands) needed to support the conditions for building *personal, relational,* and *community stamina* necessary to be present with conflict. Silence is an example of our actions (hands), more specifically our inaction when facing conflict.

Silence in the face of oppression or privilege leads an individual to avoid taking a position and hide their beliefs. In the face of privilege and oppression, silence supports the existing power structure, which supports privileges for some and oppression for others. In the epigraph, Desmond Tutu's words (as cited by Quigley, 2003, p. 8), remind us that if we stay silent in the face of oppression, we enable oppressive systems. Therefore, silence is violence because it reinforces existing social structures that support oppression and privilege. Tutu saw firsthand how being silent was one reason for the longevity of the violent apartheid system in South Africa. Violence and repression against Black South Africans began to weaken only when committed individuals spoke up and took a stand against the apartheid system.

According to Wiesel (1986), a Holocaust survivor, "We must take sides. Neutrality helps the oppressor, never the victim. Silence encourages the tormentor, never the tormented" (para. 8). In the United States, we have seen several examples of social justice movements attempting to speak about some form of injustice and the resistance they receive from the dominant group. One recent example of this would be the Black Lives Matter movement. Although some would say there are only two sides, Black Lives Matter or All Lives Matter, I believe there is a third side and that is silence. Some scholars would argue that silence is an important strategy to use when navigating through one's own intersectional privileged identities; however, I argue that silence from individuals in spaces of privilege can be extremely harmful to members of marginalized groups in our society. This position is supported by both Desmond Tutu and Elie Wiesel.

Historically, many social justice advocates have fought against a culture of silence in the face of privilege and oppression. Martin Luther King, for example, once said, "The hottest place in Hell is reserved for those who remain neutral in times of great moral conflict . . . [an individual] who accepts evil without protesting against it is really cooperating with it" (as cited in Serres, 2013, para. 22). This quote clearly illuminates the harm caused by silence and neutrality and serves as a call to build a culture of advocacy and resistance to oppression and injustice. We must create a culture that discourages silence in the face of oppression and encourages active resistance to all forms of injustice. This chapter includes a brief discussion of the culture of silence, a review of the literature on intersectionality and advocacy, a discussion of silence as privilege, compliance, and violence, and four practical recommendations on how not to remain silent in situations of injustice.

Intersectionality and Advocacy

My review of scholarship begins with Mueller and Pickett (2015) who discussed the current literature on intersectionality and advocacy in higher education and in society as a whole and the importance of intersecting identities when doing social justice work. They recommended staying on a learning curve and always being open to new perspectives when confronted with situations that involve identity differences.

In addition, Paulo Freire (1970/2000) and bell hooks (1994) emphasized the importance of everyone, both the privileged and the oppressed, working together in order to dismantle systems of oppression. Potapchuk et al. (2005) provided a similar argument when discussing the power dynamics between systemic racism, internalized racism, and White privilege. Throughout this chapter, I discuss the work of several other authors who studied silence as privilege, compliance, or violence.

In particular, Sleeter and Grant (2009) discussed different frames in which to view multicultural education. The authors gave a detailed explanation of six different frameworks that a conscious scholar-practitioner can use to frame conversations and initiatives around multicultural education. The framework that would work best for this chapter is the multicultural social justice education framework (Banks, 2004).

The multicultural social justice education framework is important for this chapter because it frames the discussion in a way that focuses on both the systemic and the individual aspects of privilege and oppression. By this I mean that it allows individuals to see how they are advantaged or disadvantaged from a specific system of oppression. This framework aligns with the theory of Being. More specifically, the theory of Being strengthens the multicultural social justice education framework because of its process orientation. The educator must reflect on how the material that they are studying influences them on an individual level. Ultimately, this approach will benefit the educator because it helps them to focus on themselves within the conversation, which is one of the main *personal ways of Being*.

Being With Silence

Before I elaborate on the idea of silence as violence, I need to first clarify why silence is seen as a form of privilege.

Silence Is Privilege

According to Watt (2013), identity privilege is a set of benefits that an individual receives due to a socially constructed identity that they possess. Watt and Linley (2013) further explained the difference between targeted and agent identities. A targeted identity group is a group that does not have privilege or power in our society, whereas an agent identity group is a group that does have privilege and power in our society. Agent identities are viewed as superior in our society, which grants individuals with these identities different forms of identity privilege. A commonly known example of identity privilege is White privilege. Peggy McIntosh (2019) described different forms of White privilege including not being followed in the store or not having her individual actions being attributed to her entire race.

In a TED Talk titled *Why Gender Equality Is Good for Everyone—Men Included*, Michael Kimmel (2015) discussed an experience where he learned that he had privilege. In his conversation with fellow graduate students, a White woman said that all women were fighting against the same oppression. A Black woman in the group disagreed and asked the White woman when she looked in the mirror, whom she saw, and the White woman said that she saw a woman. The Black woman then responded by saying that she saw a Black woman. Kimmel's realization came to fruition when he realized that when he looked in the mirror, he saw a human. Privilege is often invisible to those who have it. The White woman did not see herself as White, and the White man did not see himself as White or as a man.

As I reflect on my own intersectional identities and how they are situated within the theory of Being, I use several ways of Being to make sense of my individual experience. The theory of Being helps me focus on my own *personal ways of Being*. It invites me to think about how my identities are situated within a specific discussion. For example, if we are discussing sexism, I feel that my experience is similar, although not like Kimmel's because I identify as a male. However, if the discussion is on systemic racism, my experience would be more similar to that of the Black woman because I, too, identify as a Black person. This skill of navigating through both privileged and oppressed identities is something that everyone can further develop through their internal process with the theory of Being.

Identity privilege allows privileged individuals to remain silent when it comes to situations of injustice. During the times of the civil rights movement, most White people in the North and the South remained silent, even though they knew that the mistreatment of African Americans was wrong. The choice not to speak up is a privilege that marginalized populations do not have as an option. Historically, protests are started and supported by people who have been discriminated against. An example of this would be how transgender People of Color started the gay rights movement with the demonstrations known as the Stonewall Riots (Carter, 2004). However, their voices were lost to White gay men. Although I am advocating for speaking up in spaces of privilege, I recognize that people often use their privilege of silence instead of standing up with those who are the victims of injustice in this society.

The Other Side: Burden of Responsibility

Although it is a privilege to be able to remain silent in the face of societal oppression, the decision to remain silent is somewhat complex. In *Teaching to Transgress*, hooks (1994) discussed how individuals decide whether or not to engage in social justice work in society. An important concept that hooks brings to light is the idea of the burden of responsibility: "Whose responsibility is it to do this work?"

Although I believe that it is problematic for the oppressors to tell the oppressed how to liberate themselves, I equally find it problematic for the oppressed to have to dismantle systems of oppression on their own. Should African Americans be the ones who stop the perpetuation of systemic racism in this country that started with slavery? This question can further be explored through a discussion centered on *humanizing otherness in self*, or *personal ways of Being*. They help us remember that we are all human and we all have a responsibility to see each other's humanity. This burden of responsibility is very complex, leading to a dialogue that is based on both/and thinking, not either/or mentality. The question of Being that we must ask ourselves is, "How might I act to resolve this conflict from within?" In the next section, I discuss the burden of responsibility that helps us navigate gray areas of social justice advocacy.

The Gray Area: Humanity

Freire (1970/2000) posed a question about the importance of humanity in his *Pedagogy of the Oppressed*. Humanity is a gray area when thinking about silence as a form of privilege. If members of the oppressed group understand how oppression negatively affects them, then they are more likely to speak up against the oppression of others. Looking through the both/and lens also affects the oppressor. Once they realize that oppression negatively affects their own humanity, they are more motivated to want to do something to change the oppressive system. Similarly, Watt and Linley (2013) discussed issues of humanity when exploring identity politics and how student affairs practitioners navigate through their own privileged identities. Next, I will explain how silence can be a form of compliance.

Silence Is Compliance

Seeing why silence is a form of privilege can lead us to an understanding of silence as a form of compliance. Compliance can be defined as agreeing with a decision that is made in our society. Compliance typically happens when decisions, which are based on systems of oppression, are upheld.

In America, compliance is often perpetuated through cultural hegemony. Cultural hegemony is a set of beliefs that are held by the majority and therefore held as universal beliefs by both the majority and the minority in a society (Pharr, 1997).

Pharr (1997) explored this idea in her discussion of homophobia as a form of violence. If heterosexuality is the culturally hegemonic norm, then homosexuality is deemed "wrong" or unethical because it differs from the norm. This is only one example, but generally anytime you have a normative group you will also have another group that is seen as inferior and those are the people with the targeted identities I discussed earlier in the chapter.

Although I shared the example of the Kimmel TED Talk to help conceptualize silence as privilege, I want to share a personal story to help illustrate silence as compliance. Several years ago, I was getting a haircut from one of my friends at his house. He was very good at cutting hair, and I told him that he should get his license and open up his own business. His response was that he could cut other men's hair, but he did not want to start cutting women's hair because he did not want people to think he was gay. He used a more derogatory term for members of the LGBT community, which is why I am sharing this personal experience. When he used what I will refer to as the "F-word," I froze up.

I wanted to tell him that I thought that word was offensive. I wanted to start a dialogue on how language can perpetuate systems of oppression that harm groups of people. I wanted to ask him why he associated the LGBT community with something that was negative. I wanted to do a lot of things in that moment, but regretfully I remained silent. After a long time of processing and reflecting I believe this was the moment when my silence turned into a form of compliance. This interaction made me question whether my silence meant that I agreed with what my friend had said.

This example also ties into the theory of Being. I believe that in this moment I was struggling with exploring my own defenses. Watt (2013) highlighted several privileged identity defenses. As I reflected on this moment, I could see myself struggling with my own defenses. The question I struggled with most was, "How might I generate the capacity to stay with others while we explore the uncertainty?" I felt extremely uncomfortable in this situation and instead of confronting my discomfort, I remained silent. This experience caused me a lot of cognitive dissonance so I think it is important to explore the other side of the discussion.

The Other Side: Burden of Comfort

I consider myself to be a conscious advocate and activist, so it was really troubling to me when I did not say anything to my friend about his homophobic remarks. As I reflect on the experience, I think the reason that I did not speak had to do with the concept of a burden of comfort. I did not feel comfortable bringing it up and I did not feel comfortable calling him out on what he said. In this situation, I could have relied on several of the *ways of Being* to better understand why I was struggling with this situation so much. I think my level of comfort prevented me from recognizing my own defenses and focusing on myself. It was not something that I felt in the moment affected me personally, which is why I did not speak up in the moment.

This is interesting because in regard to racism, I quite frequently call people out on racist things they may say, but in this situation, I was in a privileged and safe space. By this I mean, I identify as heterosexual and I did not see myself to be in any danger in that environment. I did not say anything which ties into privilege as a form of silence, but it also illustrates my point about privilege being a form of compliance.

The Gray Area: True Empathy

Brené Brown (2013) suggested that the only way to create a genuine empathic connection with someone else is if we are brave enough to connect with our own internal fragilities. The gray area within, our individual fragilities, promotes silence as a form of compliance. It is through understanding the power of true empathy that frees us from silence. For example, if one of my friends was in a similar situation as myself (in my haircut example) and the barber had used a racial epithet, I would have wanted my friend to speak up in the same way that I know my friends within the LGBT community would have wanted me to speak up. So, it is necessary for me and others to rely upon our ability to empathize to speak up whenever we are confronted with any form of oppression. As King (1994) stated years ago:

> I cannot sit idly by in Atlanta and not be concerned about what happens in Birmingham. Injustice anywhere is a threat to justice everywhere. We are caught in an inescapable network of mutuality, tied in a single garment of destiny. Whatever affects one directly, affects all indirectly. (p. 1)

Silence Is Violence

Silence as privilege leads to silence as compliance. Silence as compliance leads to silence as violence. The ideas connect to one another in a staircase model where the previous concept builds on the one beneath it. The third and final step to this staircase model is silence is violence. Systemic oppression is the purposeful and strategic institutionalized discrimination against a group of people due to a targeted identity that they possess. Silence about systemic oppression serves to strengthen and give validity to the different forms of oppression. Racism, sexism, and heterosexism are all examples of social constructs that systemically oppress People of Color, women, and members of the LGBT communities. Understanding systemic oppression is important because it can connect to the everyday microaggressions that Sue (2010) argued are harmful to marginalized individuals even though they may be subtle and subconscious. The "pyramid of hate" articulates how using problematic language and participating in racist, sexist, and heterosexist behaviors perpetuate harmful norms that eventually amount to cultural genocide.

One example to illustrate silence as violence is the rise of the Black Lives Matter movement in the United States. Although leaders and supporters of this movement want to bring attention to racial discrimination and police brutality in this country, several opponents of the movement have instead supported the All Lives Matter countermovement. This countermovement deflects from the issue that the Black Lives Matter movement is trying to address—the ongoing oppression against the Black community, particularly young African American men. If someone says "Black lives matter" and your response is silence or "all lives matter," then you are continuing to perpetuate a system that has historically harmed People of Color since the beginning of American history.

The divisiveness and polarization of this discussion can point to our *community ways of Being*. It speaks to how we normalize defenses and learn together. Two questions posed by the theory are, "What other feelings (negative or positive) are present during this conflict?" and "What else can we do together while we are angry with each other?" Too often we are busy being angry at each other that we do not move forward. The theory of Being can help us center our emotions and move to solutions that help us to see each other's humanity.

The Other Side: Burden of Safety

Although I define silence as a form of violence, I believe that it is important to address an alternative perspective to this controversial argument. Individuals could choose to be silent because of a burden of safety. Historically, whenever an oppressed group made progress, there was always privileged resistance. For example, in regard to racism in this country, White abolitionists often faced the same fate as runaway slaves whenever they were caught. During the Jim Crow era, White people who supported equal rights for Blacks were shunned and sometimes physically attacked. When you stand up with a marginalized population, there is always a possibility that you could lose some of the privilege that comes with privileged identity and one of those privileges is the ability to feel safe in regard to privileged identities possessed.

The Gray Area: The Mouse

The gray area in this section of the chapter is "the mouse" introduced in the quote that opened this chapter. In his famous quote, Desmond Tutu stated that you may choose to be neutral, but if an elephant has its tail on the mouse, the mouse will not appreciate your neutrality. We all make decisions that affect other people whether we realize it or not. This quote helps us think about the importance of empathy. We should care about what the mouse thinks, because we can all relate to how it feels to have an elephant's foot on our targeted identity tail. We can all feel that pain, which should push us to react. This quote also illustrates the view on silence as violence because it shows that if you do not speak up, you are using your identity privilege to remain compliant with the systemic oppression that ultimately affects us all.

The point of this chapter is not to tell individuals how to think. Instead, I am trying to bring awareness to the privileged identities that we all hold. I argue that if we do not speak up against violence and oppression, then we are contributing to the violence. If the mouse does not appreciate your neutrality/silence, then would you appreciate the neutrality/silence of another individual if you were the mouse? The last section of this chapter provides practical suggestions to how we can remain verbal advocates when faced with our own privilege.

Recommendations: Four Practical Suggestions

Being aware of your choices around silence is a controversial topic. Navigating through your own personal privileged identities is not an easy task. However, I want to leave you with practical strategies in terms of how to be an effective advocate in regard to your own privileged identities. The four practical strategies that apply to this are multipartiality, the four R system, upstander intervention, and challenging privilege. In this section, I will also talk about how these recommendations connect to the ways of Being.

Multipartiality

According to Landerman (2013), multipartiality is a method of facilitation where the facilitator engages in balancing a dialogue where both dominant and counternarratives are present. The key to this form of facilitation is understanding the power dynamics between dominant and counternarratives. For example, in Kimmel's (2015) scenario, if he were using the multipartiality facilitation model, he would engage in a dialogue where he could speak about his experiences while still learning from the experiences of both

White and Black women. Again, the key to this strategy is understanding how White experiences are dominant and challenging that narrative by listening to and learning from the experiences of individuals who do not look like him.

Multipartiality can be explored by using *relational ways of Being*. An individual can use *humanizing otherness in relationship and idea exploration* to better understand how their own view can be enhanced by trying to understand the experiences of others. This process is introspective, so it can help someone to truly think about what they are going to say before they decide to respond. Understanding the humanity of others also helps us switch from *an us-versus-them mindset to us-and-them-exploring-it* mentality, with the "it" being the system of oppression. This recommendation takes a lot of patience, but ultimately it will help the individual to better understand themselves as they try to understand others.

The Four R System

The second strategy that can be applied to advocacy work is called the "four R system" (Garcia & Hoelscher 2010). The four Rs stand for recognize, reflect, react, and reassess. The system helps manage diversity flashpoints defined as "uncomfortable, potentially explosive situations that involve differences in attitudes, values, and behaviors of people from different multicultural backgrounds" (Garcia & Hoelscher, 2010, p. 176).

The system's key strategy is to react. For example, in the scenario where I was receiving a haircut, if I would have used the four Rs, I would have been better prepared to engage in a dialogue with my friend, which could have been beneficial to both of us. Again, the key to this strategy is understanding the importance of reacting. If you remain silent, you continue to perpetuate the systems of oppression we are trying to dismantle.

The four R system can be explored using *personal ways of Being*. An individual can focus on self to deepen their own understanding of the four Rs. When an individual can focus on themselves, then they can better explore how they recognize conflict, reflect on it, react to it, and reassess it. This way of Being is important because it teaches us how to process our decisions in a way that still challenges us not to be silent when conflict arises.

Upstander Intervention

The next strategy that can be applied to advocacy work is known as "upstander intervention." Upstander intervention occurs when an individual or a group of individuals takes a stand against an act of some injustice or intolerance. The bystander effect, also known as group silence, is a social phenomenon seen when people will not get involved because they think someone else will get involved. If everyone thinks everyone else will get involved, then ultimately no one will get involved. The practice of upstander intervention was created as a counterpractice to being a bystander.

The key to this strategy is that if you see something, you say something and then do something. It may seem easy, but as I discussed earlier, often individuals do not get involved and end up being bystanders instead. For example, the Black Lives Matter movement is led by a group of people trying to bring attention to racial injustice in this country. If we remember the strategy of upstander intervention and adopt the philosophy expressed by "If you see something, say something, do something," then we will be better equipped to fight social injustice even when it comes to identities that we are privileged in.

Upstander interventions can be further explored from the angle of *community ways of Being*. A group of people can use the strategy of *balancing dialogue and action,* one of the *community ways of Being,* to collectively decide to speak up when they see or experience conflict. This specific way of Being helps us remember not to only speak about what we are going to do, but to actually do it. This is important because if we collectively learn how to speak up then we are more likely not to allow actions that further perpetuate various systems of oppression.

Challenging Privilege

The final strategy pertains specifically to the privileged identities of an individual. I strongly believe that if we are going to dismantle systems of oppression, we must do it on both global and individual levels. On an individual level we need to challenge the privileges that we accept and benefit from on a day-to-day basis. Chávez and Sanlo (2012) discussed how to be an effective higher education professional while remaining cognizant of one's intersectional identities. The scholars cited Pete Englin, director of the Division of Student Life at Iowa State University, who described a time when he challenged his White privilege in a way that challenged systemic racism.

During the recruitment of underrepresented students and staff, Englin realized that his privilege was allowing him to be heard differently:

> There did not appear to be self-interest or advantage for me to hold these positions, so there was more time and scrutiny given by reasonable people who wished to do the right thing but were blinded by who was bringing the message rather than the content of the message. (Chávez & Sanlo, 2012, p. 74)

This is a perfect example of challenging your privilege and using your privilege to help marginalized populations of people. The key to this strategy is educating yourself on your intersectional identities so that when you find yourself in a situation involving your privilege, you can recognize it. After you recognize the situation, you can speak up and say something in a way that stands with those who are oppressed in our society.

Challenging privilege can be explored using *personal ways of Being*. An individual can *discern their motivations* to explore how they recognize their privilege and what they do to challenge their privilege in a specific situation. This practice of *ways of Being* is important because it helps the individual to reflect on why they are speaking up instead of remaining silent. In addition, this practice helps the individual resolve the conflict by getting involved in a way that is meaningful and authentic for the individual.

Conclusion: Your Voice Matters

Silence is a form of violence. Through identity privilege, compliance, and systemic oppression, we continue to perpetuate systems of oppression that harm marginalized groups of people. Although it is important to highlight these three perspectives on silence, it is equally important to highlight the burdens in advocacy work.

My hope in writing this chapter is not to persuade the reader to think one way or another. I wanted to show multiple sides of the same coin to allow the reader to decide how the coin would land in their own reflective way. Hopefully, this chapter has provided you with a new perspective on the role of silence in social justice advocacy. We all have to make a decision whether to remain silent in the face of injustice. But it was Martin Luther King Jr. who said, "Our lives begin to end the day we become silent about things that matter" (as cited in Emery, 2017, para. 1).

References

Banks, J. A. (2004). Teaching for social justice, diversity, and citizenship in a global world. *The Educational Forum, 68*(4), 296–305. https://doi .org/10.1080/00131720408984645

Brown, B. (2013, December). *Brené Brown on empathy* [Video]. RSA. https://www .youtube.com/watch?v=1Evwgu369Jw&t=94s

Carter, D. (2004). *Stonewall: The riots that sparked the gay revolution*. St. Martin's Press.

Chávez, A. F., & Sanlo, R. (2012). *Identity and leadership: Informing our lives, inform-ing our practice.* NASPA-Student Affairs Administrators in Higher Education.

Emery, D. (2017, January 16). Did MLK say *"Our lives begin to end the day we become silent"*? Snopes.Com. https://www.snopes.com/fact-check/mlk-our-lives-begin-to-end/

Freire, P. (2000). *Pedagogy of the oppressed.* Continuum. (Original work published 1970)

Garcia, J. E., & Hoelscher, K. J. (2010). *Managing diversity flashpoints in higher education.* Rowman & Littlefield.

hooks, b. (1994). *Teaching to transgress: Education as a practice of freedom.* Routledge.

Kimmel, M. (2015, May). *Why gender equality is good for everyone—men included* [Video]. TED Talks. https://www.ted.com/talks/michael_kimmel_why_gender_equality_is_good_for_everyone_men_included/transcript?language=en

King, M. L., Jr. (1994). *Letter from the Birmingham jail.* Harper San Francisco.

Landerman, L. M. (2013). *The art of effective facilitation: Reflections from social justice educators.* Stylus.

McIntosh, P. (2019). *On privilege, fraudulence, and teaching as learning: Selected essays 1981–2019* (1st ed.). Routledge. https://doi.org/10.4324/

Mueller, J. A., & Pickett, C. S. (2015). Politics of intersecting identities. In S. K. Watt (Ed.), *Designing transformative multicultural initiatives: Theoretical founda-tions, practical applications, and facilitator considerations.* Stylus.

Pharr, S. (1997). *Homophobia: A weapon of sexism.* Chardon Press.

Potapchuk, M., Leiderman, S., Bivens, D., & Major, B. (2005). *Flipping the script: White privilege and community building.* MP Associates and the Center for Assessment and Policy Development (CAPD). http://www.mpassociates.us/uploads/3/7/1/0/37103967/flippingthescriptmostupdated.pdf

Quigley, W. P. (2003). *Ending poverty as we know it: Guaranteeing a right to a job.* Temple University Press. http://www.jstor.org/stable/j.ctt14bt1jf

Serres, D. (2013, May 15). *Here's how Desmond Tutu, Elie Wiesel, Paulo Freire, and MLK approach neutrality.* Organizing Change. https://organizingchange.org/here-is-how-moral-leaders-approach-neutrality/

Sleeter, C. E., & Grant, C. A. (2009). *Making choices for multicultural education: Five approaches to race, class and gender* (6th ed.). Wiley.

Sue, D. W. (2010). *Microaggressions in everyday life: Race, gender, and sexual orienta-tion.* Wiley.

Watt, S. K. (2013). Designing and implementing multicultural initiatives: Guiding principles. In S. K. Watt & J. L. Linley (Eds.), *Creating Successful Multicultural Initiatives in Higher Education* (New Directions for Student Services, no. 144, pp. 5–15). Jossey-Bass. https://doi.org/10.1002/ss.20064

Watt, S. K., & Linley, J. L. (Eds.). (2013). *Creating Successful Multicultural Initiatives in Higher Education* (New Directions for Student Services, no. 144). Jossey-Bass.

Wiesel, E. (1986, December 10). *Elie Wiesel: Acceptance speech* [Speech audio record-ing]. The Nobel Prize. https://www.nobelprize.org/prizes/peace/1986/weasel/acceptance-speech/

PART THREE

INTRODUCTION TO
RELATIONAL WAYS OF BEING

PART THREE INTRODUCTION

Sherry K. Watt

T his part focuses on *relational ways of Being* practices. The practices involve focusing on relational awareness to sustain our Being in active, authentic, and intentional relationships with ourselves and others when experiencing dissonance during conflict. Being in a relationship with others includes attending to the emotional states related to trustworthiness, humility, patience, and consideration while also being bold, direct, hearty, and transparent. Each chapter in this section is cowritten, by design: "Interpersonal Communication" is by Audrey Scranton, Aralia Ramirez; and Brian Lackman; "Resistance" by Steve Malvaso and Kira Pasquesi; and "Boundaries" by Milad Mohebali and Janice A. Byrd. Through an exploration of their writing relationship and personal stories, the authors apply *relational ways of Being* to describe how to be present with conflict. Communication, resistance, and boundaries are three windows into the dilemmas that the chapter authors explore through *relational Being* practices.

These practices include *listening deeply, humanizing otherness in a relationship and idea exploration, exploring defenses,* and *dissenting wisely and well.* In the following list, we offer questions to invite you to reflect upon and personalize these *relational ways of Being* practices as you engage with each of these chapters. You may also use them to reflect on how the authors engage with each other in writing their personal narratives, writing together, and in engaging their (at times) diverse disciplinary and academic backgrounds.

- *Listening deeply*: What words am I hearing? What thoughts do I hear? What desires are being spoken? What do I notice in my expressions (tone of voice, body language, etc.) and those of others as we listen? How can I be here and focus on listening to hear rather than preparing to communicate?
- *Humanizing otherness in a relationship and idea exploration*: What perspectives do I share with whom I am exploring this conflict? Where can I not relate to/in: identity, experiences, age, etc.? What do I feel when

I cannot imagine the other person's view surrounding this conflict? What scares me most about this way of viewing the world surrounding this conflict? What will happen if this conflict continues? What can I (we) do to relate to this conflict differently than I (we) have in the past?

- *Exploring defenses* (PIE model): What perspective or experiences inform how I and others relate to this conflict? How can I support another while they experience dissonance? How can I be good company while exploring conflict? When have I felt this type of conflict unresolved in my life or relationships with others? How might I generate the capacity to stay with others while we explore this uncertainty?

- *Dissenting wisely and well*: How do I disagree while simultaneously maintaining regard for myself and others? How might my disagreement be devoid of dehumanizing? How can I disagree while holding my own ground and respecting that of others with whom I am in conflict? What are the actions that I can take for the sake of bettering society to work with people whom I hate or vehemently disagree with?

The authors have also provided a set of supplementary materials for application of Being practices (see Appendix F).

6

INTERPERSONAL COMMUNICATION

Audrey Scranton, Aralia Ramirez, and Brian Lackman

When someone deeply listens to you
The room where you stay
Starts a new life.

—John Fox

Humans are inherently social creatures. We create joy and meaning through giving and receiving love and care. We learn about ourselves through important relationships (Braithwaite et al., 2015). Issues of equity and inclusion are also understood through these relationships (Fairclough, 2015). When more resources or attention is given to one group relative to others, we see and experience injustice. Although it is immensely important to understand how systems and institutions contribute to inequity, it is also crucial to see and address how this works in our daily life and relationships. Using tools from the theory of Being in our interpersonal relationships allows us to correct inequities in these interactions on systemic and communal levels.

We all came to this project through shared interests in Sherry K. Watt's work, dialogue, supervision, and interpersonal communication. Audrey Scranton and Aralia Ramirez were both members of Watt's research team. Aralia Ramirez and Brian Lackman worked together at Duke University. In this chapter, we will share personal examples to show how to integrate the theory of Being in interpersonal relationships in higher education, specifically, in interpersonal communication. Inclusive interpersonal communication is a dialogue reflecting our identities and showing the role of power in discourse. Understanding power in these everyday conversations is essential to integrating practices of the theory of Being. This chapter is about how we (and you), in our many roles and relationships on campus, work to create spaces where these conversations can happen.

Power in Interpersonal Communication

Interpersonal communication refers to the way "humans create and negotiate meanings, identity, and relationships through social interaction" (Braithwaite et al., 2015, p. 5). These interactions occur in the family, among friends, amid colleagues, with strangers, live or online. For professionals working in the context of higher education, interpersonal communication can look like interactions with colleagues, students, and supervisors. These kinds of inter-actions happen across an institution in offices and classrooms, via email, in large- or small-group conversations, or as a brief exchange with someone on the street. Interpersonal communication occurs daily in our engagement with other people.

Power has an immense role in interpersonal interactions. Power is defined as the ability to create change; therefore, it is not inherently bad or good (Fairclough, 2015; Foucault, 1975). However, when power is used to suppress the voices or limit opportunities of marginalized groups, it becomes oppression (Foucault, 1975). There are two types of power to con-sider when thinking about interpersonal interactions. Fairclough (2015) distinguishes between the power behind discourse and the power within discourse. The power behind discourse is the ability of people to shape the rules of communication; it represents how social structures influence what is acceptable or unacceptable in an interpersonal interaction. In contrast, the power within discourse is how people uphold or challenge these con-ventions through daily communication. Therefore, power is contestable in every moment.

A way to disrupt the status quo is to pay attention to how language func-tions in a moment, how it makes people feel, and motivates them to take up or reject certain identities. To understand the importance of power in interpersonal interactions, we must be aware of how history affects how we and others perceive our social identities. If we do not take that history and the social structures that shape its meaning into account, we miss a lot—par-ticularly, the role of power. If we are not aware of that, we risk perpetuating oppression in our interpersonal interactions.

It is crucial to understand how power works both in the moment and behind the scenes when thinking about creating equity in our everyday relationships. The theory of Being provides several practices to help us be reflective about the role of power in our relationships with ourselves, col-leagues, supervisors, advisees, and students. These tools include *personal ways of Being* (e.g., *focusing on you*, self-awareness), *relational ways of Being* (*listening deeply, dissenting wisely and well*), and *community ways of Being* (*understanding the third thing and third thinging*, shifting from surviving to thriving). The theory of Being gives us a guide for what inclusive power within discourse can look like. Student affairs professionals are constantly interacting in a power-up relationship (supervisee to supervisor, or advisee to advisor), or power-across (colleague to colleague), or power-down (supervisor to supervisee/advisor to advisee) relationship. Through interpersonal communication, we can practice elements of the theory of Being. That means we can create environments where people can be authentic, explore their positionalities, and remain motivated to make the world socially just.

Audrey's Experience With The Theory of Being

One day at work, I needed to reserve a room for an event. I stepped into the office of my colleague who scheduled rooms for all of campus. Before I could speak, she walked up to me. "Oh! Do we have a little one here?" she said excitedly, touching my belly. I was not pregnant. My fat lay on my body in such a way that many people have assumed that I was. This has happened often enough that I had come up with a plan for what I was to say in these moments. I vowed that I would only say no, and nothing else. Let them sit in the discomfort they put me through. But the moment was so uncomfortable and my tendency to diffuse tension so strong that after she realized her mistake, a "that's okay" popped out of my mouth before I could stop it.

She did not know that I had to stay and interact with her because of the nature of our relationship, but the whole time I was shrinking inside and could think of little else but leaving as soon as possible. As soon as I left, I power walked back to my office and closed the door. I was not able to work for hours afterward as I stewed in anger and shame.

I replayed all the things that I wish I could have said in my head. I wanted to tell her that I did not owe her an explanation for what my body looks like. That nobody owed her the right to touch them because of what she believes about their body. I wish I could have told her how it made me feel and how devastating these assumptions can be. What if I had been pregnant but was not ready to tell anyone for fear of discrimination? What if I had had a miscarriage? What if I had tried but could not become pregnant? I could have told her that no one owes anyone news of their pregnancy, and when someone shares news about their body it is precious and that she should treasure that. If I had prepared for it so much, why didn't I say anything? Especially when the interaction affected me so much?

Such moments of powerlessness and shame happen frequently in the workplace. Modern professional workplaces are built on many assumptions that prevent us from engaging meaningfully with one another around topics of power. For instance, showing emotion is often seen as unprofessional (Cheshin, 2020) and directly talking about or visually indicating social identities like race, class, or sexuality and how they influence how we show up in the spaces is often discouraged (Jackson & de Koker, 2014; Rosette & Dumas, 2007). These norms perpetuate stifled silence when hurtful interactions do occur. A theory of Being practice that counters the segmented nature of modern workplaces is inviting, assuming, valuing, and knowing wholeness. This looks like seeing our whole lives and identities as present and valued in every circumstance, resisting seeing life as divided, and shifting toward seeing conflict as part of life rather than an illness to cure or fix. In this moment, I found myself wishing that the norms of our workplace had been aligned in this way so I could speak up without fear.

In this interaction, power behind and within discourse were at play. The history of expectations of what women should look like influenced my colleague to ask her question. Her inquiry echoed the myriad of media messages that say having fat or bulges on the stomach requires an explanation. Power behind discourse also showed up in the kind of relationship that we had. Because we were both White women, she may have felt this statement was going to build a positive relationship through showing care and inquiring about what she assumed to be true. The similarities in these two identities may have led her to be more forthright. We were colleagues, but she was an older woman who had control over whether I could reserve a room for my event. This was a factor that made me feel like I could not say anything. In that moment, her words had power over my feelings of self-worth, which functioned as power within discourse. I could have exerted power within discourse by pushing back against what she said, but the power behind discourse prevented me from feeling like I could because of the potential consequences.

Within a different work environment—one in which the tools of the theory of Being were used—the same interaction could have taken place with us finding a way to healing and deeper understanding. If my workplace encouraged people to reflect on their own identities and how those influence how they interact with other people, then I may have been able to speak openly about how that statement affected me. If she could have focused on herself and spoken to me about how she had made a faulty assumption and I could talk about how the media treats women's bodies, she might have learned how to be more aware of her assumptions in the future. If I thought that she would listen deeply to how the interaction had affected me, I would have felt safer to express my perspective. If these two skills were commonly used, I feel we could have embraced this moment of stickiness, hurt, and discomfort as a learning opportunity. This conversational misstep could then have been a moment of growth for both of us. The theory of Being outlines *focusing on you, listening deeply,* and *viewing missteps as developmental* and important tools for inclusion. If my colleague had known how to continue that conversation in a way that would address her privileges, the power she had over me in that situation, and how it made me feel, we could have gotten to a much deeper understanding and she could have learned from the interaction.

Brian's Experience With The Theory of Being

As educators, we are typically placed in roles and positions that require us to navigate positional power and hierarchy in all directions. Every role that I held has placed me in positions where I had to actively choose how to inhabit the space given my social identities. Professionally, I have spent my career in the southern region of the United States and at historically White institutions. These two spaces have been greatly affected by the oppression of Black, Brown, and Indigenous people impacting how I engage my identities, namely, my queerness, cognitive disabilities, my Whiteness, and cis-masculinity.

My most notable experience came from my time serving as the advisor for a university-sponsored organization at a historically White research institution in the southern United States. Many on the executive team that I served with were Black and Brown students. This role, compounded by my privileged and marginalized social identities, made me acutely aware of the power dynamics in the group settings. This situation was further intensified by the events taking place around me. Some of these events included the murder of Michael Brown in Ferguson, Missouri, decades-long efforts to address institutional connections to confederate iconography, the targeted murder of multiple Muslim students in the local community, the push for the institution to reckon with the totality of the institution's history, and more. Structurally, my role was to serve as both a supervisor and advisor, depending on the student and their role in the organization. This student group had a far-reaching impact on campus and frequently engaged with stakeholders at every institutional level (i.e., undergraduate students, graduate and professional students, staff, faculty, and upper-level university leadership).

I became aware of my need to be very intentional with my actions, given my responsibilities and the numerous ways power flowed in this setting.

This awareness went beyond the usual fulfillment of the administrative aspects of my job. It influenced how I navigated my role and positional power, my ability to provide and receive feedback, and how I built relationships. This reflection was intentional and ongoing. I found myself regularly working to ensure that I acted in meaningful and contributive ways. This work aligns with the practice of *personal ways of Being*. I tried to ensure that my thoughts, feelings, and actions focused on my self-awareness and authentic personal connections to the conflict (or in this case, my role, position, and the power over others built into the position). This self-work has not always been easy. I try to actively work to ensure that my intentions match my impact, and work to take responsibility for my actions when they are not congruent. This intentionality has been meaningful for my personal growth, and it enables me to be present in my ascribed and lived values and to be authentic in how I come across.

To develop relationships with my students and colleagues, I sought out ways to engage in deeper dialogue through formal and informal ways. The tool/framework that I felt most comfortable utilizing was the cycle of socialization (Harro, 2000). I learned about the cycle of socialization as an undergraduate student. The framework provided a dissonance-provoking stimulus (Watt, 2007) that greatly enhanced my understanding of the world. I became more aware of how I was socialized passively and actively, of the impact of that socialization on my sense of self and the world, and of the impact I had on others. The tool also helped me understand how people's lived experiences and interactions with institutions such as family, school, and work influenced their perspectives on the world.

Through my engaging with the theory of Being, I realized that the cycle of socialization makes use of the *third thing* (for details see Watt's "Part One Introduction," this volume). The use of the *third thing* can be an effective way to engage in interpersonal relationships, whether these are power-down, power-up, or power-across relationships. By placing socialization as the *third thing* at the center of my interactions, I can speak more intentionally and ask meaningful questions to create spaces for deeper communication and relationships with others. For example, I used this tool formally when facilitating educational sessions and trainings for the executive team and the officers of an organization. Informally, I incorporated some of the language from the cycle of socialization into one-on-one meetings with student leaders. This framework helped me better understand students' backgrounds and how the institution and their organizations have shaped their development.

More importantly, using the cycle of socialization as *a third thing* allows me to cocreate a space with students where we can explore our social identities, discuss how we navigate institutional systems, and find ways to empower students. To the students I advised or supervised, I tried to explain that my role was to help them navigate red tape within the university. I wanted to interact with them authentically and in alignment with their needs, which sometimes meant providing guidance on how to communicate with university administration, creating structures and protocols, strategizing how to engage in difficult dialogue, or simply providing space to process. This approach required me to engage in some combination of *listening deeply, exploring my defenses, and dissenting wisely and well.*

There were many times when I had to be the first one to go to bat for students, to advocate for their needs and potential solutions. While the solutions did not always pan out in the ways we wanted, I made sure that students were clear on the challenges confronting them and that they were equipped with the tools necessary to advocate for their needs and rights. In these conversations I learned to dissent wisely and well, which meant honoring and nurturing trust in my relationships with the students so that we could express and work through concerns and conflict. For example, we worked collectively to improve campus programming and outreach so that more voices could be heard. This required all of us to consider power dynamics, politics within the organization's membership and executive team, and my role in it. The group conversations could get heated as people were attached to certain ways of doing programming and outreach. I supported and encouraged the leadership team as they navigated these dialogues. I invited them to consider the strengths and weaknesses of their current efforts. From there, the group identified other student groups that were left out of the planning or implementation of programs, and so they reached out to other organizations and created new partnerships to connect and support more students across campus. This process also reflects the *community ways of Being* demonstrating how to shift away from centering individual survival and move toward expecting individual and community to thrive.

Aralia's Experience With The Theory of Being

During my 1st year as a graduate student, there were many times when I felt that I did not belong. I experienced microaggressions. I felt like an imposter. I questioned my ability to succeed and considered dropping out of my graduate program. As I continued to learn more about the experiences of Black, Indigenous, People of Color (BIPOC) within institutions of higher education specifically at historically White institutions, I learned that my experiences were not an anomaly and there were tools like the theory of Being to help me navigate these barriers while creating spaces for BIPOC voices.

As a graduate assistant and the only Person of Color in my office, I experienced difficult moments trying to articulate my experiences to my supervisors who were White, cisgender women. During my last year as a graduate student, I led the curriculum development for a topics course for undergraduate students with two colleagues as part of my assistantship. While developing the curriculum, I was concerned that it was not a collaborative effort; specifically, when it came to embedding content around diversity, equity, and inclusion.

I shared my concern with my supervisor saying that I hoped to collaborate more on the curriculum. A couple of weeks later, a meeting to discuss programming was put on the calendar. I assumed that we would also be discussing curriculum and was excited to share some of my ideas and collaborate with the team. As the meeting began, I quickly realized that there was a misunderstanding about the intentions for the meeting.

During meetings, I am normally engaged and conversational. This time I did not contribute much and I was frustrated with the situation. I expressed my confusion at the beginning of the meeting and was quiet most of the time because I had not brought anything prepared to share. When I was asked for my thoughts and opinions, I gave clear and direct responses. My supervisor noticed and followed up with an email after the meeting.
She asked me:

> Is everything alright? I was picking up some negative vibes from you during our meeting, and things seemed to be off. You weren't engaging as much as normal. I felt more push back from you than I typically do, and I wanted to check in.

I responded:

> Thank you for checking in. I am not sure why the meeting was more difficult than it needed to be but I sensed that as well. I did not feel like I was being heard when it came to my ideas. My intention was not to be negative, I am just frustrated that the purpose of this meeting was not clearly communicated to me, but it was communicated to [my coworker].

In her next correspondence, my supervisor asked me to verbalize my feelings up front and shared that she believed that I was contributing to a negative space and that I made the meeting challenging. She requested that we, in the future, reschedule meetings to avoid the tension and combativeness if we are feeling upset. I was upset by the assumptions made of me and specifically by the statements, "I felt more push back than I typically do," "picking up some negative vibes," and "combativeness." As I read her correspondence, there were a million thoughts rushing through my mind. I felt anger, sadness, and guilt. I wondered if I did something wrong. I worried about how these emails would affect my reputation as a graduate student and my job search since she would be a reference. I wondered how I would respond, when to respond, and I even considered just apologizing and leaving it alone to protect myself. As I was processing all my emotions, I came to realize that I could use elements of the theory of Being to navigate this conflict. My response to her email included an invitation to discuss our experiences in that meeting and the language that she had used to describe me.

To prepare for the conversation, I used *personal ways of Being* to ask myself: "What feelings arise in me as I contemplate the conflicts inherent in this issue? How can I prepare myself for the difficult dialogue?" I also used *community ways of Being* by incorporating *a third thing* and asking myself, "What do I hope to get out of the conversation?" I decided to use the poem "When Someone Deeply Listens to You" by John Fox to be the base of our conversation in hopes that it would mitigate any defensive reactions and create an authentic space for both of us to be heard. The barriers that may prevent individuals from engaging in this process are often feelings fueled by defensive reactions (Watt, 2007). I asked my supervisor if she would feel comfortable taking turns reading sections of the poem out loud to begin our conversation.

After reading the poem, I shared how I had been feeling in the office and the planning meeting, and the impact her words had on me. I shared that describing my actions as combative, contributing to negative vibes, and pushing back in the workplace plays into how Women of Color are presumed incompetent or the historical trope of being an angry Woman of Color (Harris & Gonzalez, 2012). The description my supervisor gave of my behavior as combative also tied into how we are socialized to understand professionalism and the policing of emotions. Workplace professionalism has historically been rooted in White supremacy culture, which discriminates against non-Western and non-White professionalism standards (Gray, 2019). This can also be seen in the way pushback or disagreement, especially from Women of Color, is often met with additional action from superiors to preserve the status quo within an organization.

I was nervous to share my experiences, but my supervisor was present and listened actively. She was apologetic for not understanding the context behind the language she used and for the impact it had on me. We discussed the impact language can have on Women of Color in historically White spaces. Her ability to listen in the moment, to understand, learn, and inquire about what she could do differently in the future showed me that she was open to reimagining what our workplace could look like to be a more inclusive and validating space.

The *community ways of Being* highlight the need to balance dialogue with action. Watt (2012) discusses how "the process of embracing diversity as a value requires that campus leaders find a thoughtful balance between dialogue and action (p. 132). We discussed small tangible ways we could move forward: to come together as a team to discuss and decide on curriculum more frequently, to increase the frequency of communication between us, and her commitment to continuing to educate herself on her privilege, language, and the ways it can harm others. I had a director who was open to receiving feedback, listening, sitting with discomfort, and learning. This openness is not always the case in the workplace, and I recommend talking to trusted colleagues if you are unsure about how your feedback will be received. Since the work situation can be challenging to manage, I recommend that departments implement a 360-degree feedback process so that all positions can provide feedback without fear. When we are in positions of power, it is vital to reflect on our identities, positionality, and identify the ways in which we can use our power to create environments for others.

Conclusion

Understanding the role of power in interpersonal communication through the prism of the theory of Being can help us advocate for equity in our interpersonal relationships. If we ignore the role of power behind discourse—the social conventions in our situations and social identities and their subsequent histories—we risk perpetuating oppression. We have choices to exert power through power within discourse, but the power behind discourse can make this difficult or unsafe. Understanding the roles of positional power is also important—whether we are in a power-up relationship (supervisee to supervisor), or power-across (colleague to colleague), or power-down (supervisor to supervisee/advisor to advisee) relationships. Power is not inherently good or bad, but we cannot ignore its roles in our interactions. When we hold privileges relative to others, using *personal, relational,* and *community ways of Being* can prevent us from perpetuating oppression. When we experience marginalization, there are times we may be able to change the interaction to create more equity for us or others. It takes a lot of labor to learn how to be rather than automatically do. It requires deeply reflecting and practicing these skills. But the work is well worth it.

Within each of these stories, we have provided examples of how and where the *ways of Being* can be applied so you can practice these skills in your own lives. In Audrey's story, a power across, or colleague to colleague, relationship did not guarantee that she felt the ability to speak up when marginalized. The shared gender and social identities may have led her colleague to ask about an assumed pregnancy, but the age difference and positional power the colleague held in the moment, as well as workplace norms, barricaded potential understanding or growth. This story emphasizes the importance of *listening deeply, embracing conflict as a learning opportunity*, and embracing space and emotion as common practices in the workplace to foster the opportunities for difficult dialogues.

Brian's story highlights a focus on engaging an authentic self to effectively learn more about himself and others. Utilizing tools like the cycle of socialization (Harro, 2000) helps ensure that those with privileged identities and/or positional power do not force others to do additional labor. Focusing on self is critically important; people who genuinely work at being authentic in their learning and unlearning of knowledge can be more effective team members. How we individually engage in this work can position us as strong team members and allies for the students whom we serve and educate. Individuals and groups can better assess how to create realistic and meaningful improvements while navigating institutional and other external factors.

In Aralia's story, she shares her experience utilizing *ways of Being* to engage in a difficult conversation with her supervisor. These skills are demonstrated in her preparation leading up to the conversation, the collaborative nature of the conversation, the focus on understanding the issue, and the shared understanding that it would be an ongoing process to improve the relationship and the work environment. Her positionality in this conversation is described as a power-up situation, or supervisee to supervisor, which helps us contextualize the challenges we may experience when addressing inequities in the workplace. This story begins to highlight the impact microaggressions can have on individuals and shares an example of how to engage in conversations with people in positions of power to foster engagement, learning, and accountability.

References

Braithwaite, D. O., Schrodt, P., & Carr, K. (2015). Introduction: Meta-theory and theory in interpersonal communication research. In D. O. Braithwaite & P. Schrodt (Eds.), *Engaging theories in interpersonal communication: Multiple perspectives* (2nd ed., pp. 1–20). SAGE.

Cheshin, A. (2020). The impact of non-normative displays of emotion in the workplace: How inappropriateness shapes the interpersonal outcomes of emotional displays. *Frontiers in Psychology, 11*(6). https://doi.org/10.3389/fpsyg.2020.00006

Fairclough, N. (2015). *Language and power* (3rd ed.). Routledge.

Foucault, M. (1975). *Discipline and punish: The birth of the prison.* Vintage.

Gray, A. (2019, June 4). The bias of 'professionalism' standards in the workplace. *Stanford Social Innovation Review.* https://ssir.org/articles/entry/the_bias_of_professionalism_standards

Harris, A. P., & Gonzalez, C. G. (2012). Introduction. In G. Gutiérrez y Muhs, Y. F. Niemann, C. G. Gonzalez, & A. P. Harris (Eds.), *Presumed incompetent: The intersections of race and class for women in academia* (pp. 1–14). University Press of Colorado.

Harro, B. (2000). The cycle of socialization. In M. Adams, W. J. Blumenfeld, R. Castañeda, H. W. Hackman, M. L. Peters, & X. Zúñiga (Eds.), *Readings for diversity and social justice* (pp. 16–21). Routledge.

Jackson, L. T. B., & de Koker, D. G. (2014). Negative acculturation conditions, well-being, and the mediating role of separation in the workplace. In L. T. B. Jackson, D. Meiring, F. J. R. Van de Vijver, E. S. Idemoudia, & W. K. Gabrenya Jr. (Eds.), *Toward sustainable development through nurturing diversity: Proceedings from the 21st International Congress of the International Association for Cross-Cultural Psychology* (pp. 65–80). https://scholarworks.gvsu.edu/iaccp_papers/132/

Rosette, A. S., & Dumas, T. L. (2007). The hair dilemma: Conform to mainstream expectations or emphasize racial identity. *Duke Journal of Gender Law & Policy, 14,* 407–421. https://scholarship.law.duke.edu/cgi/viewcontent.cgi?article=1119&context=djglp

Watt, S. K. (2007). Difficult dialogues, privilege and social justice: Uses of the privileged identity exploration (PIE) model in student affairs practice. *College Student Affairs Journal, 26*(2), 114–126. https://eric.ed.gov/?id=EJ899385

Watt, S. K. (2012). Moving beyond the talk: From difficult dialogue to action. In J. Arminio, V. Torres, & R. L. Pope (Eds.), *Why aren't we there yet? Taking personal responsibility for creating an inclusive campus* (pp. 131–144). Stylus.

7

RESISTANCE

Steve Malvaso and Kira Pasquesi

This being human is a guest house.
Every morning a new arrival.
A joy, a depression, a meanness,
some momentary awareness comes
as an unexpected visitor.
The dark thought, the shame, the malice.
meet them at the door laughing and invite them in.

—Jelaluddin Rumi, "The Guest House"

Imagine that you are in a challenging conversation about societal conditions with a friend, family member, peer, colleague, or neighbor. The conversation is awakening something in you that you may not know how to describe. It is an "unexpected visitor" to your guest house. It enlivens one, or more, of your senses—touch, smell, sound, taste, or sight—without notice. You can meet this visitor in a room or maybe have passed it on the street. The perception of this visitor feels deceptively new and oddly familiar at the same time. The visitor to your guest house may be resistance. This chapter explores resistance as a "visitor" in politically or socially polarizing interactions. We question what it means to be with or be in resistance as part of the theory of Being (for details on the theory of Being see Watt's "Part One Introduction," this volume). In this chapter, we first briefly introduce our relationships with resistance as authors and review relevant literature on resistance from multiple theoretical angles. Next, we situate resistance as a painful, yet productive, facet of being in difficult dialogues using reflections on one author's teaching experience. We then examine the classroom experience from *individual, relational,* and *community ways of Being,* and close with *open and honest questions* to continue the work.

Our Relationships With Resistance

It is important for us as authors to start a heart-centered conversation about resistance. Kira brings experience as a community-based dialogue facilitator and leadership educator managing difficult classroom conversations with undergraduate students. She holds a multitude of intersecting privileged identities as a White, cisgendered, heterosexual woman from an upper-class family. Her resistance often emerges as a well-meaning, at times knowingly fragile, White woman. To Kira, resistance feels like shame that can mask itself as charity lurking in the corner of a room.

Steve's experiences have primarily been in residence life, advising, and athletics, but he entered the work of Being by teaching and co-consulting for undergraduates, graduate students, and staff in educational settings. Like Kira, Steve holds several intersecting privileged identities as a White, cisgendered, heterosexual man from a middle-class family. His resistance typically takes the form of an empathetic, too frequently anxious, White man. To Steve, resistance feels like a whirlpool of self-loathing and guilt that can materialize as a benevolent desire to protect.

Kira and Steve have critically examined resistance as a facet of the process-oriented theory of Being as team members and alumni of the Multicultural Initiatives (MCI) Research Team. Resistance is always present in their work as conscious-minded scholar-practitioners and, as the great Grace Lee Boggs once said, as *human* human beings.

After 3 years of not having formally worked together on the MCI team, the authors' shared relationship with resistance certainly evolved. Kira initially introduced Steve to the research team. Kira's heart-first and Steve's head-first orientations complemented each other well and created an ideal opportunity to go on this journey together. Furthermore, the events of the global pandemic and a renewed (albeit short-lived) national consciousness about systemic injustice catalyzed their unabashed vulnerability and tried-and-true strength as a pair.

The authors' meetings consisted entirely of questions and wanderings of our streams of consciousness and exploration of a wounding experience. Our conversations were about the unmitigated honesty one of us needed to hear in a particular moment to deal with dissonance and eventually process. Fortunately, that vulnerability was felt as a warm hug from an old friend that cut through the physical disconnectedness of video calls, and that allowed us to be present with and for each other. The story that both authors share in this chapter is painful because it affected people that both of us care deeply about and we did not take that lightly. As Kira so plainly stated, "Our comfort for being in the messiness together is why we needed to write this chapter." Our hope is that our readers can find that same comfort amid the messiness of resistance.

Conceptualizing Resistance

Resistance is everywhere we turn. It surfaces within self-talk, on social media posts, through collective demands for policy change, and in response to organizational diversity efforts. It is an everyday personal and social phenomenon occurring anytime people resist ideas, feelings, fellow humans, institutions, and even themselves (Lawrence & Dodds, 2018). In this review of literature, we define resistance using a variety of theoretical perspectives and shared assumptions. We then briefly outline the ways in which resistance fuels transformation in educational contexts. We close by situating resistance within *relational ways of Being* in the context of the theory of Being.

Defining Resistance

While manifestations of resistance abound, it is not a unitary construct across fields of study and practice (Chaudhary et al., 2017). Scholarship on resistance stems from different theoretical angles, including dialogic self-theory, psychodynamic theory, and cultural psychology, among others. For example, in psychoanalytic theory, resistance is defined as unconscious avoidance of threatening material as a means to repress or manage conflicting thoughts and emotions (Arlow, 2000). Some psychologists focus on resistance as behavioral in nature, or a demonstrated resistance to carrying out therapeutic strategies or suggestions (e.g., Arkowitz, 2002). Others emphasize resistance as indicating a reluctance to changing negative inter/intrapersonal patterns or a reluctance to interact with anxiety-provoking feelings (e.g., Beutler et al., 2011).

Within the field of social psychology, resistance gained recognition under the label of reactance (Arkowitz, 2002). According to Brehm and Brehm (1981), psychological reactance is defined as a "state of mind aroused by a threat to one's perceived legitimate freedom, motivating the individual to restore the thwarted freedom" (p. 4). Additionally, from a cultural perspective, resistance is a common human phenomenon stemming from friction between social groups, whereby actions of members of society are actively and intentionally unappreciated by others (Chaudhary et al., 2017). The cultural language of resistance triggers such questions as "resistance to what?" or "resistance of what kind?" (Chaudhary et al., 2017, p. xiii). Awad et al. (2017) named characteristics, or underlying assumptions, of resistance as an everyday lived cultural experience. The authors posited that resistance is

"(1) a social and individual phenomenon; (2) a constructive process that articulates continuity and change; and (3) an act oriented toward an imagined future of different communities" (Awad et al., 2017, p. 161).

Moreover, in organizational psychology, Oreg (2006) defined resistance as a negative attitude toward change that influences affective, behavioral, and cognitive components, or the various ways people evaluate a dissonance-provoking object or situation. The affective component involves how one feels about change; the cognitive component refers to how one thinks about change; and the behavioral component emphasizes actions in response to change. Wiggins-Romesburg and Githens (2018) focused on resistance to change in organizational diversity efforts. On an individual level, resistance reflects a person's deepest held values and motivations and can be expressed as silence, inaction, stereotyping, or other forms of backlash within an organization. On an organizational level, resistance is an organizational stance, policy, or action used to resist diversity change efforts to protest the status quo of power and privilege.

Common across the multitude of theoretical frames is the concept of making meaning. Meaning-making reflects the relationship between the meaning-maker (or actor) and the object provoking the need to make meaning (a dissonance-provoking stimulus) and resolving tensions between the two (Chaudhary et al., 2017). In theorizing resistance, Chaudhary et al. (2017) explained the systemic and oppositional relationship between resistance and action. Action does not exist without its corresponding counterpart in resistance. In other words, "resistance escalates intentionality," in that it heightens one's understanding and perception of self (Chaudhary et al., 2017, p. x). Integrative perspectives on resistance highlight the idea that human beings are capable of actively changing their environments and transforming their realities through meaning-making processes (Arkowitz, 2002).

Resistance as Transformation in Education

Scholars in education posit resistance as a constructive-change process. For example, Jaramillo and Carreon (2014) theorized pedagogies of resistance rooted in the practices of Latin American social movements and guided by reciprocity, solidarity, and horizontalidad, or democratic decision-making in Spanish. Such forms of education align with Freire's (1983) concept of critical education that raises student consciousness about social inequalities perpetuating their lived experiences and existence in the world. Resistance as a pedagogical approach is aligned with larger social movements that advance more equitable visions and actions toward transformative equity and justice (Bajaj, 2015).

Relatedly, Solorzano and Bernal (2001) proposed a race- and gender-conscious model of resistance in their qualitative inquiry and a critical race counterstory of Chicana and Chicano student protests. The study offered distinctions between types of student resistance behavior, including reactionary behavior, self-defeating resistance, conformist resistance, and transformational resistance. The model considers the relationships between students' critiques of oppressive conditions and social justice motivations. Specifically, the fourth type of resistance is transformational in nature, whereby the student behavior reflects a desire for social justice alongside a critique of oppression, which offers the greatest possibility for social change.

Resistance and The Theory of Being

As articulated in the review of the literature, resistance can be observed and experienced at multiple levels, from various theoretical perspectives, and in different contexts. In this chapter, we explore a narrative of resistance in a university classroom that emerged from a conflict over a class assignment. Conflicts are inherent in the process-oriented practices within the theory of Being. For this discussion, we focus on resistance as a conflict within and among self, relationships, and communities inherent in teaching and learning settings. The educator's role is to facilitate meaning-making processes for students to unearth and resolve conflicts at multiple levels and facilitate attempts to unearth and resolve conflicts. Furthermore, we assume in this chapter that resistance contains intrapersonal and interpersonal dimensions, that it is transformational and developmental, and that it can emerge within or outside of consciousness.

Connected to these assumptions, two specific manifestations of resistance present are performative wokeness and expert-victim handcuffs. Performative wokeness is the act of projecting a heightened sense of social consciousness, not for the purpose of educating somebody, but for the purpose of gaining a personally elevated status (Gray, 2018). Within social justice circles, this is typically used as a tool to show that someone with a dominant identity is worthy of trust to gain ingroup pseudostatus with marginalized people (Davis et al., 2019). It is the disingenuous desire to fish out the proverbial "invite to the cookout," or the metaphorical/literal opportunity extended to attend an exclusive gathering of Black people, whereby the invite itself symbolically proclaims a White person as a *real* ally (Arceneaux, 2017; Johnson, 2017; Miller, 2017). While it is arguably the most zeitgeisty and apropos example in the United States, this type of status-seeking by the dominant-identity people is by no means specific to race. Placing someone in *expert-victim handcuffs* (Watt & MCI Research Team, 2014, personal communication) is the act of using personally experienced marginalization to take control of someone else's voice within a group dynamic. It implies, "I am the expert on this experience for my entire [identity] group, so I am going to dictate the terms of how you will proceed through this interaction." As the name indicates, the person receiving the attention is handcuffed until notified otherwise.

In writing this chapter, we both reflected on times when we displayed resistance and/or experienced resistance from others. Steve found himself returning to a particularly turbulent semester ("that semester" as he put it) as a teaching assistant for a graduate class on multiculturalism and student affairs. He explores this narrative next to reflect on what the experience taught him while he was grappling with resistance in this class.

A Narrative of Resistance: That Semester

Pain that isn't transformed is transmitted.

—Richard Rohr, *A Spring Within Us*

Throughout the process of rehashing that semester in my mind, I keep thinking about Rohr's (2016) quote. It is so simple, yet too often forgotten in the meaning-making associated with relational resistance. Thoughts and feelings are virtually infinite whenever an educator reflects in the moment or in the rearview. The impact that a situation has on us and others—and the thread of transmitted pain that wove its way through the fabric of this time—end up hiding in plain sight. In my first attempt at writing this section of the chapter, that reality could not have been more inconspicuously hiding from me. Because unlearning unconscious-thought processes and behaviors has continued to prove itself challenging, I want to take a narrative approach not only to reflect on that semester, but also to reflect on the very human—and very self-referential—process of resistance that happened in writing this.

Since you are probably reading this and thinking, "That semester? What does that even mean—especially in the context of resistance?" I want to take a moment to rewind and provide some context. During one semester as a teaching assistant in a multiculturalism course, one of the seminal semester-long projects required each individual student to safely invite a stranger—who held some social identity different from their own—to engage in a genuine dialogue over multiple interactions (and ideally, establish a rapport and relationship). While some version of this assignment is common across a variety of courses in student affairs programs, the distinguishing factor here was the focus on self and self-awareness through a genuinely reciprocal exchange, mostly centered in that identity difference. It was meant to initiate a transformative learning experience for students.

Maximizing that transformation requires a number of necessary conditions. Considering the "heart" aspect of the theory of Being, it requires a level of vulnerability and authenticity between students and instructors that individuals can easily resist if any part of the ground the class is on is unsettled. While the semester-long project served the purpose of practicing newly learned *relational ways of Being*, it unearthed a specific type of relational resistance that shaped the semester: the desire for justice in the form of retribution instead of justice as liberation. For the remainder of this chapter, we will anchor resistance to *relational ways of Being* to this theme.

As in many student affairs programs, master's degree students took this course to round out key aspects of their foundational field knowledge and exit with a more comprehensive set of practical skills to better prepare them for future practitioner experiences. Unique to this situation, these students were familiar with the professor and her process-oriented teaching style because of having already completed a different course with her. One of the most crucial criteria for process-oriented learning that these students carried over from the previous course was the need to set aside the motivation to reach a finite outcome. Resistance to the process is natural, given the arguably stark contrast between the process-oriented learning and the traditional knowledge-transfer pedagogy practiced in the United States (Sill et al., 2009). The stamina that the process-oriented learning can build to fuel *personal, relational,* and *community* transformation is substantial.

When our instructor group (made up of two Black women, a White woman, and me, a White man) explained the assignment and its logistics, our students' hearts engaged, but not in the way that we anticipated:

Are you kidding me?! How could you ever ask us to do this?! I can't do this!

Just because you've been doing this assignment forever, doesn't mean it still matters, or still has any relevance. Maybe it's time for you to reevaluate your teaching.

You really think I'm going to compromise my safety? I can't do something like this. This is f****** ridiculous!

When met with this elevated level of skepticism, our professor (a Black woman and a tenured professor) calmly absorbed this feedback and reemphasized the assignment's purpose to students. This assignment was an opportunity for students to practice process-oriented interactions and relationship building, increase self-awareness, and meta-analyze their *ways of Being* in relation to someone different from them vis-à-vis the theory of Being. Regardless of how she reframed it or the closing reflective activity that we used in class, our professor was unable to fully quell the emotional charge of the day. While this assignment is typically met with some level of trepidation (understandably so), this was unlike anything we had experienced. The yelling, the tears, and the near refusal to participate was a sign to us, instructors, that what we initially thought was a well-structured rollout of the assignment, was actually a house of cards waiting for a gust of wind to collapse.

We understood that the resistance manifested because of some harm that we may have unconsciously and unintentionally caused. Since this was one of the first classes of the semester, we decided to shift our next opening *third thing* activity to a more overtly restorative process. We hoped to engage in both the metacognitive and emotionally vulnerable processes that the assignment was supposed to invoke. In alignment with the concept of *third thinging*, we attempted to focus on the students' resistance and our relationships to their resistance in all their complexity, and to humanize their resistance. It was an attempt to build a community through our shared accountability, struggling through it together. An intensive assignment like this reasonably provokes feelings of discomfort, and we knew our responsibility to help them intellectually and emotionally digest that. Regardless of how students externally materialized their feelings, they were entirely valid, and we wanted to honor that.

While we tried to maintain a space for conversation and create *the us-and-them-exploring-it* dynamic, we still struggled to move away from the *us-versus-them* mindset (i.e., students versus instructors). Through the *third-thing* activity, our instructor group received a preview of the rest of the semester. We were grappling with two emotionally charged issues: performative wokeness and *expert-victim handcuffs*. Sometimes, the performative wokeness involved students' interjecting comments to prove that they knew more than other majority-identity peers, as if trying to be "woker than thou." Other times, students sought to rebuke their own or others' previous social justice failures. The rebukes all but opened the door for certain members of the class to place their classmates in *expert-victim handcuffs* related to race and social class. Instead of utilizing this time together to examine and deconstruct the systemic "isms" to experience justice as liberation, the group's acts of performative wokeness and placing others in the *expert-victim handcuffs* came across as retribution.

While there was some genuine sharing throughout that activity, the rest of the semester was a roller coaster of peaks and valleys—some good days and some bad—all with lingering reminders of the assignment rollout turned sour. Regardless of the students' adaptation to our approach, their resistance was mostly resolute. *Third thing* activities and lessons fell flat. We seldom were able to explore beyond the surface what transformation was or could be. Ultimately, outside of our creative work to grapple with teaching challenges related to resistance, that semester was mostly uninspiring.

Kira and I explored different paths to showcase stamina-building in this group, but ultimately we fell short. Since the narrative lacked a successful end, our instincts told us that we had failed. We decided that the truly instructive meaning of this story—the one that stayed truest to the maxim of the process being the outcome, in the spirit of the theory of Being—was the honest conclusion that the instructor group that semester never got to an end. We concluded that managing the tension of those two realities was innately difficult, yet it was vitally important to do this work authentically (and as a community).

As important as we thought it was to tell a story with a fully achieved resolution, it is so much more important to tell the story that actually happened. Why? Because you, readers, deserve to know that despite our best efforts, not every group can be inspired to build stamina when they are not ready to build. Thinking in terms of group dynamics evolution (Tuckman & Jensen, 1977), we did our best to develop the group stamina before we gave up at the end of the semester. Inevitably, we were left with one question: How could we have better taught and modeled *relational Being* skills for our students to cultivate the stamina to persist?

Reflecting on Our Process

In hindsight, there were several aspects of our approach that, if changed, would have provided an opportunity for us to shift the group dynamics. We would have shifted away from the tactics of performative wokeness and *expert-victim handcuffs* to achieve justice through retribution toward developing the stamina to sustain difficult dialogues together to achieve justice as liberation. Most significantly, a redistribution of effort and approach was needed to effectively and explicitly employ *third things*.

Liberation as a concept inherently presents challenges. We do not actually know what liberation looks like since we have never truly seen it, yet it exponentially amplifies the process-as-outcome nature of this type of work. Retribution, however, is not only readily conceivable, but has a potentially concrete end point. When marginalized people inherit generational oppression, and then experience their own, who are those with privilege to deny the cognitive dissonance and genuine emotional deflation, resulting from the vague response to systemic oppression, "We're not entirely sure, but we need to trust the process, because we'll know when we get there"? On its surface, that explanation could have been received by our students as a blatant denial of their opportunity to transform their pain and find some healing. In turn, that may have removed some of the fuel to the performative wokeness fire and allowed them to be more authentically and emotionally available. In addition, *third thinging* on our instructor group's resistance to our students' resistance would have provided an opportunity to shift away from the *us-versus-them* (i.e., students versus instructors) dynamic toward the *us-and-them-exploring-it* dynamic. Speaking from our personal experience, how could we, in good faith, possibly ask students to authentically engage in this work, if we were just as responsible for resisting? If that is not a complicated matter of the heart, we are not sure what is.

More explicitly examining that resistance could have served as a cornerstone for us to revisit further instances of resistance throughout the semester. When the pain felt like it was bubbling up (and over), we would have had a common place to return to, and wrestle with that pain as a community.

Individual, Relational, and Community Resistance

In the moment, our instructor group did not capitalize effectively enough on the opportunity to identify and hang onto those resistant instances, but reflecting on the individual, relational, and community levels of resistance that occurred was quite meaningful. The theory of Being notes that at the individual level, *personal ways of Being* require people to focus on themselves and recognize their defenses. By definition, capitalism rewards individuals not for who they are, but for what they do, and so students are not conditioned to qualitatively focus on and openly discuss areas for their growth. That may explain why several students tried to change the assignment to something that resembled an interview. Their PIE model *deflection or intellectualization* (Watt, 2015) shifted focus away from themselves. I (Steve) also realized that I failed to directly intervene or explain how my own home base defenses prevented me from completing a similar assignment as a master's student. If I had leaned into my own and the students' discomfort, perhaps we (instructors) could have established genuine trust with students and *humanized the otherness in ourselves and each other*. Normalizing my resistance and vulnerability could have made an important difference.

At the relational level, two of the most important *ways of Being* are *listening deeply* and *dissenting wisely and well*. Identifying resistance to these *relational ways of Being* is complex. For example, the teaching assistants facilitated small-group discussions where students frequently paired off. A lack of trust emerged as a catalyst for resistance. Regardless of the common coursework in the program, the students entered that space with some life experience that consciously or unconsciously informed certain unique beliefs and approaches to diversity, equity, and inclusion work. The practice of *listening deeply* should have given students opportunities to engage in difficult conversations; yet seldom did we, as instructors, hear something other than a strong cosign for their partner's opinions. One possible source of this not trusting their partner to respond in a humanizing way or with feedback that did not strike a nerve connected to an insecurity (i.e., a dearth of wokeness). Even though they were physically present, some portion of them checked out. Despite my alignment with the other teaching assistants and our professor, we could have modeled how to *dissent wisely and well* with one another. Openly working through a disagreement by using a *third thing* or *exploring our defenses* (and what they meant for us) could have normalized that type of engagement.

Additionally, our instructor group's utilization and integration of *third things* in the course almost exclusively occurred at the community level. This potentially put undue pressure on students to feel as though quality participation was about being "right" in relation to their reflections on the *third thing*, instead of focusing on the process of sustaining engagement with their dissonance (or, getting it right). Again, we observed an attempt at the personal elevation through retribution instead of the collective elevation through liberation. Incorporating several more relational *third things* as primers for breakout-group dialogue in small groups—some with members of the instructor group facilitating and some with students facilitating—may have reduced students' anxiety around this type of engagement and provided them with opportunities to celebrate missteps as important successes in their learning process and learn from conflict. Perhaps, these modifications could have also fostered the practice of focusing on themselves in relation to "it," as opposed to in relation to each other, which is a major barrier to trust.

At the community level, this group struggled to *view missteps as developmental* as well as to *embrace conflict as a learning opportunity*. While the previously mentioned restorative circle applies here, a later lesson about how to achieve racial justice also demonstrates this. One student who identified as a racial minority took a particularly firm stance that power needed to be reclaimed by People of Color and outlined several ways in which White people needed to "fall in line." While making these statements, this student shifted their eye contact to several different White students around the room. Many of those faces displayed obvious nervousness, but the few who spoke sheepishly agreed with this stance and declined to engage with the reading we used as *a third thing* to prime the conversation.

Then the professor spoke up to introduce a counterpoint related to cultivating liberation. This shift was an attempt to redirect the student's energy from flipping the script of the power differential to reimagining it. The place of painful, lived experience from which that student spoke resonated with the professor, so she wanted not only to humanize the student, but also to humanize their thought process in a way that helped them aspire to wholeness, instead of a different flavor of division. Although the professor held some of the same underrepresented identities as this student, the student fervently attempted to put their *expert-victim handcuffs* on the professor, due to the discrepancies in their educational and social class privileges. The student was determined to dictate the terms of "truth" and what was "right" related to racial justice, by any means necessary, arguably, the most direct resistance to process-oriented problem-solving.

As the conversation about the *third thing* further derailed, none of the teaching assistants attempted to embrace conflict in that moment. We missed an opportunity to find a key to the handcuffs and divert some energy into another task that may have reenergized and reengaged other students. Through that redirection, our students could have built up stamina to revisit this conversation in the latter portion of the class period to steer them toward the *us-and-them-exploring-it* thinking.

While it may not have bonded our group more closely, perhaps the act of more overtly providing opportunities to examine ourselves would have increased the likelihood that our students gained more stamina to work through their discomfort. Not all groups perfectly coalesce, regardless of how hard we work as instructors. Even though that can be discouraging and damaging to the ego, the reality of this work, regardless of background, is that it is challenging for almost all people, instructors included. One of the pillars of dominant American culture is the finality and satisfaction associated with crossing a finish line, and higher education is arguably one of the most egregious perpetrators of that paradigm. Overcoming the elimination of a finish line is hard enough, let alone postulating the need to strive toward liberation; readiness and willingness to suspend disbelief are hard to come by. Almost all of us would be lying to ourselves if we said that we easily started to engage with this work. Of course we owe it to those in the community to be in the struggle with them together, especially if we hope to collectively start to take action toward shifting our environment.

The Work Continues

In closing, we are left with many more wonderings and critical inquiries about resistance. Specifically, we recognize the centrality of our privileged identities in advocating for *ways of Being* with resistance as a productive struggle. Throughout the writing process, we called this the hopeful-White-person perspective to help keep these significant limitations in perspective. We continue to question: How might calls to humanize resistance give people with privileged identities a pass? Who might be unintentionally silenced by giving space to resistance? What is the role of healing for individuals and groups? In what ways is resistance experienced differentially by bodies, hearts, and minds? What knowledge, skills, and dispositions are needed to be with resistance in more critically conscious ways?

In revisiting the epigraph at the start of the chapter, Rumi's poem "The Guest House," we can say that perhaps resistance is not an "unexpected visitor." Rather, resistance is an expected visitor in Being human and Being in relationships with others. Welcoming and inviting resistance can be painful, but also transformational in a process-oriented approach that engages the head, heart, and hands. This chapter explored resistance in relevant literature and reflected on the classroom dynamics and the role of resistance within the theory of Being. We invite readers to be with resistance, whether their own or others', in the name of liberation.

References

Arceneaux, M. (2017, February 16). *White folks can't just come to the cookout because they perform blackness*. The Root. https://www.theroot.com/white-folks-can-t-just-come-to-the-cookout-because-they-1792357577

Arkowitz, H. (2002). Toward an integrative perspective on resistance to change. *Journal of Clinical Psychology, 58*(2), 219–227. https://doi.org/10.1002/jclp.1145

Arlow, J. A. (2000). Psychoanalysis. In R. J. Corsini & D. Wedding (Eds.), *Current psychotherapies* (6th ed., pp. 16–53). Peacock Press.

Awad, S. H., Wagoner, B., & Glaveanu, V. (2017). The street art of resistance. In *Resistance in everyday life* (pp. 161–180). Springer.

Bajaj, M. (2015). 'Pedagogies of resistance' and critical peace education praxis. *Journal of Peace Education, 12*(2), 154–166. https://doi.org/10.1080/17400201.2014.991914

Beutler, L. E., Harwood, T. M., Michelson, A., Song, X., & Holman, J. (2011). Resistance/reactance level. *Journal of Clinical Psychology, 67*(2), 133–142. https://doi.org/10.1002/jclp.20753

Brehm, S., & Brehm, J. (1981). *Psychological reactance: A theory of freedom and control*. Academic Press.

Chaudhary, N., Hviid, P., Marsico, G., & Villadsen, J. (Eds.). (2017). *Resistance in everyday life: Constructing cultural experiences.* Springer.

Davis, C. H. F., Harris, J. C., Stokes, S., & Harper, S. R. (2019). But is it activist? Interpretive criteria for activist scholarship in higher education. *The Review of Higher Education 42*(5), 85–108. https://muse.jhu.edu/article/724912

Freire, P. (1983). *Education for critical consciousness.* Seabury Press.

Gray, J. M. (2018, October 1). *Performing wokeness: Signaling you've got the "social justice know-how" for the sake of your own self-image.* The Harvard Crimson. https://www.thecrimson.com/column/better-left-unsaid/article/2018/10/1/gray-performing-wokeness/

Jaramillo, N., & Carreon, M. (2014). Pedagogies of resistance and solidarity: Towards revolutionary and decolonial praxis. *Interface: A Journal for and About Social Movements, 6*(1), 392–411. http://www.interfacejournal.net/wordpress/wp-content/uploads/2014/06/Interface-6-1-Jaramillo-and-Carreon.pdf

Johnson, G. P. (2017, October 12). *Why Eminem is always invited to the cookout.* Houston Press. https://www.houstonpress.com/arts/eminems-bet-hip-hop-awards-performance-earned-him-a-permanent-invite-to-the-cookout-9828600

Lawrence, J. A., & Dodds, A. E. (2018). Toward a psychology of resistance. *Integrative Psychological and Behavioral Science, 52*(1), 67–76. https://doi.org/10.1007/s12124-017-9411-9

Miller, I. (2017, October 17). *Invitations to the cookout have now been rescinded.* Huff Post. https://www.huffpost.com/entry/invitations-to-the-cookout-have-now-been-rescinded_b_59e644e4e4b0e60c4aa365ad

Oreg, S. (2006). Personality, context, and resistance to organizational change. *European Journal of Work and Organizational Psychology, 15*(1), 73–101. https://doi.org/10.1080/13594320500451247

Rohr, R. (2016). *A spring within us: A book of daily meditations.* CAC Publishing.

Rumi, J. (1997). *The illuminated Rumi* (C. Barks, Trans.). Broadway Books.

Sill, D., Harward, B. M., & Cooper, I. (2009). The disorienting dilemma: The senior capstone as a transformative experience. *Liberal Education, 95*(3), 50–55. https://www.aacu.org/publications-research/periodicals/disorienting-dilemma-senior-capstone-transformative-experience

Solorzano, D. G., & Bernal, D. D. (2001). Examining transformational resistance through a critical race and LatCrit theory framework: Chicana and Chicano students in an urban context. *Urban Education, 36*(3), 308–342. https://doi.org/10.1177/0042085901363002

Tuckman, B. W., & Jensen, M. A. C. (1977). Stages of small-group development revisited. *Group & Organization Studies, 2*(4), 419–427. https://doi.org/10.1177/105960117700200404

Watt, S. K. (Ed.). (2015). *Designing transformative multicultural initiatives: Theoretical foundations, practical applications, and facilitator considerations.* Stylus.

Wiggins-Romesburg, C. A., & Githens, R. P. (2018). The psychology of diversity resistance and integration. *Human Resource Development Review, 17*(2), 179–198. https://doi.org/10.1177/1534484318765843

BOUNDARIES

Milad Mohebali and Janice A. Byrd

We shared gentle moments that reawakened the poetic,
finding strength in each other's spaces;
meeting lines but never crossing them.

—Yolanda Sealy-Ruiz

We have both been members of the Multicultural Initiatives (MCI) Research Team, and while we had been in the same work spaces together, writing this chapter collaboratively brought us into a new relationship. In fact, people live in a network of voluntary and involuntary relationships with one another and with varying entities in society at the microlevels (e.g., siblings) and macrolevels (e.g., schools; Belgrave & Allison, 2018). These relationships are, but are not limited to, personal, professional, educational, medical, and spiritual. They can also vary in closeness; intimate with a partner, communal with a neighbor, professional in a writing project, or with a larger entity like a community or a nation. Relationships are inherently unavoidable as these bonds signify what it means to be human and play a pivotal role in how we view ourselves and one another. To us, from our very first meeting, it was clear that we both wanted the writing of this book chapter to be a humanizing experience. Particularly given that centuries of European settler-colonialism and racism have completely unformed, reformed, and deformed our human relationships by scaling up Whiteness against the "other"—Indigenous, Black, and Asian peoples—in a racialized system (Loomba, 2015; Said, 2014; Smith, 2012). How can we live well in a relationship with one another in the afterlives of slavery, genocide, and economic deprivation? We believe that the theory of Being is one way to think about this question, and in this chapter we ponder the *relational ways of Being* and the boundaries around them.

Exploring the Nuances of Boundaries in Forming and Maintaining Relationships With Anti-Blackness

Developing and maintaining positive relationships is one of the indicators that one is functioning well psychologically (Huppert, 2009). However, given our precarious lives, people miscommunicate, misunderstand, and may not fully see the worth of the people or things they are in relationships with over time. And yet, some of the issues that occur in voluntary and involuntary relationships are due to an inability to engage productively across Difference (Watt, 2015). In this chapter, we discuss anti-Blackness as one current example of an ongoing breach in relationships in the United States and globally. We draw from our personal and professional backgrounds to think about relationship-building techniques to effectively engage across Difference.

We started writing this chapter a couple of weeks after George Floyd's violent murder by police officers encouraged people across the world to collectively examine the experiences of Black people in the United States' carceral system and nation. It is apparent that cross-racial relationships among Black people and individuals and institutions form persistently unhealthy conditions that result in emotional and physical damage. George Floyd's case is not isolated. Only halfway through 2020, our nation witnessed many other anti-Black extrajudicial killings at the hands of police officers and White vigilantes to include, but not limited to: Ahmaud Arbery, Rayshard Brooks, Tony McDade, Breonna Taylor, and countless others who unfortunately remain nameless. Simply relegating the cause of these murders to unhealthy cross-racial relationships without acknowledging the historical systemic oppression and anti-Blackness that plagues our nation would be extremely negligent and ignores the root of the problem.

Anti-Blackness is a direct outcome of the White supremacy ideology and is inherent in the fabric of our nation (Bell, 1992; Browne-Marshall, 2013). Wilderson (2010) stated, "Anti-Blackness manifests as the monumentalization and fortification of civil society against social death" (p. 90), which relegates the humanity of the Black community to nonbeing, socially dead, and regarded as the antagonist in the story of America. This causes us to pause. As we previously described, people are in a relationship with each other and with other nonhuman entities (e.g., governments, school systems, criminal justice systems, etc.) that are foundationally anti-Black. Anti-Blackness posits that the relationship that Black people have with others in America is fundamentally flawed because since its inception people of African descent were not viewed as deserving of respect or as human.

Therefore, to nurture a positive relationship under such societal conditions, there must be a mutual belief that the other person is inherently worthy, deserves respect, and is entitled to the same rights and privileges. Notably, encapsulated within anti-Blackness is not merely the thought that Black is synonymous with inhuman, undeserving, and inherently flawed; it is coupled with the idea that White means one is superhuman (i.e., has more feelings) and inherently deserving of grace. Also, there is a presumption that Black death and pain are somehow sacrificial in our collective journey to becoming better human beings.

For example, Nancy Pelosi, democratic speaker of the United States House of Representatives said, "Thank you, George Floyd, for sacrificing your life for justice" after the conviction of Derek Chauvin for the murder of George Floyd. In response, Ahmad Washington (2021) said on Twitter, "Black people don't aspire to be the world martyrs and this country's racial miners canary." There is much to be explored about how non-White people are viewed in a relationship with individuals and with systems that are inherently abusive and problematic. While improving relationships is not the cure to racism, sexism, homophobia, transphobia, and the like, the cancers that plague our society (Watt, 2015), this exploration can plant the seeds that can, over time, improve how we understand and care for each other through being authentic, extending unconditional positive regard, and maintaining accountability-driven respect.

How can we be with each other and with (anti)Blackness to humanize systems that benefit from logics of dehumanization and unworthiness? How can we achieve what Sealy-Ruiz (2020) notes in her poem, "finding strength in each other's spaces; meeting lines but never crossing them"? How can we be in authentic relationships with each other that encourage accountability while extending unconditional positive regard?

Throughout this chapter, we practice *third thinging* by wrestling with these questions from our lived positionality and disciplinary socialization. Janice is trained as a counselor educator and Milad studies higher education. We come from different countries and background, but our lives are affected by Whiteness and racism, one way or the other. This practice of *third thinging* helps us engage our Differences in speaking of the issue of anti-Blackness while practicing *listening deeply, humanizing otherness in relationships and idea exploration, exploring defenses*, and *dissenting wisely and well*.

As we each developed our narratives, we met several times, and each time we discussed the ways in which we were impacted by anti-Blackness using the *ways of Being* (see Watt's "Part One Introduction," this volume). Therefore, our writing is a product of this rich process of explorations in a relationship with each other and with anti-Blackness as the *third thing*. Given our interest in literature and poetry, we each start our segments with a quote that helps us think more deeply through the dilemmas we are wrestling with.

The quote serves as *a third thing* that assists us in exploring our relationship to systems of oppression while maintaining our distance from it to avoid reliving the violence as we explore these systems deeply. As we share our perspectives on these dilemmas with each other and with you—our reader—we also invite you to practice *relational ways of Being*, that is, *listen deeply, explore defenses, humanize otherness* in relation to the dilemma, and *dissent wisely and well*. At the conclusion of our chapter, we posed each other *an open and honest question* to invite each other into further exploration (see Appendix F).

Janice: Explorations of Me—Across Time, Across Space— In Search of Authenticity

> *No, I do not weep at the world—I am too busy sharpening my oyster knife.*
>
> —Zora Hurston, *How It Feels to Be Colored Me*

At a young age, I became aware that I was viewed as an alien in spaces, notably academic spaces. Although I am not just the sum of being Black and a woman, I have over time learned through experiences that when people see me—sometimes that's all they see. I always knew I looked different from others. Be it skin tone, facial features, body type, intense introspective perspective, or being shy; I am always just different. I continue to unravel my thoughts to make meaning of the ways in which my sheer presence is an act of resistance against racism, sexism, misogynoir and how oppression robs me, a Black woman, of my individuality. Misogynoir, a term coined by Moya Bailey (2021), captures the unique bias Black women face at the intersection of race and gender within and outside our racial community. We are generally regarded as too loud, too Black, too independent, not light enough, too angry, and at every turn we face rules on how we should be or not be, which creates limitations, voids us of our humanity, and impacts our quality of life. We are also expected to take care of everyone else before ourselves, but very few are in line to reciprocate. The ways in which Black women are rendered invisible have been well-documented across history and are evident in the murder of Ma'Khia Bryant by police officers in Columbus, Ohio. Like many murders of Black people, public officials spent time proclaiming that Ma'Khia was deserving of what happened to her and that she was inherently a threat and/or not deserving of life.

While I am aware that I am very much alive and what I experience cannot be compared to what led to the murder of Ma'Khia, I'm astutely aware, however, that Ma'Khia and I exist in the same narrative about how our lives are meaningless. My existence as a Black girl and woman has been replete with experiences that I am somehow not worthy of life, happiness, or protection. My childhood shaped many relationships (i.e., familial, community, and school) that determined who I am, how I view others, and how I view myself. These relationships presented spaces where I could feel whole without repercussions (i.e., be authentic and held in unconditional and positive regard) and environments where I did not feel safe (e.g., out of fear of persecution if I did not perform as a good Black girl).

Authenticity, also known as genuineness, is a fundamental element that guides counselors in forming meaningful relationships with their clients. Gelso and Carter (1994) define authenticity as "the ability and willingness to be what one truly is" (p. 297) with someone in a mutual relationship centered on growth. As a counselor, I use my honesty, openness, and sincerity to make the client feel that they are in a relationship and environment where they can be free to communicate without judgment. However, authenticity is not always positive, and it does not mean "anything goes." For example, the relationship should include boundaries, or agreed upon limits, established by the counselor to ensure the client's safety. While authenticity within a helping relationship is created by the counselor, many therapies, if utilized appropriately in a cross-cultural relationship, could make for a more meaningful connection. Listening to understand is a big component of conveying authenticity that constitutes one of the *relational ways of Being*, that is, *listening deeply*.

Because the core components of the therapeutic relationship are intertwined, here I briefly introduce the concept of unconditional positive regard defined as acceptance and support of another person without judgment (Rogers, 1957). Rogers (1957) stated that unconditional positive regard, combined with other essential characteristics such as authenticity, listening, and empathy, supports an environment that fosters growth. Unconditional positive regard does not suggest you must like someone or be kind to them, but means that you are open to listening to someone regardless of differing opinions (Rogers, 1957). In fact, sometimes, dialogues related to topics directly connecting to one's core values, one's lived experiences, or reminding of current or historical pain, can cause what Fanon (1967) called cognitive dissonance that can make communication difficult. Unconditional positive regard would suggest that one remains in potential discomfort and actively listens to the other without judgment. The theory of Being suggests that dissonance can invite self-exploration in relation to the conflict while allowing to stay with others exploring the uncertainties.

If individuals are able to employ empathy and meet in a place that allows them to extend unconditional positive regard, they can convey genuine understanding and mutual respect (see also chapters 2, 9, and 10, this volume).

Across many cross-cultural dialogues, this disposition can help us increase understanding and awareness of different perspectives. However, this is not as easy as conveyed. James Baldwin once said, "We can disagree and still love each other unless your disagreement is rooted in my oppression." Individuals can feel exhaustion if they have tried to engage in authentic relationships with others while patiently extending unconditional positive regard, yet results are not just a difference of opinion, but ongoing oppression. Young (2004) conveys that there are five "faces" or types of oppression: violence, exploitation, marginalization, powerlessness, and cultural imperialism. So, while authenticity and unconditional positive regard are powerful tools that can help facilitate positive cross-cultural dialogue, they are not enough. If we are committed to maintaining healthy relationships, then accountability is needed.

In my case, across many years in personal and educational environments, individuals and society have at every turn attempted to restrain me, use me to fill the cups of others, but not to shield me from pain. The sad reality is that I have been socialized to maintain these restraints on my own and some-times find purpose in being a vessel of comfort for others while suppressing my own pain. This manifests as showing extreme empathy, even if it means silencing my own hurt because I want everyone else to feel okay. It can also look as if I am convincing myself and others that their efforts to stop being oppressive are sufficient, even if the effort is not sustained. Because hey, "they are trying," and I should meet them where they are or extend graciousness without remembering that accountability is a form of love.

Also, it can appear as if I am purposely engaging in conversations with others committed to viewing me as inferior to them to somehow convince them that I am worthy of regard. I walk away wondering, "Was I trying to convince them or myself?" In actuality, I am attempting to regain control and power over a situation that constantly makes me feel powerless (gendered racism). It causes a form of madness, you know, facing individual turmoil, navigating the margins created by oppression, and observing an epic mani-festation of the same violence play out each day with each murder and the ongoing disregard for the human life of people who look like me.

Shortly after the murder of George Floyd, I found myself in professional spaces with mostly White women. Conversations included their admissions of not knowing that racism was "so bad," an unawareness of prominent his-torical events that document the ongoing violence against Black people, a plea for People of Color to teach them how to be better, and then ending in tears. These tears were generally followed by comforting words from others (notably White people and Black men), offers to help them not feel so sad, or even just silence to provide them space to process. Initially, when leaving these environments, I felt angry. Not because I felt the attention should be on me, but because of an awareness that the space intended for healing centered Whiteness, decentered the violence against Black people, rendered our feelings unimportant, and reminded me that historically White women's tears would initiate violence against Black people and undermine the experiences of Black women.

Also, it was as if they were inherently viewed as more human (hyperhumanization of sorts), deserving of care, and in need of protection I would never be afforded. Fortunately, I am aware that this phenomenon is not an individual problem, but I am reminded that it is a product of White supremacy and the fog it creates that we all consume and maintain to certain degrees. It creates a psychological strain, and just like everyone is encouraged to commit to a lifelong journey of exploring individual bias and privilege, one should also constantly assess the psychological toll of gendered racism. It causes me to question who one can trust, how to develop and maintain relationships, and how to see self and others.

Defining race-based trauma helps me understand my internal and external responses. Race-based traumatic stress (RBTS) acknowledges that racism is a stressor that can injure or harm its targets and negatively impacts their mental and physical well-being across their lifetime (Carter et al., 2020). People experiencing RBTS may display behavioral and emotional expressions that include but are not limited to aggression, irritability, self-blame, confusion, shame, guilt, and avoidance (Carter et al., 2020). Previously, I shared the anger I felt after engaging in optional healing spaces where White women expressed their feelings, but I failed to share that later on I purposefully avoided these spaces to ensure I had the mental stamina to attend to my students or participants in equity-focused workshops. Because I was in a leadership role, I felt responsibility to my students but not to my colleagues/peers being in spaces where I sought an opportunity to share and heal.

The compilation of facing my own internal struggles caused by daily oppression, awareness of current and historical violence against Black people, navigating the symptoms of racism (e.g., White guilt/fragility of White people, internalized oppression exhibited by Black people) and the ongoing erasure of Black women's feelings ignited an awakening for me to consult the work of my muses (e.g., Audre Lorde, Toni Morrison, bell hooks, Zora Neale Hurston, etc.) for clarity, guidance, and notably hope. Although much of their work is transformational, Hurston's words offer an escape from the boundaries that society tries to force on me as a Black woman and serve as a reminder that I am inherently wholesome, and give hope for myself and those who look like me or those who face oppression. Hurston (1928) stated:

> I am not tragically colored. There is no great sorrow dammed up in my soul, nor lurking behind my eyes. I do not mind at all. I do not belong to the sobbing school of Negrohood who hold that nature somehow has given them a lowdown dirty deal and whose feelings are all hurt about it. Even in the helter-skelter skirmish that is my life, I have seen that the world is to the strong regardless of a little pigmentation more or less. No, I do not weep at the world—I am too busy sharpening my oyster knife. (pp. 215–216)

Although my feelings do not fully align with Hurston's thoughts that somehow being strong can preclude you from experiencing the realities of racism, I do, however, choose not to view my race, gender, or any parts of me called "marginalized" by White people or men as flawed because they are not socialized to see my wholeness (e.g., physical, intellectual, and emotional) and my contributions. Like Hurston, I'd rather spend time sharpening the tools (i.e., natural gifts, skills, and knowledge) that I have to contribute to dismantling oppression and experiencing the beauty that exists in the world. Empathy, unconditional self-regard, and radical love for myself is essential for self-preservation (Lorde, 1988) and necessary before you can extend it to others. For me, spending time weeping over what others do not acknowledge about me is their problem, not mine.

Milad—Dissonance and Relational Exploration of an Entangled Self

> That, too, is why this epidemic has taught me nothing new, except that I must fight it at your side. I know positively . . . that each of us has the plague within him; no one, no one on earth is free from it. And I know, too, that we must keep endless watch on ourselves lest in a careless moment we breathe in somebody's face and fasten the infection on him. What's natural is the microbe. All the rest—health, integrity, purity (if you like)—is a product of the human will, of a vigilance that must never falter. The good man, the man who infects hardly anyone, is the man who has the fewest lapses of attention. And it needs tremendous will-power, a never ending tension of the mind, to avoid such lapses. It's a wearying business, being plague-stricken. But it's still more wearying to refuse to be it. (Camus, 1948, chapter 24)

I was sitting and working at a coffee shop with two dear friends one of whom was Black, Casey, and the other White (passing), Jordan. I remember having this conversation with them about a statistics course Casey and I were taking. I had practiced some of the homework with Casey a previous day where I explained a question and its answer by elaborating on the very detailed mathematical logic of it. This is how I was trained as a former engineer, which allowed me to best make sense of learning and teaching statistics. I do not recall what Casey noted in our coffee-shop conversation, but I have a faint memory that it had a questioning undertone for the ways I was trying to explain the statistics homework. I then clearly remember hearing my friend Jordan say "White people" in reference to the situation and implicitly in reference to me. Now both of them nodded and smiled in agreement. It always makes me wonder about past events that I remember clearly and the ones that remain faint memories. The snippets I remember are the ones closest to my sense of self: I don't completely remember what was said afterwards, but I remember I was already implicated. I clearly remember my dizziness.

Looking back, I understand how my ways of explaining statistics had to do with the tropes of racism engrained in the United States and its educational system. I also understand why the term White people can be a harmless joke to direct attention to the racial aspects of the scene involving friends. The whole situation, however, created an uneasiness in me as I was clearly implicated in racism and was placed in a racial category that I had difficulty identifying with. Although I have come to recognize how colorism impacts the way I am perceived as White in some situations and as Brown, Middle Eastern, or Iranian in others, I also understand that my on-the-ground experience does not match the legal category of White for Iranians and Iranian Americans in the United States (Maghbouleh, 2017). However, I was never White or a Person of Color before coming to the United States. My first goal in noting this story is to highlight the unease with the situation and, second, the unease with writing about the situation: what is my positionality in speaking about Whiteness and anti-Blackness as an Iranian international student currently immigrating to the United States?

Unlike a U.S. citizen of my age, I do not have an extensive lived experience with racism, and I am not Black or White. I would even argue that I still struggle with my own racial identity. Some advocate for Middle Eastern and North-African as a racial category in the United States census, but the category itself is problematic. These categories are products of colonizers dividing the world, people, and natural resources. Hence, I write this as a person conscious of his racialization and the shifting position around Whiteness and anti-Blackness in the United States and globally. Not surprisingly, this also explains why I am drawn to the theory of Being as it principally deals with racism as an ever-present but always shifting system of power that superhumanizes the White man and dehumanizes everybody else.

My second goal is to expand the unease as an entry point into thinking what it means to be in a relation with self, others, and anti-Blackness when confronted with dissonances in dialogue. How can unease invite the use of *relational ways of Being*? Of course, the coffee-shop conversation I noted previously was neither difficult (I knew and still know that my friends deeply care about me) nor intentional (it happened in a casual conversation about a course). What made that dialogue difficult for me was to stay with the uneasy dissonance it created for me; or rather, to take the unease as being in a relation to a disease—of Whiteness and anti-Blackness in this case (I'm inspired to make this connection reading Patel, 2015). I have not resolved the previous dissonance for myself. In some ways, I have resisted doing so, wanting to stay with the unease that I hope can help me be more wary of the cancer that is racism (Watt, 2015). In this section, I specifically think about the boundaries of being in a relationship with others while holding on to the dissonance. How do I stay in a relationship when in conflict, meeting lines but not crossing them (Sealy-Ruiz, 2020)? Moreover, I am still unsettled by the dissonance as my defensive mechanisms muddy the grounds of reflection. Thinking of the defensive mechanisms in the privileged identity exploration (PIE) model (see Watt, 2007, 2015 and Appendix E), I recognize that I have experienced a series of reactions as I have dealt with the dissonance produced by the coffee-shop conversation with my friends: *denial, deflection, rationalization and intellectualization, and benevolence* (charity).

The story I described also helps me highlight the impacts of racism on bodies that bear the mark of it one way or another; the air that we breathe leaves us exhausted for the "wearying business [of] . . . being plague-stricken" (Camus, 1948, chapter 24). As an educator, I am on a thin thread of hope that transformation is possible, that a dissonance can someday spark a revolutionary becoming. I ask how can I/we stay with dissonance? Staying with dissonance may sound overwhelming, tiring, even unnecessary. I think staying with dissonance is like "staying with the trouble" (Haraway, 2016), "being in the wake" (Sharpe, 2016), as in caring to stay in relationships with self, others, and racism that is in the air. PIE defenses arise for the underlying sense of fear and entitlement (Watt, 2007, 2015). Why go to uncertain grounds? Why leave the safety and the fullness of breath I feel entitled to?

To care, to stay in the wake, to stay with the trouble is thus to explore places to which defensive mechanisms open doors that we would not otherwise dare to enter. When I fear something, I find myself short of breath;

similar to when I recall the video of Ahmaud Arbery's death. While the media found that George Floyd's murder was a more profitable video to repeat over and over—in absolute disregard for the trauma it caused to Black people and People of Color—Ahmaud's death was moved to the background. Since the day I saw the video of his murder by White vigilantes, I have recurring dreams of the video and feel my breath pattern changing. Short of breath, my body reveals itself, making me see marks of oppression in its various mani-festations on/in/from it. And as I take a deep breath and let it out, I wonder about the conditions for learning when one is short of breath. If shortness of breath gets us closer to death (death as running out of breath), maybe short-ness of breath itself has a pedagogy, even if momentarily, to bridge life and death in a global society that observes, consumes, "likes," and retweets videos of death that resurface on news cycles every day. How can we sustain life, not death, from dissonances that cut our breaths short?

I think of being short of breath as a pause on the "spacetime" of racism. It allows me to "intra-act" with self and "diffract" the many ways oppression is mapped onto my own body (for details on the notions of feminist mate-rialism, see Barad, 2007). I ask, "What would it mean to be in a relation-ship with self (i.e., diffraction), others, and Whiteness and anti-Blackness in order to live in the world that implicates me in all its various manifes-tations of its unfolding?" To me, that is a question of how to "live into" response-ability, which demands from us to respond to what matters (Barad, 2007). My note on response-ability is not about the notion of individual reasonability in Western civics that relies on individualism, rationality, and enlightenment ideals. Rather, I think of response-ability as a way in which my Being is entangled with the world's becoming with all its beauty and violence. In moments of dissonance, as I touch myself (Barad, 2012), there lies a pedagogy of openness, vulnerability, and entanglement.

> Entanglements are relations of obligation—being bound to the other—enfolded traces of othering. Othering, the constitution of an "Other," entails an indebtedness to the "Other," who is irreducibly and materially bound to, threaded through, the "self"—a diffraction/dispersion of iden-tity. "Otherness" is an entangled relation of difference (différance). (Barad, 2007, p. 265)

As Barad's previous quote highlights, traces of othering exist in such entan-glements of breath/short-of-breath, self/other, Black/People-of-Color, Blackness/anti-Blackness. Response-ability means thus to remain in a rela-tionship with self, the "other," and most importantly with the structural systems of othering.

The point of staying with the dissonance is more than trying to resolve the conflict between subjects: it is to stay in an uneasy relationship with the "gratuitous violence that occurs at the level of a structure that constitutes the Black as the constitutive outside" (Sharpe, 2016, p. 28). As I think about the coffee-shop scene, I recognize how my own practices have been violent to Casey (I stick with the word "violent" to emphasize the structural component that the action constitutes but is not necessarily manifest in the action). Deep inside, I want closure. I think of reaching out to Casey and having a dialogue about the situation but then pause and wonder if it really needs to become their issue. Who and what does my closure implicate? This brings me into the question of response-ability, boundaries, and accountability.

More often than not, reliance on self-reflection through relationships demands an Other that has to be the source of dissonance. Intergroup dialogues, for example, have entailed bringing people from conflicting identity groups into dialogue with one another to promote justice. In doing so, intergroup dialogue relies heavily on the powerless to entice the empathy of the powerful and for the structurally powerful to humanize the structurally powerless and grant them what has previously been taken via depersonalization (Buckley & Quaye, 2016; Gurin et al., 2013; Zuniga et al., 2016). However, it is important not to cross the line when coming to meeting the line (Sealy-Ruiz, 2020). In my relationship with Casey and Jordan, I do not position them as being there for my transformation. I have loved them for all the care they provided to/for me as I entered a new school, new city, and navigated life in a still new country. I have tried to be there for them when they were facing problems but also when they celebrated life achievements. As one of the characters in Camus novel points out, "for the plague-stricken their peace of mind is more important than a human life" (Camus, 1948, chapter 24), and for me, that means staying with the unease and the ways it implicates me with the disease that is racism, even if I may not have the closure I want to achieve through my friends' labor.

Way too many social justice trainings rely on Black bodies to tell White people or other People of Color how not to be racist (or more recently how to be antiracist), emphasizing one's comfort over caring for the "inner life" of Black folks (Love, 2019). Fewer among them invite self-exploration as caring, caring for living an interdependent life in joy. I resist responsibility that relies on some sort of guardianship and charity that often manifest in the liberal moral logic of "reducing harm" (Haidt, 2013a, 2013b). Rather, I think of response-ability in terms of staying with the trouble, "as a *process* [emphasis added] . . . becoming—with each other in surprising relays" (Haraway, 2016, p. 3). I ask, "caring when and where?" Far too often,

I find myself avoiding difficult dialogues about anti-Blackness with those with whom I am already in a comfortable relationship. Who do I care for when I refuse to engage in difficult dialogues about anti-Blackness with people with whom I feel safe and comfortable? How do I live with the unease of tracing othering within self to overcome the disease of Whiteness and anti-Blackness? If response-ability is an obligation to the Other in a relationship, it thus requires embracing our interdependencies. To care is thus to be accountable to "the nurturing of all that is necessary for the welfare and flourishing of life" (Chatzidakis et al., 2020, p. 5). The dialogue that does not nurture life comes short of addressing anti-Blackness, even if it is done with the best of intentions. Thus, at a personal level, accountability is to stay in the wake with the uneasiness and shortness of breath, even if that is uncomfortable. On a relational level, accountability relies on boundaries of not using others for one's comfort and ease, as well as staying in nurturing and caring relationships, even when dissenting and disagreeing. On a community level, accountability involves staying with the unease as it connects us with the disease of Whiteness and anti-Blackness in us and in our institutions.

Janice and Milad: Toward Accountability

As we discussed in this chapter, racism creates a global systemic reality that highly values White lives and treats Black lives, and lives of other People of Color, as deficient of worth. As a result, before anyone considers the aforementioned *ways of Being* to support the formation and maintenance of positive relationships, they must explore their own bias and beliefs related to the humanity of people that are different from themselves (e.g., gender, race, religion, sexuality, etc.). However, an observation across the history of the United States provides evidence that racism is insidious, in view of the current agenda to dismantle scholarship like critical race theory. Critical race theory (CRT) encompasses a body of legal scholarship with varying, but related perspectives, established in the 1970s and 1980s by individuals such as Derrick Bell, Kimberlé Crenshaw, Patricia Williams, Mari Matsuda, and Charles Lawrence III, and many others (Crenshaw et al., 1991). In the vein of accountability, CRT has grown to be a lens in many environments (e.g., education, sociology, healthcare, etc.) that provides the language to dissect and name the nuanced manifestations of racism. When someone can name the conditions that harm them, they have a better chance of identifying ways to stop the harm and to hold individuals/systems accountable. However, the current dismissal and attack on CRT, and the White supremacist insurrection mounted at the United States Capital building on January 6, 2021 proves that many are still resisting accountability (Sawchuk, 2021). Much like CRT, the PIE model (Watt, 2015) provides the language to name the defenses that arise within us for self-exploration and in others for humanizing otherness in relationships with individuals who are confronted with an awareness of privilege.

When considering accountability, a magic wand to influence people to believe that non-White lives are also valuable clearly does not exist. The dehumanization of People of Color is embedded in the history of the world as evident in the history of eugenics, racial genocide, enslavement, and colonization (Dunbar-Ortiz, 2014; Yakushko, 2019; Zinn, 1980). So, we call for accountability in the hopes of reaching a place where people can exist in a space that celebrates differences and views accountability as a "love language" that maintains healthy relationships among all people.

Conclusion

We each wrote from our own positionalities and came into a relationship with each other in this chapter through *third thinging* the dilemmas we introduced early in the chapter. Here in the conclusion, we offer some reflections on our own processes. Rather than trying to come up with some universal checklist on how to resolve the dilemmas that we introduced earlier, we offer what a process-oriented approach to Being in a relationship looks like. It is tempting to bring our narratives together and present their transcendental lessons here. It is not equally comforting to note how reading each other's sections may have brought up some uneasiness for the other. Further, we practice setting boundaries by meeting the line but not crossing them (Sealey-Ruiz, 2020). We can bring our sections in dialogue with one another, but it is by no means possible to give some conclusion on the content without flattening our experiences, positionalities, identities, and even our relationship.

In resisting to provide a conclusive remark on the "doing" of relationships, we shift our focus on the processes of Being in a relationship with one another. As we invited you—our reader—to practice *relational ways of Being*, we also *deeply listened* to one another in reading each other's sections, we *turned to wonder* on why each said what they said, we *recognized our defenses*, and we offered an open and honest question to one another as a way of *dissenting wisely and well* (See Appendix F).

References

Bailey, M. (2021). *Misogynoir transformed: Black women's digital resistance*. NYU Press.

Barad, K. (2007). *Meeting the universe halfway: Quantum physics and the entanglement of matter and meaning*. Duke University Press.

Barad, K. (2012). On touching—the inhuman that therefore I am. *Differences, 23*(3), 206–223. https://doi.org/10.1215/10407391-1892943

Belgrave, F. Z., & Allison, K. W. (2018). *African American psychology: From Africa to America*. SAGE.

Bell, D. (1992). *Faces at the bottom of the well: The permanence of racism*. Basic Books.

Browne-Marshall, G. (2013). Stop and frisk: From slave-catchers to NYPD, a legal commentary. *Trotter Review, 21*(1), 98–119.

Buckley, J. B., & Quaye, S. J. (2016). A vision of social justice in intergroup dialogue. *Race Ethnicity and Education, 19*(5), 1117–1139. https://doi.org/10.1080/13613324.2014.969221

Camus, A. (1948). *The plague*. Modern Library.

Carter, R. T., Kirkinis, K., & Johnson, V. E. (2020). Relationships between trauma symptoms and race-based traumatic stress. *Traumatology, 26*(1), 11–18. https://doi.org/10.1037/trm0000217

Chatzidakis, A., Hakim, J., Littler, J., Rottenberg, C., & Segal, L. (2020). From carewashing to radical care: The discursive explosions of care during Covid-19. *Feminist Media Studies, 20*(6), 889–895. https://doi.org/10.1080/14680777.2020.1781435

Crenshaw, K. (1991). Mapping the margins: Intersectionality, identity politics, and violence against women of color. *Stanford Law Review, 43*(6), 1241–1299. https://doi.org/10.2307/1229039

Dunbar-Ortiz, R. (2014). *An Indigenous peoples' history of the United States*. Beacon Press.

Fanon, F. (1967). *Black skin, white masks*. Grove/Atlantic.

Gelso, C. J., & Carter, J. A. (1994). Components of the psychotherapy relationship: Their interaction and unfolding during treatment. *Journal of Counseling Psychology, 41*(3), 296–306. https://doi.org/10.1037/0022-0167.41.3.296

Gurin, P., Nagda, B. (Ratnesh) A., & Zuniga, X. (2013). *Dialogue across difference: Practice, theory, and research on intergroup dialogue*. Russell Sage Foundation.

Haidt, J. (2013a). Moral psychology for the twenty-first century. *Journal of Moral Education, 42*(3), 281–297. https://doi.org/10.1080/03057240.2013.817327 http://jeffco.axis360.baker-taylor.com/Title?itemid=0009839976

Haidt, J. (2013b). *The righteous mind: Why good people are divided by politics and religion*. Vintage Books.

Haraway, D. J. (2016). *Staying with the trouble: Making kin in the Chthulucene*. Duke University Press.

Huppert, F. A. (2009). Psychological well-being: Evidence regarding its causes and consequences. *Applied Psychology: Health and Well-Being, 1*(2), 137–164. https://doi.org/10.1111/j.1758-0854.2009.01008.x

Hurston, Z. N. (1928, May). How it feels to be colored me. *The World Tomorrow*, *11*(5), 215–216. https://search.proquest.com/docview/1797170085? accountid= 13360

Loomba, A. (2015). *Colonialism/Postcolonialism*. Routledge.

Lorde, A. (1988). *A burst of light: Essays*. Firebrand Books.

Love, B. (2019). *We want to do more than survive: Abolitionist teaching and the pursuit of educational freedom*. Beacon Press.

Maghbouleh, N. (2017). *The limits of whiteness: Iranian Americans and the everyday politics of race*. Stanford University Press.

Patel, L. (2015). *Decolonizing educational research: From ownership to answerability*. Routledge.

Rogers, C. R. (1957). The necessary and sufficient conditions of therapeutic personality change. *Journal of Consulting Psychology*, *21*(2), 95–103. https://doi.org/10.1037/h0045357

Said, E. W. (2014). *Orientalism*. Knopf Doubleday.

Sawchuk, S. (2021). *What is critical race theory, and why is it under attack?* Education Week. https://www.edweek.org/leadership/what-is-critical-race-theory-and-why-is-it-under-attack/2021/05

Sealey-Ruiz, Y. (2020). *Love from the vortex & other poems*. Kaleidoscope Vibrations.

Sharpe, C. E. (2016). *In the wake: On blackness and being*. Duke University Press.

Smith, L. T. (2012). *Decolonizing methodologies: Research and Indigenous peoples* (2nd ed.). Zed Books.

Washington, A. [@DrARWashington]. (2021, May 25). *Black people don't aspire to be the world's martyrs and this country's racial miner's canary* [Tweet]. Twitter. https://twitter.com/DrARWashington/status/1397167771046354946?s=20

Watt, S. K. (2007). Difficult dialogues, privilege and social justice: Uses of the Privileged Identity Exploration (PIE) model in student affairs practice. *College Student Affairs Journal*, *26*(2), 114–126. https://eric.ed.gov/?id=EJ899385

Watt, S. K. (Ed.). (2015). *Designing transformative multicultural initiatives: Theoretical foundations, practical applications, and facilitator considerations*. Stylus.

Wilderson, F. B. (2010). *Red, white & black: Cinema and the structure of U.S. antagonisms*. Duke University Press.

Yakushko, O. (2019). Eugenics and its evolution in the history of western psychology: A critical archival review. *Psychotherapy and Politics International*, *17*(2), e1495. https://doi.org/10.1002/ppi.1495

Young, I. M. (2004). Five faces of power. In L. L. Heldke & P. O'Connor (Eds.), *Oppression, privilege, and resistance: Theoretical perspectives on racism, sexism and heterosexism*. McGraw-Hill.

Zinn, H. (2015). *A people's history of the United States*. HarperCollins.

Zuniga, X., Lopez, G., & Ford, K. A. (2016). *Intergroup dialogue: Engaging difference, social identities and social justice*. Routledge.

INTRODUCTION TO
COMMUNITY WAYS OF BEING

PART FOUR INTRODUCTION

Sherry K. Watt

This part focuses on *community ways of Being* practices. The practices involve facing the conflict by shifting away from centering on just individual survival and moving toward expecting community thriving. In this section's chapters "Truth" by DaVida L. Anderson, "Otherness" by Duhita Mahatmya and Saba Rasheed Ali, and "Research" by Kari E. Weaver and Amanda L. Mollet, the authors explore how their social identities show up when sharing space with others across Difference and conflict. The authors provide specific examples of how they applied *community ways of Being* in higher education environments to practice aligning their thoughts, feelings, and actions to focus on community awareness as a group about a conflict. Truth, otherness, and research are three windows into the dilemmas that the authors explore at the intersection of their personal stories and their work in and with various communities. Further, the authors imagine what it means to thrive together in a community while centering on Difference and conflict. In doing so, the authors bring their personal narratives, relational dilemmas, and community practices into conversation with related scholarly areas to highlight *community ways of Being* practices.

These practices include *understanding the third thing and third thinging, balancing dialogue and action, normalizing defenses, embracing trouble as a learning opportunity,* and *viewing missteps as developmental.* In the following list we offer questions to invite you to reflect upon and personalize these *community ways of Being* practices.

- *Understanding the third thing and third thinging*: What do you notice about the way this conflict weaves in and throughout your life and the life of this community? What threads are present here in this community? If you had to pick a thread, what is the single thread that is ever-present as you explore this conflict—for you? for others? for the community? What thread saved you and the community? What thread nearly snuffed the life out of you and the community? What threads interconnect? What are the threads related to this conflict that need to die in order for the community to thrive? How do these threads connect with the purpose and intent of life—as you see it? as others see it? How do these interconnecting threads align with the action the community wants to take in the face of this conflict? What ways can the community counter the conflict by actively seeking what it wants rather than solely resisting what it does not want?

- *Balancing dialogue and action*: What information does the community need to discuss that is related to this conflict? How can we avoid our dialogue getting derailed when we face this conflict? What preparation is needed as we enter this dialogue and face this conflict? What are the commitments we want to make to each other as a community about how we talk to each other while in and around this conflict? What actions can I take in my role to undo the distress this conflict causes for the community? What thoughts drive my behavior when I interact around this conflict with others? What are the barriers that perpetuate harm to this community? What are the salves already present that foster health and prosperity for this community? How can we take time to explore while attending to taking action to change the negative consequences the community is enduring around this conflict? What will we do when dialogue does get derailed?

- *Normalizing defenses* (PIE model): What are the various ways in which we generally interact around this conflict? What feelings are present with us as we explore the ways in which this conflict impacts each of us and the community? When have we seen community conflicts erupt or go wrong? What happened during these eruptions? What was the source of the eruption? What happened if/when the community moved through the conflict? How might we stay with our feelings of angst? What other feelings (negative or positive) are present during this conflict? What else can we do together while we are angry with each other?

- *Embracing trouble as a learning opportunity*: What do we hope for around this conflict? Do we have a plan (a vision for solving the conflict, expectation about the conflict, feeling about the origins of the conflict) in mind? How is the plan different than the reality as we experience this conflict? What is our way of being with the uncertainty of life? What do we fear? How do we want to be with uncertainty? What can we learn together (about the issues, each other, our institutions, society, etc.) as we explore this conflict? How can what we learn together inform the actions we take surrounding this conflict?

- *Viewing missteps as developmental*: What informs this conflict? Is it how we were socialized? What role has supremacy, *us-versus-them*, domination played in our understanding of this conflict? How has supremacy, *us-versus-them* domination played in how we interact surrounding this conflict? How does the idea of winning or of "survival of the fittest" influence the way we see this conflict? How does "winning" or "survival of the fittest" influence the way we work together to shift this conflict? How can we simultaneously embrace what we know and understand about each other and hold the possibility for ourselves to evolve? How might we embrace our failings as lessons rather than seeing the other as fatally flawed? What if we focused on the possibilities that might come from this conflict rather than its limitations? What if we welcomed and celebrated the revealing of blemishes? What does it look like when we use shame and guilt as correction? What are the practices we will embrace that offer generative connections that are generative rather than reductive interactions?

The authors of each chapter have also provided a set of supplementary materials for application of Being practices. These supplementary materials are listed in Appendix F.

9

TRUTH

DaVida L. Anderson

I believe that unarmed truth and unconditional love will have the final word in reality. This is why right, temporarily defeated, is stronger than evil triumphant.

—Martin Luther King Jr.

I remember the first time some of my classmates challenged me about my belief in Santa Claus. When I was growing up, my family celebrated Christmas, and every year my older brother and I would set aside cookies and milk for Santa Claus. I believed that we had to go to sleep for Santa Claus to deliver presents to our house. That was my truth until one day I went to school and overheard two kids talking about how their parents got them their Christmas presents. One of the kids said that Santa Claus did not exist because he did not celebrate Christmas. So, I entered my first debate over the truth about Santa Claus. I believed Santa Claus was real because every year Santa Claus stopped by my house, left presents, ate the cookies, and drank the milk I had left for him. I had over 9 years of evidence that Santa Claus was real and yet the confrontation made me examine myself on a personal level. How could my truth be wrong? I did not want to hear nor believe their reality because that would mean everything that I knew to be true about Santa Claus would be questioned. Reflecting years later, I recognize that both of my classmates had a history of their parents telling them something different from what my parents told me. My classmates' parents either provided their gifts every year instead of Santa Claus or Santa Claus did not exist because they did not celebrate Christmas due to their religion or nonreligious beliefs. This experience showed me how our understanding of truth is formed by our parents, teachers, media, or respected sources that provide us with social constructs that inform our ideas and beliefs.

The way that our truth is socially constructed can also influence our behavior. Think about our buying habits. My parents purchased Jif peanut butter. As an adult, I have purchased Jif peanut butter as well. It was not until later and after much introspection that I recognize that this preference regarding peanut butter stemmed from my childhood. Unconsciously, Jif peanut butter became the staple or definition of peanut butter for me. I am sure that if I surveyed a group of people, there would be a wide range of peanut butter brand preferences. I am sure we could debate better price points, taste, quality, and other differences and the like. However, one kind of peanut butter does not devalue any other peanut butter from being peanut butter. This highlights our socialization and foundational perspectives of what we accept as our preference, or in this case, truth. This precondition, socialization, or foundational perspective is not only embedded in the childhood legend of Santa Claus from my childhood or what influences our consumer behavior. These preconditions, socialization, or foundational understandings show up in and perpetuate oppressive narratives for minoritized and marginalized groups.

The truths that we develop as children can be harmful to our development by creating otherness. It can be dangerous when we fail to acknowledge that interpersonal values are rooted in socially constructed perspectives that influence children's development (Bronfenbrenner, 2005; Montgomery, 1992; Overton & Müller, 2012). Dualistic thinking can create additional consequences by eroding the possibility that other truths can exist simultaneously. Debates about Santa Claus or the best peanut butter turn into disputes about race, gender, social class, and other differences (Watt, 2015) that align with our socially constructed truth.

So, what is the truth among these differences? I propose that truth is composed of a big "T" and a little "t." The big "T" is a collective interpretation of truth and captures how the dominant society makes meaning of social, political, economic, and other values that are formed over time and are deemed to be true. It is socially constructed from dominant (e.g., White, hetero, cisgender, ableist, etc.) ideologies and epistemologies (Leigh, 2015). The little "t" is how individuals manifest their own truth, usually informed by their lived experiences that include their upbringing and human interactions. Little "t" truth is constructed from the intersections of people's race, religion, socioeconomic status, gender, sexuality, and other characteristics of our identity. In either definition, the T/truth is viewed as an absolute, with a right and wrong side, and only one side prevailing. Viewing truth in terms of *us-versus-them* limits the opportunity to explore truth more deeply. Furthermore, when someone challenges what you believe to be accurate, you may be left feeling frustrated, upset, or perhaps internally questioning your truth, especially if your truth conflicts with more than one of your identities or sense of Being.

The purpose of this chapter is to be a guiding post for facilitating difficult dialogues where dissonance may arise when one or more persons in the conversation are vehemently opposed to what the other people believe is the truth. Master narratives have become monuments in societies that uphold a narrow perspective while ignoring counternarratives. Counternarratives are essential for the cultural context in considering our relationships to ourselves, others, and communities.

Identity and Humanizing Otherness When Being With Truth

The intersection of identity plays a critical role in creating the conflict that we feel in ourselves and when situating ourselves within otherness. Kimberlé Crenshaw (1991) developed the idea of intersectionality to explore how social identities relate to power and oppression. The concept of intersectionality highlights the idea that people have multiple social identities, such as race, gender, social class, and sexuality, which can contradict or complement each other within an individual. These identities can also compete across individuals in such a way that interacting with people who hold privileged identities erases others' identities (Case, 2016). Further research and theory extend the development of identity intersectionality and the interplay of power; in particular, understanding intersectionality helps reveal the ways in which identity serves as a function of the individual Being, historical and social narratives, and the tension among them (Crenshaw, 1987). It is also important to consider the role of empathy (see chapter 3, this volume) as it cues us to explore intersectionality while examining privileged and oppressed identities. Empathy requires vulnerability and an acknowledgment of your privileged and minoritized identities and how they all interact.

Have any of your salient identities ever conflicted with another? Two of my most salient identities are my racial identity and my spiritual/religious identity. Since I could remember, my Black identity spoke in a room before I could talk. When I was in kindergarten, to help us identify our colors, the teacher asked us daily to stand up if we were wearing the day's color. One day was brown, and I proudly stood up in my pink dress and pink shoes. She said, DaVida, where is your brown? I said, "I am Brown." Similarly, at the young age of seven, I was baptized in a Baptist church. My parents introduced me to Christian practices and traditions in a Black Baptist Church. As a result, I developed a strong connection to my social identities as an African American/Black woman who has a deep relationship with God. I learned from research and shared knowledge that Baptist Christianity has historical consequences for my identity as an African American/Black woman. Jones (2021) outlines that after the Confederacy lost the Civil War, it fought to keep Black people enslaved. They fought to maintain White supremacy ingrained in the Southern Baptist Convention during the late 19th century to control the southern culture. The Southern Baptist Convention grew into one of the largest Christian denominations in the country, which built a foundation for influence regarding social norms.

My relationship with God is the foundation for my Being. I recall the first time someone told me to question my Christian identity; the under-lying tone of the question was—how I could embrace Christianity when Christianity has been weaponized as a tool of power to oppress Black people historically? Did that mean that I should reject Christianity? No. My spiritual connection to God is irrefutable. I experienced firsthand the protection, peace, and power of God's word and how it positively influenced my life. As I dealt with the tension of my two most salient identities, I came to a place that allowed me to be with both identities by situating them within other-ness. The theory of Being centers on self in coexistence with other social identities that a person holds and societal conditions (racism, sexism, het-erosexism, genderism, classism, etc., and their intersections) connected to the long-lasting historical traditions and practices coded in supremacy. The tension between my two salient identities has persisted throughout my life. And yet, I cannot examine my role in a conflict until I have explored my positionality or how the conflict targets one of my salient identities.

Thinking about my racial and religious identities later as an adult, I experience conflict as I watch White Christians share ideologies that normalized White supremacy during political debates and discuss social issues and social inequities. For example, how could they, on the one hand, proclaim Christian principles for some in society but exclude some of God's children while discussing voting rights and creating laws to oppress some of God's children by targeting suppressing their vote. Their behav-iors nod to remnants of Jim Crow laws that enforced racial segregation. Acknowledging the impact of others' actions and the consequences of internal conflict due to historical implications, I eventually shifted my focus to humanizing the tension by stepping back from my own prejudg-ments and finding synergy in my internal conflict as it related to my social identities and others' ideologies. Working toward a place where more than one experience, idea, perspective can be in concert with those of others helps to create space where all can coexist. It allows room for us to remain with ourselves when unpacking internal conflicts and external conflicts and when entering into dialogue with others.

Vaes and Bastian's (2021) research highlights how interpersonal harm can create a breakdown in humanizing each other when one experience, perspective, or idea conflicts with those of others. Their integrative framework offers an approach to a "tethered humanity hypothesis" (Vaes & Bastian, 2021, p. 377). The hypothesis asserts that perpetrators or survivors (of interpersonal conflict) can reclaim their full humanness by establishing the other person's humanness. Two parties are "tethered" (Vaes & Bastian, 2021, p. 378) when they stop seeing each other as fully human in the face of interpersonal harm. Their results showed that both perpetrators and survivors self-dehumanize due to interpersonal harm but were able to rehumanize the other person. However, the process of rehumanizing did not work when one of the parties did not accept the opportunity for reconciliation.

The theory of Being is rooted in the ideas of transformation and liberation to help participants engage in critical reflection while transforming dehumanizing spaces so that people within them can be more fully human (for details, see Watt's "Introduction to Part One," this volume). The theory of Being also suggests that when people align their intellect (heads), emotion (hearts), and action (hands) and simultaneously work together, their being becomes transformed in the process of addressing a dissonance-provoking social issue. It is essential to shift one's mindset to *third thinging* and exploring ways to practice and facilitate social and restorative justice practices, inclusive of multiple perspectives that can coexist instead of colliding with each other. For a person to deal with self or others, one must engage in storytelling to unpack the concept of truth.

Using the *Third Thing* With Truth

Parker J. Palmer (2009) argues that "truth is an eternal conversation about things that matter, conducted with passion and discipline" (p. 8). Being with T/truth can be exhausting when only master narratives are present, and counternarratives are ignored or co-opted (Patel, 2015; Tuck, 2009). Subsequently, an individual may experience internal and external conflicts when their truth interacts or collides with another person's truths about ideologies (Watt, 2015).

The higher education classroom is a space where this type of conflict can arise during a difficult dialogue. Classroom controversy usually ensues when students share conflicting truths, beliefs, or values. The classroom should be a space to help students and student affairs educators increase their comfort level with conflicting perspectives that can create tension on college campuses. The classroom becomes a place to practice *ways of Being* through conversations. Engaging in challenging dialogues is no longer optional but a requirement to advancing social justice (Watt, 2007) and fostering critical and conscious reflection of oneself. However, individuals with marginalized identities may experience macro- and microaggressions when engaging in difficult dialogues that reverberate beyond the conversation (Love et al., 2016; Sue et al., 2009; Warner, 2019). For example, some professors may want to engage with topics that challenge individuals' intersectionality of identities, while others may be reluctant to engage. bell hooks (2003) stated:

> Teachers are often among the group most reluctant to acknowledge the extent to which white-supremacist thinking informs every aspect of our culture including the way we learn, the content of what we learn, and the manner in which we are taught. (p. 25)

Faculty, student affairs professionals, and students should be able to engage in honest dialogues without having a confrontation, but this skill must be taught and practiced. Cocreating a classroom includes a "reciprocal leadership" role rather than a "leader-follower" relationship between student and teacher (Follett, 1970, p. 137). Therefore, everyone becomes "simultaneously teachers *and* students" (Freire, 2011, p. 72). Using this framework, power must be diffused when engaging in multiple truths because everyone is a teacher and student simultaneously. This type of dialogue becomes less oppositional because there is an exchange and recognition of shared authority.

While engaging in this reciprocal relationship, it is helpful to understand and use *third thinging* to help facilitate difficult dialogues in the classroom. *Third thinging* repositions the focus onto an idea or concept that can act as a mediator when engaging across Difference. For example, it is helpful for people to use music, poetry, or another medium as a *third thing* to invite multiple experiences, ideologies, or perspectives into the conversation.

Conversations that utilize *third thinging* create a space for listening, sharing, introspection, and truth-telling rooted in authentic storytelling. Through storytelling, people can interrogate issues and engage with diverging truths rather than with an individual. This storytelling, or truth-telling experience, will not always be easy to express or embrace, but it does challenge us to use our heads, hearts, and hands. Utilizing all three—head, heart, and hands— is challenging, especially when we are used to only using one. For example, I remember my childhood pastor, Reverend Dr. William H. Curtis, preaching on thinking through your emotions to make better decisions from a more comprehensive perspective. I reflect on the times when it was hard to engage in diverging truths. Often, it was when I did not think through my emotions or allowed my emotions to direct the conversation. However, as my social and emotional intelligence increased, I started to engage head, heart, and hands to examine my own experiences, ideas, and perspectives before engaging with others.

Viewing truth itself as a *third thing* also helps to focus on listening and holding space for diverging and sometimes colliding truths. *Third thinging* provides an opportunity to focus on the issue (truth) without attacking the person and to focus on listening to an authentic exchange of experiences. *Third thinging* relies upon an understanding that multiple truths can coexist not to activate defenses but to create an opportunity to examine multiple truths and identify how they relate in the context to self and others. Rather than seeking external or societal evidence to prove what the other person says is true, invite yourself to pause your thoughts, listen with appreciation, and practice reflection when encountering dissonance. Before practicing this type of engagement, one must understand the existing types of truths.

We must acknowledge and understand the role of power dynamics when being with truth as well. The privileged identity exploration (PIE) model (Watt, 2015; see also Appendix E) helps uncover where power is held and applied in dialogue. The PIE model describes why identity matters when inserting truth and how privilege can interrupt how people engage with truth. For example, utilizing my example earlier about Christianity, Christians can justify their ideas, experiences, or actions by suggesting that it is the Christian thing to do (which is one of PIE defenses, *principium*). However, to engage with truth, we must consider and reflect on the opposing viewpoints, even when the topic is particularly heated, especially when making decisions about a group of people different from us. Inviting multiple perspectives into the conversation encourages us to move through difficult dialogues and reach respect; it humanizes truth despite diverging ideologies.

Being Practices for Confronting Truth

Confronting truth is not easy because it can challenge everything that we protect, cherish, or value. The theory of Being offers an approach to acknowledge and being with multiple truths. When we can enter a conversation and *practice aligning our thoughts (head), feelings (heart), and actions (hands)*, we are better able to engage in an honest exploration of our truths. The goal of dialogue, then, is not for individuals to share their truth to win over the other side, but for individuals in relationship with one another to share their truth and be willing to listen across the difference (Watt, 2013). As illustrated in Figure 9.1, truth does not have to be a tug of war. Instead, it can be a bridge we cross to unpack each other's socially constructed realities and examine the implications or harms of those truths. It acknowledges that everyone owns a truth that combines their socialization, dissonance, privileged identities, and experiences. Moreover, truth is not always shared. Therefore, creating a container for multiple truths to exist can only be done if people focus on humanizing truth instead of dehumanizing the person speaking the truth. As follows, I describe how *personal, relational,* and *community ways of Being* invite us to explore ourselves first before extending our hands to Being and investigating our positionality to others.

Figure 9.1. Capacity-building bridge.

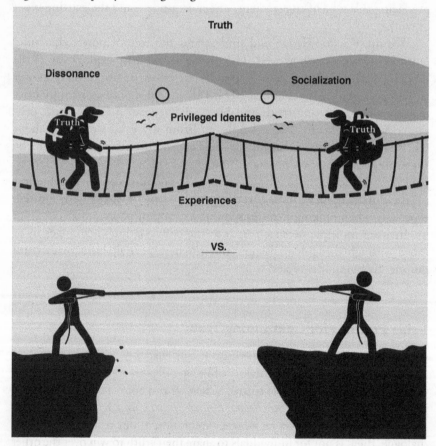

Note: Image is an original creation of chapter author.

Personal and Relational Practices

Where do we have opportunities to develop these skills when multiple truths are tested? One opportunity arises when we develop our personal value systems. We can become conditioned to view and adopt different truths. Intrapersonal communication and interpersonal communication are connected; the messages that we communicate to ourselves influence our communication with other people (Abubeker, 2019). Scholars suggest that self-talk is a critical component in concert with self-concept, self-reflection, internal monologue, and self-love, influencing intrapersonal communication (Berko et al., 2007). Therefore, focusing on ourselves (or practicing *personal ways of Being*) and being conscious of the messages that we communicate to ourselves is a critical part of developing and understanding truth.

As I reflect on my childhood stories about Santa Claus and Jif peanut butter, I realize how social interactions and experiences create the pathways for knowledge to become a truth. For example, interpersonal interactions contribute toward developing truth when shared knowledge is consistently reinforced over time or experiences substantiate our knowledge. Interpersonal interactions can also shape our truth by limiting our capacity to understand how our truth has been constructed and how it influences our interactions. I remember teaching a class where one of the students, a middle-aged White woman, shared that her truth about Black people being lazy and thieving was passed down from her grandparents. She grew up in a historically White space and her only experience with Blackness was through media portrayals. She did not realize that her truth was invalid until she went to college and interacted with Black people. She then evaluated the truth that her grandparents passed onto her. She found out that her grandparents worked at a bottling company, and up until the company started hiring Black people, her parents had job security. She shared that her grandparents were upset to see positions that were once occupied by White employees being filled by Black employees. Over the years, the discontent became a damaging truth in her family. The reality is that the bottling company could hire Black people and pay them less than what her grandparents made. Did it make Black people who worked in the factory lazy? Did it make them thieves because the company took advantage of paying a group of people less than another group of people? What does the theory of Being say regarding multiple truths?

Watt's (2015) privileged identity exploration model suggests that defensive reactions come from interactions with others when confronted with dissonance-provoking stimuli. My student's grandparents' privileged identities shielded them from a different reality rooted in a constructed master narrative that contributed toward a belief system shared between generations in their family. Their knowledge transitioned to truth and created intergenerational implications. She experienced dissonance when she found out that her grandparents' truth was at odds with her own experiences with Black people on her college campus. Thus, recognizing and exploring our defenses (via *personal* and *relational ways of Being*) are the practices that help build our stamina when engaging with multiple truths.

Community Practices

Where is another place that we have opportunities to develop these skills when multiple truths are tested? Another place where we are tested is in our community while interacting with others. Triandis (1979) shared that interpersonal values are rooted in strong beliefs about a particular behavior and that these beliefs become the lens people use to interpret societal issues. Looking closer at the landscape of our college campuses, we see evidence of multiple competing truths. For example, a popular debate in the 21st century suggests a divide between what is considered "freedom of speech" and "hate speech" (Tontodimamma et al., 2021). Student affairs educators frequently face the responsibility of facilitating two or more diverging sides that divide their college campuses. Restorative justice circles and other forms of mediation are one resource to address multiple truths. Leadership first needs to practice, then role-model institutional restorative justice. One step toward connecting diverging viewpoints is to create small communication circles to address an issue about inequality or hate speech that occurred on campus. The next step is to *use a third thing* that can invite synergy into the conversation.

Regardless of whether either person's truth is convenient or empirical, all parties need to meet on the bridge (Figure 9.1). Meeting halfway means not only *listening deeply, a relational way of Being* but also hearing and not shutting down the other person's truth. I admit this practice can be challenging, especially when the truth unsettles one of your core values. For example, I strongly identify as Black before any of my other invisible or visible identities, partly due to how White supremacy ideologies have cultivated my lived experience. My Blackness is something that I cannot hide, nor do I choose to hide. I embrace my Blackness despite what predominantly White spaces impose over non-White bodies or ideologies. Therefore, when engaging in difficult dialogues surrounding race, I am aware that I must pause my presumptions to hear someone's truth about them not appreciating Black culture. I am not suggesting taking abuse from anyone's truth that emboldens their power to create intentional or unintentional harm. Rather, I suggest that embracing the theory of Being can move us beyond simply identifying the problem to dismantling the systemic oppression embedded and reinforced in truths. The theory of Being challenges us to hear multiple truths, face the tension in the truths, and explore actions that can reduce harm in these truths (*community ways of Being*).

Another example of multiple truths is when conservative students and faculty believe they are being threatened on a liberal campus or when the President of the United States threatens to take away federal funds from public institutions if deemed too liberal (Graham, 2020). Since the 2016 election, some may argue that a Trump flag with "Make America Great Again" is nothing more than showing support for a political figure. Others may say that the flag represents insurrection or a hostile and racist ideology that sends a message of intolerance toward non-Trump supporters and People of Color. So, what happens when a Deferred Action for Childhood Arrivals (DACA) student walks on a college campus and sees a Trump flag hanging from another student's window, and the student who owns the flag sees nothing wrong?

A college campus should be the teaching ground for experiences across Difference and difficult dialogues (Watt, 2015). There should be room for conservative and liberal students on campus to share their truths. But how? Using *a third thing* and the bridge framework (Figure 9.1) might be a way to invite opposing parties into a conversation that explores the complexity of their truths. The truths exist at the center and the conversation focuses on what we can learn together (about the issue, each other, and society) as we explore these truths. Without the willingness to meet on the bridge, we forfeit the purpose of higher education, which is creating a holistic education experience inside and outside the classroom. Focusing on transformative learning and dismantling systemic oppression embedded in each other's truth constructs a more generative way to coexist and creates more welcoming and inclusive campus environments.

This example helps to demonstrate that it is not the content of dialogue alone that liberates us. How we treat one another in a dialogue liberates us as well. The process of *listening deeply* to others (*relational way of Being*) liberates us from dehumanizing ourselves (*personal way of Being*) and others (*relational and community ways of Being*) and unveils the many realities of oppression. Instead of working to protect ourselves from the attacks of others, to prove others wrong, or to build legitimacy from external sources, we should embrace our shared humanity. We must turn from seeing others as the enemies of our liberation (a reduction of their humanity to defend our humanity) to seeing their experiences as ways in which they have been tangled up in the same systems of oppression. This type of dialogue is an act of love for the world, love of ourselves and of others. It shows our commitment to be free from systems of power that limit us all (Freire, 1970/2018). Freire (1993) wrote, "Love is an act of courage, not fear . . . a commitment to other . . . [and] to the cause of liberation" (p. 78). As we describe experiences that extend beyond our roles as institutional producers and performers, the listener(s) form a more human model of us across time and space.

Conclusion

This chapter's description of *third thinging* demonstrates the importance of exploring ways of constructing truth, capacity building for opposing truths, and rectifying harmful truths perpetuated and protected in society. To practice *ways of Being*, we must first sit with ourselves. By *focusing on you*, we can learn to authentically examine how our own knowledge transforms into truth. Then, perhaps we can practice the skills that embrace the *us-and-them-exploring-it* mindset.

Entering difficult dialogue requires people to meet on a bridge of truth. Creating space for multiple truths to be heard creates an opportunity for community-minded and inclusive solutions that address multiple perspectives. We must be willing to have an open dialogue and humanize the other person with which we are engaging in dialogue. Keep an open mind and heart. Reflect on the parts that trigger you after the dialogue and examine why they trigger you. Enter a dialogue prepared to listen and share, not debate; but also know when to walk away if others are being defiant of the process or causing psychological or emotional harm.

Imagine a suspension bridge (see Figure 9.2). I remember attempting to walk over a suspension bridge in the state of Washington overlooking Ross Dam. As I walked toward the middle, I could feel the bridge shake slightly as I looked 600 feet down. That was a scary task, not because I am afraid of heights but because it was a feeling of uncertainty as it continued to shake. When we engage in difficult dialogues about race, gender, sex, politics, organizational dilemmas, or any other topics that cultivate diverging experiences, it is like walking on a suspension bridge. However, the goal is not to get to the other side of the bridge. It is just to meet in the middle. Meet the other person or persons in the middle of their truth. Not to walk

Figure 9.2. Image of suspension bridge.

Note: Image is an original creation of chapter author.

them back over to your side of the conversation, but to stand in the middle and deconstruct and reconstruct the truth. Even if you have questions about the other person's truth, it should not be an interrogation. Instead, interrogate the problem and not the person. The goal is not to poke holes in someone else's truth, but rather to engage in thoughtful questioning that opens deeper dialogue and possibilities for personal growth when we face the conflict.

Fundamentally, one must be open to evaluate and participate in the iterative process of understanding truth. Unpacking socialization, privilege, dissonance, and harmful ideologies that impede growth to embrace the theory of Being is helpful to understanding truth. Facilitating and participating in difficult dialogues is a way to practice *ways of Being*. Operating in the theory of Being allows us to move from adversarial approaches to hearing a truth that is not our own but someone else's truth. Then we can explore together the implications of our truth. We can sit with the dissonance in ourselves and then connect with others across the bridge. Remember this will require you to do the work shared in the last and preceding chapters with your heart, head, and hands.

References

Abubeker, N. (2019). *The Influence of intrapersonal communication on interpersonal communication. Perceptions of journalism and communication students.* GRIN Verlag.

Berko, R. M., Wolvin, A. D., & Wolvin, D. R. (2007). *Communicating: A social and career focus* (10th ed.). Houghton Mifflin.

Bronfenbrenner, U. (2005). *Making human beings human: Bioecological perspectives on human development.* SAGE.

Case, K. A. (Ed.). (2016). *Intersectional pedagogy: Complicating identity and social justice.* Routledge.

Crenshaw, K. W. (1987). Race, reform, and retrenchment: Transformation and legitimation in antidiscrimination law. *Harvard Law Review, 101,* 1331.

Crenshaw, K. (1991). Mapping the margins: Intersectionality, identity politics, and violence against women of color. *Stanford Law Review, 43(6),* 1241–1299. https://doi.org/10.2307/1229039

Follett, M. P. (1970). The teacher-student relation. *Administrative Science Quarterly, 15*(2), 137–148. https://doi.org/10.2307/2391484

Freire, P. (1970). *Pedagogy of the oppressed.* Seabury Press.

Freire, P. (1993). *Pedagogy of the city.* Continuum.

Freire, P. (2011). *Pedagogy of the oppressed* (D. Macedo, Trans.). Continuum.

Freire, P. (2018). *Pedagogy of the oppressed.* Bloomsbury.

Graham, D. A. (2020, July 10). What a direct attack on free speech looks like. *The Atlantic.* www.theatlantic.com/ideas/archive/2020/07/trump-universities/614038/

hooks, b. (2003). *Teaching community: A pedagogy of hope.* Routledge.

Jones, R. P. (2021). *White too long: The legacy of white supremacy in American Christianity.* Simon & Schuster.

Love, J. M., Gaynor, T. S., & Blessett, B. (2016). Facilitating difficult dialogues in the classroom: A pedagogical imperative. *Administrative Theory & Praxis, 38*(4), 227–233. https://doi.org/10.1080/10841806.2016.1237839

Montgomery, D. E. (1992). Young children's theory of knowing: The development of a folk epistemology. *Developmental Review, 12*(4), 410–430. https://doi.org/10.1037/0012-1649.29.2.337

Overton, W. F., & Müller, U. (2012). Metatheories, theories, and concepts in the study of development. In R. M. Lerner, M. A. Easterbrooks, J. Mistry, & I. B. Weiner (Eds.), *Handbook of psychology: Developmental psychology* (2nd ed., pp. 19–58). Wiley.

Palmer, P. J. (2009). Transforming teaching and learning in higher education: An interview with Parker J. Palmer. *Spirituality in Higher Education Newsletter, 5*(2), 1–8.

Patel, L. (2015). *Decolonizing educational research: From ownership to answerability.* Routledge.

Sue, D. W., Lin, A. I., Torino, G. C., Capodilupo, C. M., & Rivera, D. P. (2009). Racial microaggressions and difficult dialogues on race in the classroom. *Cultural Diversity and Ethnic Minority Psychology*, *15*(2), 183–190. https://doi.org/10.1037/a0014191

Suppe, F. (1973). Facts and empirical truth. *Canadian Journal of Philosophy*, *3*(2), 197–212. https://doi.org/10.1080/00455091.1973.10716876

Tontodimamma, A., Nissi, E., Sarra, A., & Fontanella, L. (2021). Thirty years of research into hate speech: Topics of interest and their evolution. *Scientometrics*, *126*(1), 157–179. https://doi.org/10.1007/s11192-020-03737-6

Triandis, H. C. (1979). Values, attitudes, and interpersonal behavior. *Symposium on Motivation*, *27*, 195–259.

Tuck, E. (2009). Suspending damage: A letter to communities. *Harvard Educational Review*, *79*(3), 409–428. https://doi.org/10.17763/haer.79.3.n0016675661t3n15

Vaes, J., & Bastian, B. (2021). Tethered humanity: Humanizing self and others in response to interpersonal harm. *European Journal of Social Psychology*, *51*(2), 377–392. https://doi.org/10.1002/ejsp.2744

Warner, T. V. (2019). Racial microaggressions and difficult dialogues in the classroom. In J. A. Mena & K. Quina (Eds.), *Integrating multiculturalism and intersectionality into the psychology curriculum: Strategies for instructors* (pp. 37–47). https://doi.org/10.1037/0000137-004

Watt, S. K. (2007). Difficult dialogues, privilege and social justice: Uses of the privileged identity exploration (PIE) model in student affairs practice. *The College Student Affairs Journal*, *26*(2), 114–126. https://files.eric.ed.gov/fulltext/EJ899385.pdf

Watt, S. K. (2013). Designing and implementing multicultural initiatives: Guiding principles. In S. K. Watt and J. L. Lindley (Eds), *Creating Successful and Multicultural Initiatives in Higher Education and Student Affairs* (New Directions for Student Services, no. 144, pp. 5–15). Jossey-Bass. https://doi.org/10.1002/ss.20064

Watt, S. K. (Ed.) (2015). *Designing transformative multicultural initiatives: Theoretical foundations, practical applications, and facilitator considerations.* Stylus.

OTHERNESS

Duhita Mahatmya and Saba Rasheed Ali

I urge each one of us here to reach down into that deep place of knowledge inside herself and touch that terror and loathing of any difference that lives there. See whose face it wears. Then the personal as the political can begin to illuminate all our choices.

—Audre Lorde, "The Master's Tools Will Never Dismantle the Master's House"

Who would we be without our otherness? Otherness is the familiar feeling in the pit of our stomach. The feeling arises when we notice how teachers and peers form relationships so easily with one another, but we can't quite figure out where we fit. It is that feeling that allows us to anticipate what people around us care for and need from us. Otherness is the complicated feeling of wanting to both be seen and be invisible when we are around others. Perhaps that feeling became an imaginary friend. A friend whom we sometimes fought with and didn't trust; and then, as we grew older, a friend whom we learned to listen to for guidance on how to navigate life and be okay with the complex emotions of being human. Alone with our otherness we sift through our anxieties, anger, and frustrations only to be reminded that nothing is wrong with us. Our otherness is part of our hidden wholeness (Palmer, 2004). Together in our otherness we realize we are not alone.

The theory of Being invites us to be with the discomfort that arises as we explore otherness within ourselves in order to transform how we engage in the community more effectively. The theory of Being humanizes the process of giving meaning to the otherness that exists, "for as long as any difference between us means one of us must be inferior, then the recognition of any difference must be fraught with guilt" (Lorde, 2007, p. 118). If we consider Difference, or biodiversity, as natural and inherent in the human condition, then it is when we give power to and weaponize Difference that we create an inferior other, even when the other is within us. If we allow ourselves to engage in "the hard work of excavating honesty" (Lorde, 2007, p. 128), understanding the origins of our otherness could invite us on the path to individual and organizational transformation.

This chapter explores some of the psychological foundations of the theory of Being and how *individual, relational*, and *community* Being practices can support our exploration of otherness and belonging. In writing this chapter, we leaned into the theory of Being to understand how to name, notice, and *humanize otherness* in us (*personal way of Being*), *in our relationships* (*relational way of Being*), *and ideas* (*community way of Being*). The guiding question of the chapter is as follows: What process invites back humanity and the stamina to transform (not just tolerate) otherness in self and communities?

Naming Otherness

Before centering and interrogating the guiding question, we (Duhita Mahatmya and Saba Rasheed Ali, the chapter authors) want to begin with a story of how this chapter emerged. In the spirit of the theory of Being, writing this chapter was an iterative process that brought together our intellectual understandings of Being with a recognition that our thoughts were fundamentally shaped by our lived experiences. This process brought further questioning and exploration of how and where we held these experiences in our memories and bodies, how and where we experienced pain and wounding, and how and where we experienced solidarity and joy. Our stories are grounded in our experiences as immigrant, Muslim-raised, Brown girls wanting to fit in predominantly White spaces. Despite different geographical contexts, we both had a strong desire to be "normal," which we equated to being a White, Christian American (Hong, 2020; Tippett, 2020). The words you read here arise from multiple conversations over the years that we had in our own heads, with each other, and in trusted communities. We do not claim to know the answers, and instead offer these stories as an invitation to understand when the seeds of otherness are planted, the way it burrows and shifts within individuals, relationships, and communities, and the futures that are possible if we are willing to live into that otherness.

Duhita's Story

I grew up in a predominantly White college town in Colorado in the 1990s and as a student in the K–12 system became well-acquainted with my status as a noncitizen, Southeast Asian women. My otherness emerged when learning about American history ("Is this for me to learn?"), and I dealt with it through acting like a model student ("I am not represented in the materials, but I can look like a compliant, academically successful American/White student."). I felt like a visitor in these educational spaces; just as eager to get invitations to my friends' birthday parties as I was to be invited to learn other people's history—on their terms. The feelings of self-doubt and shame brought on by the sense of otherness was resolved through doing academic things to feel a sense of belonging. Complicating matters was the fact that my family immigrated to the United States to get higher education, which heightened that pressure to achieve academically. Up to and including my doctoral training, I adopted a positivist orientation that reinforced the idea that knowledge can be studied objectively because my social identities and subjectivity were never invited into educational spaces. Part of the reckoning I experienced during my time as a faculty member was the division between the intellectual and emotional appraisals of my work. The work passed the peer-reviewed tests but left me wondering "so what?" and more importantly feeling a deep disconnect between what I was doing and who I wanted to be. Missing in my academic experiences was the importance of our humanity and wellness when building relationships and community with others.

Saba's Story

I experienced a similar *way of Being* as Duhita growing up in a rural coal mining town in West Virginia. The main difference is that the context in which I was raised was a mining town in the 1970s and 1980s with high rates of poverty. The town where I grew up was about 20% Black, and the majority was White. Protestant Christianity was a dominant force in this region of Appalachia (as it is for most parts of rural Appalachia). I grew up as a South Asian Muslim American during the Iran hostage crisis. This was a time when most Americans in the area were not very familiar with Muslims and relied mostly on what they understood from the conflicts between the United States and Iran. Further, understandings of race were mainly based on distinctions between Black and White people, so many of my White peers had a hard time "placing" me in the racial hierarchy. Thus, my desire to be normal was really a desire to be Christian. I do not think I understood that I conflated Whiteness and Christianity at the time, but I perceived Christianity to be "normal." I often felt invisible in spaces where I was growing up, but also learned to crave that sense of invisibility because when I was seen, it was because I was being mocked by some of my peers. Invisibility became a way of being safe and still to this day is how I sometimes try to cope with pressure or fear. What I also learned to crave was a sense of belonging in that invisibility. It is easier to hide in a crowd of people who share a common goal. When I am able to see the benefits of this *way of Being*, I have been able to recognize that invisibility can lead to decentering oneself and trying to find commonality with others for the sake of a shared value or goal.

Being Skills to Humanize Otherness

Ways of Being encourage us to focus on self and how and why we relate to ourselves, others, and ideas in certain ways. Such reflection brings critical thought and emotion together so that we can build the stamina to engage with Difference and explore a full spectrum of equitable and liberatory solutions. In the sections that follow, we focus on *humanizing otherness*, which is a specific skill that spans across *individual, relational, and community* Being practices. We describe how using the privileged identity exploration (PIE) model (Watt, 2015), reengaging the *us-and-them-exploring-it* mindset, and *understanding the third thing* can build the stamina to *humanize otherness*.

Humanizing Otherness in the Self

When facing dissonance due to controversial social differences, individuals are motivated to ease the discomfort that the dissonance creates; this is a normal part of the human experience (Harmon-Jones & Mills, 2019). The PIE model describes the defensive reactions that commonly emerge for individuals when confronted with a dissonance-provoking stimulus (DPS). The PIE model directs us to focus on ourselves, our relationship to our social identities, and how the DPS disrupts our sense of self and identities. The defenses are grouped into three broad categories—*recognizing, contemplating, and addressing privileged identity*—with each group describing how cognitive and emotional processes "animate the reaction" (Watt, 2015, p. 46). For example, when individuals express defensive reactions in the *recognizing* category (*denial and deflection*), they most often are not conscious of their cognitive or emotional processes. Cognitive processes become more conscious in defensive reactions characterized as *contemplating* privileged identity (*minimization, rationalization,* and *intellectualization*), but emotion is still suppressed. Cognitive and emotional processes merge in defensive reactions characterized as *addressing* privileged identity. Ultimately, in the PIE model, defensive reactions reflect the managing of cognitive and emotional responses to dissonance. The model acknowledges that while everyone will experience discomfort when confronted with dissonance, the key is to practice learning how to name and locate the dissonance in what we think and how it makes us feel.

As we reflect on the defenses we employ, we realize that different defenses arise depending on the identity and sense of self (especially otherness) and our desire to belong. For me (Duhita), *intellectualization* is my default defense when confronted with a dissonance-provoking stimulus presented by someone with *a privileged identity*; however, I tend to use *false envy* if the same stimulus is presented by someone with whom I perceive to have a similar identity or benevolence when I hold *a privileged identity*. For example, when a White person says something that is the source of dissonance, I respond by citing theories I learned in my doctoral program; when People of Color raise the issue, I slip into saying how I envy their community activism or mention my own volunteer work. As I reflect on why I engage differently depending on who activates my dissonance, I realize that it stems from the educational privilege that intersects with my immigration story and the sense of otherness that I have with both White Americans and Asian Americans (I am not enough of either). My defensive reactions arise from being afraid to explore further (Watt, 2015) and expose the pain of otherness that I feel in that moment or from acknowledging that despite the financial hardship that my family experienced in the United States, in their home country they held class privilege.

For me (Saba), I often use *false envy* and *benevolence* as well. One piece of the cultural landscape in the United States is being placed in a category. We tend to have categories or boxes to complete on applications that help us know our place in U.S. society (race/ethnicity, age, etc.). One defense mechanism that I believe I engage is *false envy*—the idea that I envy someone else's place, category, or box because they have more status. I also believe that I envy others' "boxes" who have more of a legitimate right to claim oppression. While I may have faced marginalization, mine is not really important or certainly pales in comparison to Black and Native American experiences. This defense mechanism can lead to *benevolence*. I had class privilege growing up in rural West Virginia. That class privilege buffered me and provided me with advantages, but I also felt guilt about that status. My guilt leads me to use *benevolence* as a defense, which I see as different from practicing and building solidarity. It is easy to engage in *benevolence* to assuage guilt or distance oneself from proximity to Whiteness. I can give money to worthy causes or I can "help" someone who needs my time or effort. However, that is different than being in solidarity to others, which is about seeing our lives as interconnected and our oppressions as linked.

The theory of Being is useful to consider when a dissonance-provoking experience arises that contradicts one's way of viewing the world or others. It invites individuals holding multiple social identities into a space where otherness resides in ourselves and others. However, considering individuals who have been consistently othered because of certain social identities, what becomes of the person who constantly confronts experiences that contradict their worldview? Does the self forsake its own discomfort to ease the discomfort of others? For us the answer is yes, but that does not mean that it is the only answer.

One way to understand this negotiation might be to turn to psychological literature on stereotype threat (Steele & Aronson, 1995). The research on stereotype threat has been widely replicated (Pennington et al., 2016) and highlights how priming individuals from stigmatized groups to think about stereotypes about their group affects performance on cognitive tests. The classic study by Steele and Aronson (1995) demonstrated that when Black students were primed to think about their racial identity and negative stereotypes related to their racial identity, they reported more concerns about their ability and tried to avoid having their performance tied to their identity. Even when confronted with positive stereotypes, such as the model minority stereotype for Asian students, the internalization of the stereotype can lead to psychological distress (Gupta et al., 2011; Wong & Halgin, 2006). When confronted with a stereotype, regardless of valence (positive or negative), individuals from stigmatized groups fear the confirmation of the stereotype and expend cognitive resources to diminish the emotional arousal and deal with the dissonance (Ozier et al., 2019). Psychological interventions that present individuals with descriptions to help them think differently about the tasks have been found to diminish the negative effect of stereotype threat (Good et al., 2003; Shapiro & Neuberg, 2007). In this way, cognitive reappraisal strategies (Gross & John, 2003) favor cognitive change to modify emotional responses to dissonance; thought is activated before emotion. And yet so often the feelings that accompany the sense of otherness are overwhelming.

The theory of Being acknowledges that we must engage the head (cognitive), heart (emotion), and hands (practice). It is not enough to change thought and not emotion. A full Being practice must integrate rather than separate cognitive and emotional responses. *Humanizing otherness in the self* is a practice of intellectual and spiritual growth that heals the dualism many of us experience in our academic socialization (hooks, 1994). To *humanize the otherness in the self,* we must be critically engaged and be curious about our thoughts and the full range of our emotional responses that bubble up so that we can truly explore our otherness and, ultimately, our Being. The PIE model is a tool that helps us explore our Being. And practicing *personal ways of Being* helps us build the stamina to make sense of the complexity of our Being and work through its messiness.

Humanizing Otherness in Relationships to Others

The work of excavating and *humanizing otherness* comes into high relief when we are in a relationship with other people. Part of *humanizing otherness in our relationships with others* is to bring awareness to the idea that in the pursuit and construction of knowledge, we bring our own experiences and motivations and must "hold space" (i.e., be present for someone with whom we are in a relationship) for the experiences and motivations of others during the process. It moves us beyond finding immediate solutions to controversial social differences; instead, we can focus on sustained processes that allow us to reveal our privilege and otherness and deal with the discomfort that emerges when we are confronted with privilege and otherness. Fundamentally, humans are social beings (Fiske, 2018), and we rely on each other to meet our hierarchy of needs (Neel & Lassetter, 2019). Therefore, *humanizing otherness* is an act of solidarity in the acknowledgment that each of us carries an otherness or a wounding.

A key principle of the theory of Being is *us-and-them-exploring-it*. This principle invites us to reposition ourselves not just in how we perceive ourselves to be different from each other, but with each other against the larger systems and infrastructure that fuel these group differences (Watt et al., 2021). *Humanizing otherness in the self* and *in relationships with others* means more than the gift of individuation that folks from dominant identities enjoy. To be humanized and human is to have the chance to center your story on your own terms; it is honoring the complexity of who you are (Tuck, 2009) and disrupting the two-dimensional renderings that satisfy the dominant gaze.

As we reflected on our PIE defensive reactions, we realize that our default defenses tap into our socialization in White majority (supremacist) environments. Because we live and work in systems that "do not include (our) heritage and the practices go against (our) experiences and expressions of (our) identity" (Watt, 2015, p. 19), we learn the rules to ensure our survival and sustenance (Brown, 2018; Kaur, 2020). How we learned to navigate our internalized otherness required learning to deal with the shame, guilt, anger, and frustration of feeling invisible, ignored, or tokenized, but through our persistent otherness, we gained the power of observation. Like a musician with perfect pitch, in our otherness we become attuned to the silence and sounds of dominant culture. In this way, when and how we deploy our PIE defenses is as much a part of our inner work as it is our relational work with others.

It does make us wonder about the defenses of folks who hold nondominant and privileged identities, that is, whether our PIE defenses are used to protect ourselves from questioning our own privileged identities or whether we use our PIE defenses to gain proximity to a privileged (e.g., White) identity. We cannot divorce our internal reactions from what the dissonance is and from whom it is spoken because our sense of self has always been defined in relation to dominant groups. In our own personal and professional spheres, we know that we fervently depend upon relationships where we have the psychological safety and trust to explore our otherness in search for belongingness. Further, the defenses that we experience are rooted in systems. In the United States, we are steeped in a culture that often values individual achievement and goals over collective good. Historical forces shape these values with an overreliance on the Protestant work ethic or neoliberal ideologies. These forces are known to serve as barriers to collective power and community engagement that rely on relationship-building over time. However, relationship-building is key to our practice despite the barriers we may experience. Perhaps that is why some of our favorite research experiences often involve drives across Iowa to meet with teachers and students. While we recognize the looks from local people when we walk into rural spaces as two Brown women and have grown all too familiar with the pits in our stomachs as a result, we appreciate the opportunity to build relationships and trust with folks in different communities.

The psychological literature on stigma and intergroup conflict provides one way to think about the skill of *humanizing otherness when in relationships* and repositioning from the *us-versus-them* principle to the *us-and-them-exploring-it* approach. Psychologists have researched strategies for conflict resolution especially in the context of challenging intergroup relations (e.g., Halperin et al., 2013). A theme emerging from the literature is the role of social motives in shaping attitudes and behaviors (Neel et al., 2016). The concept of motivated reasoning hypothesizes that people want to experience emotions consistent with their ingroup's goals and ideologies and will engage in behaviors accordingly (Porat et al., 2016). Here, an *us-versus-them* attitude functions as a guide for action that ensures cognitive and emotional consonance.

Psychological interventions on conflict resolution have focused on how to change the meaning of a conflict situation and the emotional reaction to the other; results show that statements used to elicit empathy or more positive emotional responses toward the outgroup increase support for de-escalation (Halperin et al., 2013; Porat et al., 2016; Tamir & Ford, 2012). When there are multiple outgroups, or multiple groups that hold stigmatized identities, in relationship with one another, the social psychological literature points to the importance of shared experiences of discrimination (Cortland et al., 2017; Craig & Richeson, 2016) to create positive intraminority intergroup relationships. Having shared goals, especially seeing each other as relevant to our goals for a more just, equitable, and inclusive society, may also diminish a sense of invisibility and otherness (Neel & Lassetter, 2019; Sanchez et al., 2017). The "it" becomes our shared experiences and goals so that the *us-and-them-exploring-it* approach resituates our relationships to each other within relationships to the systems of dominance and oppression. The practice of seeing and feeling shared pain and joy can act as a bridge toward disrupting the otherness that we carry in us and project it on the larger and more complex social issues.

As we wonder about and continue to build our practice on how to *humanize otherness in relationships to others*, we invite you to consider a situation where you felt defensive and how othering manifested in that situation. For anyone engaging in Being practices, a greater discernment of our roles in defining *us-versus-them* helps to prepare us to reposition our motivations toward targeting the it rather than each other. Just as *humanizing otherness in the self* requires our thoughts (head) and feelings (heart), *humanizing otherness in relationships* tends to lead to the cognitive and emotional arousal (Sanchez et al., 2017) that comes with experiencing stigma and prejudice. In other words, if we only practice *ways of Being* as an intellectual exercise (head), we run the risk of altering our beliefs about others for the sake of diminishing our own sense of discomfort (heart) as opposed to transforming systems of oppression. Staying in the realm of the head may keep the energy and focus on doing something to fix the controversial social difference rather than being with the uncomfortable emotions that the otherness poses in a sustained way.

Humanizing Otherness in Relationship to Ideas

When in relationships with ourselves, others, and complex ideas, we are invited by the theory of Being to suspend a sense of urgency for external action and instead take time for internal contemplation and the work of Being. In particular, the *community ways of Being* involve *humanizing otherness in relationship to ideas*, which requires an orientation that resists the urge to create solutions, especially when we have not spent time defining the complex problem. It invites a questioning that goes beyond *intellectualization* (Watt, 2015) of the dissonance and rather questions how the idea lands within us. What are our reactions to the idea? Where do we feel those reactions? What is the source of those reactions? How do we tap into those reactions to dream up more equitable and liberatory solutions?

The *community ways of Being practice* involves *a third thing* used to refocus the critical analysis of an idea through engaging with our thoughts and feelings around the idea. Using *a third thing* repositions each of us so that we balance our relationships to each other with the relationship to the idea or charged social issue. With the idea or issue at the center of the conversation, we can work together to dissect the controversy to inform our actions. Importantly, the disagreement is not with each other. In using *a third thing*, we learn to "live into" and move through our otherness; in *third thinging* as community members, we are with all others in the service of exploring the idea. Rather than pointing fingers toward an individual when dissonance arises, we turn to curiosity and wonder how we each arrived at our understandings, whose understanding holds power, and why. In sharing an otherness to the it (*third thing*), we live into our common humanity. And while dealing with it is difficult, we create space for folks to share our joys and pains together to transform our notions and actions around *the third thing*.

The research on intergroup conflict, especially when there is a clear *us-versus-them* dynamic, suggests that it is possible to shift the dynamic when individuals become more aware of their cognitive and affective responses to the idea. When confronted with dissonance, individuals must reconcile their thoughts with emotional responses (e.g., empathy) to develop more authentic reactions and reflections. Reflection forces the self to turn inward and name the emerging emotions that inform the engagement with the idea and with others around the idea. This self-awareness heals the "dualistic separation of public and private" (hooks, 1994, p. 16) so that the pursuit of knowledge and being fully human become part of the same endeavor (Alschuler, 1986).

The Antiracism Collaborative

To create space for this fuller and more humanizing exploration of complex problems, particularly in the context of charged social issues like racism, the University of Iowa College of Education created the Antiracism Collaborative (ARC). The ARC started in the Fall of 2020, amid the COVID-19 pandemic, rapid awakening around racial justice in the United States, and a polarizing presidential election season—all ingredients with the potential to create a heated social space. However, the ARC provided a refuge for all of us in the college to listen, share, and make mistakes in the process of learning how to be antiracist as people and as an organization (Watt et al., 2021).

The *third thing* for the ARC was the issue of racism, and the structure of the collaborative provided a container in which we could do our inner and relational work in service toward uncovering the ways we could create systemic change in our organization. Finding multiple ways for people to engage, no matter the roles they had or their familiarity and comfort with diversity, equity, and inclusion work, was foundational to the ARC structure. Everything was invitational. Structurally, a steering committee was made up of the college's dean and associate deans, directors of human resources and the Baker Teacher Leader Center, and lead by Will Coghill-Behrends and alumnus Rusty Barcelo and Sherry K. Watt who coordinated various ARC gatherings.

The gatherings included monthly college-wide open forums where participants explored current issues facing the college community or discussed missteps and lessons learned from doing antiracism work. We offered monthly skill-building sessions with other scholars, alumnae, and community members and ongoing small-group discussions and activities within college units. In all formats of the gathering, participants learned and practiced *touchstones* to guide development of relational trust (see Appendix B). The *touchstones* are intentional guidelines for collaboration that include *listening with authenticity and depth and practicing confidentiality, grace, and reflection.* Common across the practices of *touchstones* is recognizing the incompleteness and complexity of everyone in the organization and understanding that transformational efforts require that we aim to be in relationships with one another in all their complexity.

Unlike institutional task forces or action plans that push for organizational transformation, the ARC offered a sustained and process-oriented approach to preparing individuals to take steps for meaningful systemic change. The process-oriented approach encourages communities to consider not only what they are doing but how they are in a relationship with each other in those actions. It also acknowledges that every community member can contribute to our shared organizational values, but contributions might look different depending on where we are in our own inner work and our social identities.

As College of Education employees, we participated in the ARC open forums and skill-building sessions where we had opportunities to notice our PIE defenses (*personal way of Being*) and interact in cross-racial small-group dialogue (*relational way of Being*). It invited us to humanize the otherness in ourselves, each other, and together as members of the organization. The discussion of defenses within the PIE model also allowed us to give each other latitude as we work together on building an antiracist coalition. When we put our own defenses into perspective, then we are often able to see others from a perspective of the human condition rather than from a perspective of alienation or otherness. This perspective-taking provides us with space to give freedom or grace to make mistakes, work on those mistakes, and to recover from those mistakes. This process is critical to relationship-building as mistakes are inevitable when working across and with Difference (Watt, 2013). Practicing *community ways of Being* is grounded in our capacity to sustain self-awareness and focus on our own preparation in service to collective ideas and actions. When humans face cognitive dissonance, we take the path of least resistance to decrease our psychological (and sometimes physiological) discomfort. This may mean engaging in defensive reactions that animate our thought more than our emotions or reappraising both our cognitions and emotions in relation to the dissonance-provoking stimuli and creating the other. The theory of Being asks that we choose a more laborious approach, which involves noticing, nurturing, and naming our responses (Hare & Leboutillier, 2014) and reactions to the dissonance. Experiencing dissonance and discomfort should encourage deeper learning and reflection of our misconceptions (McGrath, 2020).

Dissonance and discomfort can reinforce histories of trauma. Watt and the MCI Research Team have sat with participants' feedback about resistance to "being" when a sense of psychological and community safety is missing, such as when there is a fear of harm when sharing power among individuals from the oppressor and oppressed groups. Going back to the research on intergroup conflict, people are motivated to feel a certain way about others that in turn informs attitudes and reactions. However, the research also finds that a way to build solidarity across groups is to make "salient the ways in which other groups' struggles with discrimination and prejudice may be experienced similarly to one's own" (Cortland et al., 2017, p. 560). Or, making salient the ways in which we have shared humanity.

The hyper-individualistic culture of the United States is a threat to seeing our shared humanity, but experiences like the ARC can start to provide environmental conditions that catalyze and cultivate more generative relationships, dialogue, and action. Thus, the theory of Being, including its *individual, relational, and community ways of Being*, helps prepare us to be more engaged contributors in our communities. It creates an ethos that fosters collaboration rather than competition and encourages us to bring our whole selves into the spaces we inhabit.

Conclusion: Being With Otherness

Even in naming our otherness, we (authors) know that it is not always invited into spaces or spaces are not inviting enough for us to reveal our full selves. In our experiences of otherness growing up and in our professional lives, we have confronted and understood the rules of engagement in White, cis, hetero, and patriarchal contexts. The theory of Being has given us the language and stamina *to notice (and affirm) our experiences and environments, normalize our defensive reactions, and attempt to humanize the otherness in ourselves and in relationships with others and ideas.* The theory of Being offers an approach that gives us the skills to take the otherness out of ourselves and place it in the center to understand the various systems of oppression and threats to Being that create the conditions for otherness. As is custom from our academic training, we turned to scholarly literature to understand how otherness manifests itself and what we can do to deal with it. Recent research acknowledges that human thoughts and emotions can be reappraised and modified to reduce discomfort with Difference. The theory of Being, however, has us question these outcomes in search of process-oriented and humanizing practices that do not ask that we fix otherness or reduce otherness or simply see otherness as an intellectual exercise. Instead, the theory of Being asks that we feel otherness deeply, speak it into existence, and move through the otherness that we each hold and judge and see what comes out on the other side. In the theory of Being, it is not only what we think about otherness but how we hold onto otherness in our bodies that paves the way toward the transformation of self and communities.

References

Alschuler, A. S. (1986). Creating a world where it is easier to love: Counseling applications of Paulo Freire's theory. *Journal of Counseling & Development, 64,* 492–496. https://doi.org/10.1002/j.1556-6676.1986.tb01179.x

Brown, A. C. (2018). *I'm still here: Black dignity in a world made for whiteness.* Convergent Books.

Cortland, C. I., Craig, M. A., Shapiro, J. R., Richeson, J. A., Neel, R., & Goldstein, N. J. (2017). Solidarity through shared disadvantage: Highlighting shared experiences of discrimination improves relations between stigmatized groups. *Journal of Personality and Social Psychology, 113*(4), 547–567. https://doi.org/10.1037/pspi0000100

Craig, M. A., & Richeson, J. A. (2016). Stigma-based solidarity: Understanding the psychological foundations of conflict and coalition among members of different stigmatized groups. *Current Directions in Psychological Science, 25*(1), 21–27. https://doi.org/10.1177/0963721415611252

Fiske, S. T. (2018). *Social beings: Core motives in social psychology* (4th ed.). Wiley.

Good, C., Aronson, J., & Inzlicht, M. (2003). Improving adolescents' standardized test performance: An intervention to reduce the effects of stereotype threat. *Journal of Applied Developmental Psychology, 24*(6), 645–662. https://doi.org/10.1016/j.appdev.2003.09.002

Gross, J. J., & John, O. P. (2003). Individual differences in two emotion regulation processes: Implications for affect, relationships, and well-being. *Journal of Personality and Social Psychology, 85*(2), 348–362. https://doi.org/10.1037/0022-3514.85.2.348

Gupta, A., Szymanski, D. M., & Leong, F. T. L. (2011). The "model minority myth": Internalized racialism of positive stereotypes as correlates of psychological distress, and attitudes toward help-seeking. *Asian American Journal of Psychology, 2*(2), 101–114. https://doi.org/10.1037/a0024183

Halperin, E., Porat, R., Tamir, M., & Gross, J. J. (2013). Can emotion regulation change political attitudes in intractable conflicts? From the laboratory to the field. *Psychological Science, 24*(1), 106–111. https://doi.org/10.1177/0956797612452572

Hare, S. Z., & Leboutillier, M. (Eds.). (2014). *Let the beauty we love be what we do: Stories of living divided no more.* Prose Press.

Harmon-Jones, E., & Mills, J. (2019). An introduction to cognitive dissonance theory and an overview of current perspectives on the theory. In E. Harmon-Jones (Ed.), *Cognitive dissonance: Reexamining a pivotal theory in psychology* (pp. 3–24). American Psychological Association. https://doi.org/10.1037/0000135-001

Hong, C. P. (2020). *Minor feelings: An Asian American reckoning.* One World.

hooks, b. (1994). *Teaching to transgress: Education as the practice of freedom.* Routledge.

Kaur, V. (2020). *See no stranger: A memoir and manifesto of revolutionary love.* One World.

Lorde, A. (2007). *Sister outsider: Essays and speeches.* Crossing Press.

McGrath, A. (2020). Bringing cognitive dissonance theory into the scholarship of teaching and learning: Topics and questions in need of investigation. *Scholarship of Teaching and Learning in Psychology, 6*(1), 84–90. https://doi.org/10.1037/stl000016

Neel, R., Kenrick, D. T., White, A. E., & Neuberg, S. L. (2016). Individual differences in fundamental social motives. *Journal of Personality and Social Psychology, 110*(6), 887–907. https://doi.org/10.1037/pspp0000068

Neel, R., & Lassetter, B. (2019). The stigma of perceived irrelevance: An affordance-management theory of interpersonal invisibility. *Psychological Review, 126*(5), 634–659. https://doi.org/10.1037/rev0000143

Ozier, E. M., Taylor, V. J., & Murphy, M. C. (2019). The cognitive effects of experiencing and observing subtle racial discrimination. *Journal of Social Issues, 75*(4), 1087–1115. https://doi.org/10.1111/josi.12349

Palmer, P. J. (2004). *A hidden wholeness: The journey toward an undivided life.* Jossey-Bass.

Pennington, C. R., Heim, D., Levy, A. R., & Larkin, D. T. (2016). Twenty years of stereotype threat research: A review of psychological mediators. *PLOS One, 11*(1), e0146487. https://doi.org/10.1371/journal.pone.0146487

Porat, R., Halperin, E., & Tamir, M. (2016). What we want is what we get: Group-based emotional preferences and conflict resolution. *Journal of Personality and Social Psychology, 110*(2), 167–190. https://doi.org/10.1037/pspa0000043

Sanchez, D. T., Chaney, K. E., Manuel, S. K., Wilton, L. S., & Remedios, J. D. (2017). Stigma by prejudice transfer: Racism threatens White women and sexism threatens men of color. *Psychological Science, 28*(4), 445–461. https://doi .org/10.1177/0956797616686218

Shapiro, J. R., & Neuberg, S. L. (2007). From stereotype threat to stereotype threats: Implications of a multi-threat framework for causes, moderators, mediators, consequences, and interventions. *Personality and Social Psychology Review, 11*(2), 107–130. https://doi.org/10.1177/1088868306294790

Steele, C. M., & Aronson, J. (1995). Stereotype threat and the intellectual test performance of African Americans. *Journal of Personality and Social Psychology, 69*(5), 797–811. https://doi.org/10.1037/0022-3514.69.5.797

Tamir, M., & Ford, B. Q. (2012). When feeling bad is expected to be good: Emotion regulation and outcome expectancies in social conflicts. *Emotion, 12*(4), 807–816. https://doi.org/10.1037/a0024443

Tippett, K. (Host). (2020, June 4). Resmaa Menaken 'notice the rage; notice the silence' [Audio Podcast]. In *On Being with Krista Tippett.* The On Being Project. https://onbeing.org/programs/resmaa-menakem-notice-the-rage-notice-the-silence/

Tuck, E. (2009). Suspending damage: A letter to communities. *Harvard Educational Review, 79*(3), 409–428. https://www.proquest.com/scholarly-journals/suspending-damage-letter-communities/docview/212268515/se-2

Watt, S. K. (2013). Designing and implementing multicultural initiatives: Guiding principles. In S. K. Watt & J. Linley (Eds.), *Creating Successful Multicultural Initiatives in Higher Education and Student Affairs* (New Directions for Student Services, no. 144, pp. 5–15). Jossey-Bass. https://doi.org/10.1002/ss.20064

Watt, S. K. (Ed.). (2015). *Designing transformative multicultural initiatives: Theoretical foundations, practical applications, and facilitator considerations.* Stylus.

Watt, S. K., Mahatmya, D., Coghill-Behrends, W., Clay, D. L., Thein, A. H., & Annicella, C. (2021). Being with anti-racism organizational change efforts: Using a process-oriented approach to facilitate transformation. *Journal of College Student Development, 62*(1), 130–133. https://doi.org/10.1353/csd.2021.0011

Wong, F., & Halgin, R. (2006). The "model minority": Bane or blessing for Asian Americans? *Journal of Multicultural Counseling and Development, 34*(1), 38–49. https://doi.org/10.1002/j.2161-1912.2006.tb00025.x

11

RESEARCH

Kari E. Weaver and Amanda L. Mollet

He drew a circle that shut me out—
Heretic, rebel, a thing to flout.
But Love and I had the wit to win:
We drew a circle that took him in!
—Edwin Markham, "Outwitted"

The theory of Being is a humanizing frame; it aims to *humanize otherness in oneself (personal way of Being)* and *humanize otherness in relationships and idea exploration (relational way of Being)*. It is therefore important to understand how humanity is compromised, particularly in the contexts of higher education and research. In our chapter, we offer our own experiences of (de)humanization in research and explore other ways in which dehumanization is readily supported in the context of higher education and in research-related practices. Next, we provide an overview of the concept of dehumanization and related ideas of infrahumanization, moral exclusion, and superhumanization. Then we juxtapose these frames with the norms and structures of academic research to examine the application of the theory of Being within institutionalized systems. Our chapter concludes with an overview of how the theory of Being and skills associated with the theory's ideas of *third thinging* and framing issues through an *us-and-them-exploring-it* perspective provide pathways for humanization in self, ideas, and relationships in the process, dissemination, and expansion of research. By using the skill of *third thinging* and the *us-and-them-exploring-it* frame, scholars can work to redefine our relationships to research participants, collaborators, and knowledge in ways that invite vulnerability, authenticity, and compassion. This transformative approach to research resists the notions of neoliberalism and the constraints that perpetuate the search for objective truth through narrowly defined parameters that merely reinforce the status quo of dehumanization in process and product.

Situating Dehumanization and Academic Research

In academe, the means for measuring individuals' worth are often reduced to tallying publications, assessing grant dollars, and counting the number of credit hours generated through instruction. Under these neoliberal norms, desire for maximizing individual human capital reduces people to objects of production and profitability (Vasquez & Levin, 2018). The reduction of individuals to metrics has devolved substantially from hooks' (1994/2014) conceptions of education as a practice of freedom focused on "providing [students] with ways of knowing that enhance their capacity to live fully and deeply" (p. 22). In research, the foundations for research and the production of knowledge are embedded in power dynamics, oppressive systems, and colonial structures (D'Ignazio & Klein, 2020) that contribute to dehumanization in the production, dissemination, and validation of knowledge in the field of higher education. If much of the research shows a propensity toward dehumanization, what are the implications for what is known and what is taught based on this research?

Kari's Reflection

During my doctoral studies, I was part of a research team that explored issues of socialization using critical frameworks that helped us focus on pursuing questions of equity and inclusion. For one project, a subgroup of the team decided to analyze a set of interviews of White undergraduate students in leadership positions. We all shared White racial identities, and we decided to cultivate a deeper understanding of our own Whiteness and the institutionalization of Whiteness through a careful program of shared readings and reflection. I was eager for this collaboration and learning opportunity, as it occurred during a presidency that emboldened White supremacist logic and supporters (Anti-Defamation League, 2019). After many engaging and vulnerable discussions, we started analyzing transcripts. During one of our discussions of this analysis, I had a moment of discomfort and dissonance when I noticed that the interviewed students had become a target of our critique of Whiteness. There was collective eye-rolling at the blatant Whiteness and lack of insight displayed in their stories of navigating leadership positions. I paused to recognize the discomfort: I wanted to examine manifestations of Whiteness, not weaponize critical frames against others. It was dehumanizing to the study participants; it was dehumanizing to participate in this weaponization.

For me, the experience demonstrated our power over others' stories as researchers and the ease with which we slipped into practices of othering and dehumanization. It revealed the problematic position of being the knowers, the privileged position of being in higher education, which distanced us from our own Whiteness. Examining this situation through the lens of Being versus doing, the pressure to produce valuable outcomes (as defined by the neoliberal context, e.g., peer-reviewed publications, conference papers) promotes an orientation on doing. This context of production kept us focused on identifying problems and offering evidence and solutions, engendering an *us-versus-them* position in our data analysis. We were the expert tools of analysis, and by learning critical aspects of Whiteness, we could now leverage those frames to identify problematic acts of White people. We shifted from understanding aspects of the system of Whiteness to seeing manifestations of these aspects to the objectification and dehumanization of individuals who displayed these manifestations. How did this shift occur and how could an orientation to Being have provided meaningful humanization of our research participants, ourselves, and the audience of our research?

Amanda's Reflection

A good friend, who is also a brilliant scholar, recently asked if I could provide feedback regarding an upcoming conference research presentation that he was preparing. Supporting each other's scholarly activities is part of our friendship and a commonality between us. I was enthusiastic about seeing the presentation and hoped to share generative feedback. As he started presenting, I found my mind immediately wandering, thinking, "Where did this come from? Where is this presentation going? This is interesting, but how do these ideas fit together?" I took more than a page of notes, and I largely focused my feedback on structure and organization. Conference research presentations always have a similar structure, format, and organization. At the end, he explained his decision to "start from the middle" to intentionally resist the normative structures reflected in my detailed feedback. His decision to approach the presentation differently caught me by surprise, generated dissonance, and led to benevolent thoughts, "I teach students strategies for engaging research that pushes against norms." He was constructing knowledge through his words and his process. I fell back into my research socialization and began performing toward shaping his thoughts and process into an outcome-oriented 12-minute talk that aligned with what a research talk is "supposed" to be.

When I engage my research, I can envision my plan and approach for generating authentic scholarship that resists norms. Similarly, when I teach graduate students about the importance of process and focusing on Being within the development of research, I work toward constructing the environment for those conversations and our research together; but others in the shared space still enter with their socialization background. During my friend's presentation, I entered the space with certain assumptions that inhibited me from listening fully, being present in the moment, and exploring the thoughts and ideas he was sharing. I was unable to journey together in wrestling with big ideas because of the ways I had fallen back into internalized ways of engaging research. For him, his presentation was more than an opportunity for adding another line on his CV; he saw the presentation as an opportunity for dialogue where the audience could join in the experience of collectively generating new knowledge and emergent questions beyond the confines of his presentation. How did I shift so rapidly to my neoliberal ways of socialization without being aware of it, and why did I assume that I had the proper lens for providing feedback? What would it look like to honor the developmental nature of our missteps in research by extending our reflective dialogues as products that invite sustained engagement? Might this practice further humanize our generation of knowledge while supporting critique and development of ideas as eternal conversations?

Norms of Dehumanization in Research

We come to this chapter centering critical and post-structural epistemic approaches that not only blur existing bounds but also provide space for questioning and reimagining the possibility of humanizing research norms. Explicitly naming and identifying oppressive norms represents an important step toward deconstructing and reimagining. As follows we define dehumanization and affiliated forms and then we share a few specific examples of the dehumanizing norms that exist within the status quo of research production within and beyond our field in order to identify potential areas for transformative work.

Dehumanization is the perception and/or treatment of people (including one's self) or groups as less than fully human (Haslam & Stratemeyer, 2016). This may involve attributing animalistic characteristics to people, such as a lack of self-restraint, irrationality, coarseness, or lack of culture; or through the relation of mechanistic characteristics, such as lack of emotion and ability, rigidity, passivity, and coldness (Haslam, 2006). Dehumanization does not always result in overt acts of aggression or violence; it takes many forms, spanning areas such as cognition, emotion, language, and behavior and manifesting on spectrums from covert and subtle to egregious (Haslam & Loughnan, 2014). However, it would be dangerous to assume that the more subtle forms of dehumanization are any less pernicious. The prevalence and cloaked nature of less overt manifestations of dehumanization can make them harder to recognize and change. By describing various forms of more subtle dehumanization, we can begin to recognize these ideas and actions in our own conceptions of humanity in ourselves and others.

Covert forms of dehumanization include infrahumanization, moral exclusion, and superhumanization. Each form is unique, yet they share a denial of human characteristics and attributes. *Infrahumanization* involves denying uniquely human qualities to outgroups vis-à-vis ingroups (Haslam & Stratemeyer, 2016). Ideas of deficiencies often concern intelligence, language, and emotions. For example, one could deny the capacity of others to have warmth, emotionality, and deep emotions (a mechanistic characteristic), or may assume that the outgroup experiences emotions in an animalistic way, such as an uncontrollable rage or a simplistic form of contentment (Leyens et al., 2007). Both characterizations deny the capacity of outgroup members to experience a full range of nuanced human emotions, and excuse the display of certain "immoral" and "highly uniquely human" emotions such as abhorrence and disrespect by the ingroup toward the outgroup (Leyens et al., 2007).

Moral exclusion can engender dehumanization by excluding others from a moral community, locating them outside boundaries of moral values, rule, and ideas of fairness (Opotow, 1990). This allows people to narrowly apply a scope of justice, seeing those outside of that scope as "eligible for deprivation, exploitation, and other harms that might be ignored or condoned as normal, inevitable, and deserved" (Opotow et al., 2005, p. 305). Symptoms of moral exclusion include the blaming of victims for their own harms, attitudes of condescension and bias, holding double standards of different norms for different groups, and the deflection of any personal responsibility for the mistreatment of others (Opotow, 1990; Opotow & Weiss, 2000).

Superhumanization is uniquely problematic, as it can appear to have positive and complementary qualities, yet it works to maintain the denial of human qualities for others. Waytz et al. (2014) define superhumanization as characterizing people as beyond human, by representing them as having supernatural, magical, or extrasensory mental and physical qualities. In five studies of undergraduate students, Waytz et al. found that White individuals attribute these superhuman qualities to Black people relative to White people. These concepts have deep roots in American history and media including the denial of Black slaves' ability to feel pain and the depiction of

Black individuals as magical healers or the embodiment of a god (Westervelt, 2014). This perception of superhuman qualities can work in similar ways to moral exclusion by placing people outside of the scope of justice and fairness and justifying the denial of aid and reduction of empathy (Waytz et al., 2014).

As aforementioned, heightened research expectations and the push for greater research productivity in higher education environments (Kuo et al., 2017) reward the separation of public and private spheres, which dehumanizes scholars by necessitating that their personal selves, identities, and experiences do not emerge in their work or scholarship. Gatta and Roos (2004) acknowledge that it is "not just a formidable task, it's virtually an impossible task" (p. 125). Valuable research is also often defined as objective (Gardner et al., 2017) where the authors "neutralize" (Weiss, 1994) any personal connection, emotions, or thoughts about the work. Data are often collected, analyzed, and disseminated without providing context of the "social, cultural, historical, institutional, and material conditions under which that knowledge was produced" (D'Ignazio & Klein, 2020, p. 152). The suggestion that data exist with neutrality ignores the human influence within the research process.

The impossibility of separating self and research emerges prominently in studies that examine academic productivity and metrics of success (e.g., citations, annual evaluations, promotion and tenure) and demographic characteristics. For example, faculty of color face epistemic exclusion (Dotson, 2012) as a form of racial prejudice from colleagues who devalue their scholarship (Settles et al., 2020). Gender differences also exist across multiple disciplines including men having more publications than women in medicine (Warner et al., 2017), women's publication rates decreasing significantly more than men in clinical psychology during the COVID-19 pandemic (White et al., 2021), and women in tenure-track positions in social work having lower measures of impact and productivity (measured by the h-index) compared to men (Carter et al., 2017). In the field of higher education, two Black women, Joan Nicole and Brittany M. Williams, started a social media movement called #CiteASista in response to the pervasive Whiteness they learned about during their doctoral studies. The group exists "to uplift and center the voices and contributions of Black women in the USA and abroad" (Cite A Sista, n.d.). Despite intentional labor from scholars like Nicole and Williams, the culture of dehumanization persists.

Much like other aspects of the research process, determining the order of authorship—or who receives "credit"—for the work comes with extensive norms and guidance from professional associations, institutions, and even publishers with a focus on reducing the influence of power and prestige in authorship decisions (Macfarlane et al., 2017; Newman & Jones, 2006). Still, in many ways the system "involves staking and maintaining territorial rights, colonization, and empire building" (Scott, 1997, p. 744) focused on individualistic ownership over the generation of knowledge. When doctoral students or junior scholars are included as authors, they are commonly listed further in the order such that their names are literally erased with in-text citation guidelines. American Psychology Association (APA, 2019) writing guidelines specify that when there are three or more authors, citations should include only the first author's name followed by "et al." Acknowledging the inequality of this practice, San Pedro, Murray, Gonzales-Miller, Reed, Bah, Gerrard, and Whalen (2020) intentionally avoided the APA style expectation of using et al. in their citations. They acknowledged that later authors were likely those with less power and so they intentionally included all authors' names in their citations.

These examples of the norms and expectations of academic research begin highlighting the deeply ingrained nature of research culture in education research. Other models for research (e.g., feminist research, critical quantitative research) exist, but they exist on the margins and as intentional resistance to some of the aforementioned norms. Returning to the prior reflections from the authors, we can see how dehumanization manifested in individual, intrapersonal, interpersonal, and environmental ways within the research process. We revisit these reflections to examine them through a lens of diminished humanity for ourselves and others and ask: how could Being transform these interactions and experiences? Finally, we end with imagining the transformative possibilities for Being within research to change the production of knowledge.

Kari's Return to Reflection

In my reflection, I recognized a moment when I felt dehumanized by our condescending treatment of participants in our research study. An in-depth exploration of dehumanization and related concepts, particularly infrahumanization and moral exclusion, helped me examine my dissonance with greater clarity. I noticed how easily a group of thoughtful, kind, and well-intentioned individuals slipped into the position of academic researchers who were distanced from their own Whiteness and developmental journeys. From this "superior" position, we exonerated our shared act of disdain and openly treated our research participants without empathy. Why did we do this? What aspects of research and our shared identities enabled this? What contextual elements were at play? Why should we pay attention to these seemingly small acts of disrespect?

First, our dehumanizing actions may have allowed us a sense of moral superiority and distance, reassuring us of the importance of our perspective as social science researchers (Haslam, 2006). Our work as critical scholars who interrogate racial injustice and other forms of inequality feels isolating and frustrating at times, particularly in the context of historically White institutions (HWIs) where social justice initiatives are often under-resourced and undermined (Patton et al., 2019). This situation can have a marginalizing and/or demotivational effect on critical scholars. We may have also gained distance from our own Whiteness, signifying our separation from "ignorant" White people through our mockery of their ideas and actions. We defined ourselves as an ingroup and these others as an outgroup based on a perception of dissimilar values and a lack of prosocial values, further permitting a dehumanization of "bad" Whites (Schwartz & Struch, 1989).

How would the theory of Being have helped in this moment of dissonance? My discomfort was a signal for the need to pause and reflect. While I have taken time since that moment, it would have been beneficial for my collaborators and I to have stopped for a shared dialogue. I might have stated my discomfort and asked to be with the dissonance so I could explore the issue with others. I could have worked to name the issue so that we could relate to it as a *third thing*. I might have described the issue as an *us-versus-them* dynamic that positioned us as knowing subjects, as "good," "woke," White people. Relating personally to that issue as a *third thing*, I might have described how I could have easily been that undergraduate student leader, ignorant of how my understanding of issues of race and equity were potentially harmful and narrow. I might have said that I felt ashamed of how long I lived with this ignorance, of how easily I navigated life with my uninterrupted White privilege. I might have wondered about my educational privilege, of the time I had to spend with critical theories within a community that valued social justice; how I used that educational privilege to dehumanize others who had not had the same opportunities. I might have heard my collaborators' stories of their own experiences of Whiteness and academia. We might have built a deeper understanding of one another as vulnerable, empathetic, and fully human individuals, and we might have looked at our research participants with greater care and compassion.

Amanda's Return to Reflection

As I reflect further on the incident described previously, I first needed to work through the defensiveness that emerged. I found myself rationalizing my behavior. "It was late on a Friday afternoon. I spent much of the day focused on outcome-oriented projects before our meeting." Instead of listening to understand, my focus was on providing feedback to help my friend improve. After years of dialoguing, discussing ideas, developing research, and creating space for valuing each other's contributions, in that incident, I let go of those *ways of Being* with him. He was engaging authentically and creating an environment for exploring enduring questions. I missed the opportunity that he intended for using the presentation as a *third thing* that provided space for exploring the ideas together. My approach was reductive and dehumanizing as I narrowly aligned his brilliance with seemingly arbitrary expectations that I associated with research conferences.

The experience and reflecting upon it reinforced the importance of continual awareness and attention. Having transformational experiences or working toward transforming a culture is a continual journey. *Being with* is more than learning and naming the skills and applying them in the spaces that I have created or the spaces where I know it is safe for engaging research with these tools. This experience created substantive dissonance precisely because of the way that I was reminded of the importance of continually attending to my journey and the ways that I show up. As a junior faculty member, pursuing tenure, and experiencing continual reminders of neoliberal expectations for productivity and research, I lost sight of the liberatory potential of research and the joy that comes from authentically sharing space, Being with others, and daring to explore ideas without a specified destination in mind.

Thinking forward from this experience, I acknowledge the importance of taking pause before entering an environment. How do I want to be in this space? How can I contribute toward an environment that humanizes our time together? What else is happening in my head or heart that may inhibit me from Being fully present, and how can I bring those intentions authentically while also learning from my own inner teacher?

Humanizing Research Through *Third Thinging*

This exploration of what might have been testifies to the humanizing potential of the theory of Being's approach and its practice of *third-thing* dialogues. Dehumanization thrives on the objectification of others and their reduction to abstract, essentialized positions that make them seem too distant to be understood or cared for (e.g., Haslam, 2006; Leyens et al., 2007). To reverse patterns of dehumanization, we can engage in intergroup contact (e.g., Allport, 1954; Pettigrew & Tropp, 2006) that allows us to appreciate others' thoughts, feelings, and intentions (Fiske, 2009) and see them with empathy, forgiveness, and increased humanity (e.g., Halpern & Weinstein, 2004; Leyens et al., 2007). This helps to expand our scope of justice, as we move from moral exclusion to moral inclusion, leading to the extension of resources for well-being to a broader audience (Opotow et al., 2005).

To combat infrahumanization, intergroup contact should be deprovincialized, or done in a way that allows for the recognition of others' points of view (Leyens et al., 2007). *Third thinging*, which is the process of exploring an idea or issue with others, facilitates this recognition of individual accountability and subjectivity (Watt, 2015). Akin to Mezirow's (1993, 2003) concept of effective discourse, in a *third thing* dialogue we focus on creating a situation where all participants feel free of coercion, work to reflect critically on their assumptions and beliefs, hold empathy and openness for others' perspectives, and learn from dialogue to guide their decision-making and actions. However, this dialogue of Being diverts from Mezirow's modernist, constructivist tendency to seek common ground and allowance of every participant to advance their own beliefs and judge arguments.

While every dialogue participant should engage in personal reflection, they are not invited to dispute the reality of oppression. This practice follows Freire's (1970/2018) argument that:

> Dialogue cannot occur between those who want to name the world and those who do not wish this naming—between those who deny others the right to speak their word and those whose right to speak has been denied them. Those who have been denied their primordial right to speak their word must first reclaim this right and prevent the continuation of this dehumanizing aggression. If it is in speaking their word that people, by naming the world, transform it, dialogue imposes itself as the way by which they achieve significance as human beings. (p. 88)

As Freire (1970/2018) notes, by centering the reality of oppression we reject the possibility of further dehumanization through others' denial of this truth. Instead of working to deny another person's truth or experience of the world, we listen to seek understanding.

When structural oppression is at the center of these conversations, we can form a more complex idea of the multidimensional and fluid nature of power (Pietrykowski, 1996). For example, if my colleagues and I were engaging in a *third thing* dialogue that centered on sexism, I would not have to argue for the existence of structural oppression against women that pervades every institution. Instead, I could explore my thoughts about intersections of motherhood and the academy that I felt limited my success or ability to thrive in a culture rooted in patriarchy and class privilege.

Figure 11.1 helps to demonstrate that it is not the content of dialogue alone that liberates; the way we treat one another in the dialogue liberates

Figure 11.1. Visual conception of *third thing*.

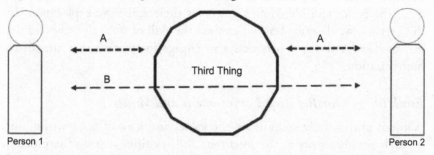

A. Interaction between the individual and the third thing allows one to understand their own experiences and socialization.

B. Seeing another person's reaction to the third thing allows for the humanization of the other, and the realization that others may experience the world in different ways.

Note: The image is an original creation of the chapter's authors.

as well. The process of *listening deeply* to others both liberates us from patterns of dehumanization within ourselves and toward others and helps us unveil the many realities of oppression. To defend ourselves from the attacks of others to prove them wrong, we build legitimacy from data or other sources that they might recognize as holding objective truth; however, to defend our own humanity, we reduce their humanity. By *listening deeply*, we turn from seeing others as enemies to our liberation to seeing their experiences being tangled up in the same systems of oppression. This type of dialogue is an act of love—for the world, for ourselves, and for others—as it is a commitment to be free from systems of power that limit us all (Freire, 1970/2018). As we describe experiences that extend beyond our roles as institutional producers and performers, the listener(s) form a more human model of us across time and space. We are not just coworkers; we are children, partners, caregivers who experience doubt, hope, joy, fear, and other emotions. Our ideas are not monolithic and unquestionable but have roots of formation, of experience, of questioning or reinforcement, and thus have the potential for change.

Being With Research

This chapter's description of *third thinging* demonstrates the importance of maintaining an orientation toward oppressive systems of power that limit our humanity. This facilitates a shift from an *us-versus-them* (or ingroup versus outgroup) orientation to the *us-and-them-exploring-it* angle, closing the psychological distance between the groups and focusing on how hegemonic forces affect all of us. As described, this power orientation validates the issues considered and promotes their authentic exploration. In this section, we describe how we can use the skill of *third thinging* and the *us-and-them-exploring-it* perspective to engage in research that attends to humanization.

Establishing Our Research Environment and Values

Without purposefully establishing the values and *ways of Being* within our research environments at the forefront, and revisiting during the process, the pull of our normative socialization can easily emerge. Transformational engagement that seeks to shift ingrained socialization requires continual attention and focus. One tangible strategy for maintaining accountability includes the approach used by D'Ignazio and Klein (2020) in their research. They started their research project by collaboratively generating a list of values and metrics proposing an "example or theorist in every chapter about Indigenous knowledges and/or activism," and asking to "feature and quote people directly impacted by an issue versus those who study or report on the phenomena from a distance" (D'Ignazio & Klein, 2020, p. 219). As a *third thing*, their list of values and metrics provided an *us-and-them-exploring-it* dynamic where they examined and worked toward the methods of research that invited collaborators into dialogue and honored their multiple ways of knowing and Being as valid, important sources of knowledge.

Another example of engaging *ways of Being* in research examines the outcome-oriented emphasis on the clear demarcation of research projects through a seemingly linear process including a beginning, middle, and end. Instead, a focus on Being in research acknowledges the intertextuality of dialogue and knowledge generation through sustained engagement. Watt et al. (2021) provided a demonstration of this environmental transformation by the inclusion of the Multicultural Initiatives Consortium as one of the publication authors, inclusive of current and alumni members of the research team who contributed toward the enduring ideas that manifested in the specific manuscript. This seemingly small act of authorship amplifies the realities of the environment of Watt's research team that values and acknowledges members' insights and contributions beyond the moment of utterance or the limited context of a specific project or manuscript.

Setting Our Research Questions

Research questions catalyze our academic and reflective efforts. They guide our knowledge development around subjects and offer a potential for knowledge creation that contributes to improved understanding and practice

(Alvesson & Sandberg, 2013). While we may arrive at our research interests by various entry points, such as pressing social issues or personal interests, we can use *ways of Being* to deepen our understanding of our motives for these questions or to determine the final form of these questions in our research project. What if we began with our research subject as a *third thing* for exploration? We might start with Patel's (2015) questions of relationality in educational research: "Why this? Why me? Why now?" (p. 57). These questions feed into areas of answerability, or our responsibility for the stewardship of ideas and learning in particular contexts. I ponder Rowan's (2019) questions of relationship-centered education: "Whose interests do my decisions serve? To whom do I offer hope?" (p. 17).

We can also engage in *third thing* dialogues with others to help shape our research questions. This collaborative exploration of an issue serves as a problem-posing educational experience which has the potential to offer hope and possibility of social transformation (Freire, 1970/2018). We might center our subject of research as a *third thing* and could ask questions that seek to uncover ways in which people feel limited or dehumanized. One question might be: What aspects of this issue make you feel constrained in your full humanity? Or, taking cues from Okello's (2020) work on self-love, we might ask: How are you existing in your body in relation to this subject? By centering social issues, norms, and oppressive forces in this dialogue, we can open a pathway for intersubjective communication of social suffering through critical empathy. This is a particular type of empathy that provides opportunities to name experiences of social issues, providing critical solidarity and raising consciousness (Lobb, 2017).

As we engage in these dialogues around our research questions, we need to pay attention to any tendencies of defining issues in *the us-versus-them* dynamic. If this occurs, we might take time to recognize any establishing of outgroups and ingroups. We might ask ourselves if we project any aspects of limited humanity upon these groups, such as a narrow emotional range, a lack of prosocial values, or a constrained intellectual capacity. We should work to recenter these elements in systems of oppression as an *us-and-them-exploring-it* dynamic.

Being With Other Research Activities

While setting our research questions is a crucial area for Being, we might utilize this approach in all areas of our research activities. We may think about the interview protocol as a *third thing* dialogue inviting our research participants to explore social issues or other problems alongside us. In order to keep this from being a shared exercise of venting, there must be a pointed effort of information-seeking, undergirded by curiosity and a desire to uncover greater understanding (Freire & Macedo, 1995). In data analysis, we should remain attuned for evidence of *the us-versus-them* dynamic and explore the possibility of shifting to an *us-and-them-exploring-it* framing. In sharing our findings and suggesting practices or application, we might ask if we have limited our scope of humanizing and justice to certain ingroups and consider expanding this scope.

Conclusion

Through the research process, continual reflection, and open dialogue about *ways of Being*, we can foster the conditions necessary for humanizing the self, collaborators, and individuals involved in the process of knowledge generation. Feeling self-dehumanized is associated with unethical behavior, leading to deeper feelings of dehumanization and continued acts of immorality and dishonesty (Kouchaki et al., 2018). Moving toward a humanizing process of Being in research, instead, presents opportunities for authenticity, sustained engagement, and transformational change as individuals in the research that we create to help inform others. We share our experiences as demonstrations for using personal reflection as a tool for enhanced understanding and development in research. May the ideas, examples, and questions presented here and in Appendix F offer prompts that can continue these dialogues toward shifting research norms that can contribute to humanizing knowledge generation.

References

Allport, G. W. (1954). *The nature of prejudice.* Addison-Wesley.

Alvesson, M., & Sandberg, J. (2013). *Constructing research questions: Doing interesting research.* SAGE. https://dx.doi.org/10.4135/9781446270035

Anti-Defamation League. (2019, March 5). *White supremacist propaganda and events soared in 2018.* https://www.adl.org/news/press-releases/white-supremacist-prop-aganda-and-events-soared-in-2018

Carter, T. E., Smith, T. E., & Osteen, P. J. (2017). Gender comparisons of social work faculty using h-index scores. *Scientometrics, 111*(3), 1547–1557. https://doi.org/10.1007/s11192-017-2287-0

Cite A Sista. (n.d.). *About us.* https://citeasista.com/about/

D'ignazio, C., & Klein, L. F. (2020). *Data feminism.* MIT press.

Dotson, K. (2012). A cautionary tale: On limiting epistemic oppression. *Frontiers: A Journal of Women Studies, 33*(1), 24–47. https://doi.org/10.5250/fronjwomestud.33.1.0024

Fiske, S. T. (2009). From dehumanization and objectification, to rehumaniza-
tion: Neuroimaging studies on the building blocks of empathy. *Annals of the
New York Academy of Sciences, 1167,* 31–34. https://doi.org/10.1111/j.1749-
6632.2009.04544.x

Freire, P. (2018). *Pedagogy of the oppressed.* Continuum. (Original work published 1970)

Freire, P., & Macedo, D. (1995). A dialogue: Culture, language, and race. *Harvard Educational Review, 65*(3), 377–403. https://doi.org/10.17763/haer.65.3
.12g1923330p1xhj8

Gardner, S. K., Hart, J., Ng, J., Ropers-Huilman, R., Ward, K., & Wolf-Wendel, L.
(2017). "Me-search": Challenges and opportunities regarding subjectivity in
knowledge construction. *Studies in Graduate and Postdoctoral Education, 8*(2),
88–108. https://doi.org/10.1108/SGPE-D-17-00014

Gatta, M. L., & Roos, P. A. (2004). Balancing without a net in academia: Integrating
family and work lives. *Equal Opportunities International, 23,* 124–142. https://
doi.org/10.1108/02610150410787765

Halpern, J., & Weinstein, H. M. (2004). Rehumanizing the other: Empathy and
reconciliation. *Human Rights Quarterly, 26,* 561–583. https://heinonline.org/
HOL/Page?handle=hein.journals/hurq26&id=571

Haslam, N. (2006). Dehumanization: An integrative review. *Personality and Social Psychology Review, 10*(3), 252–264. https://doi.org/10.1207/s15327957pspr1003_4

Haslam, N., & Loughnan, S. (2014). Dehumanization and infrahumanization.
Annual Review of Psychology, 65, 399–423. https://doi.org/10.1146/annurev-
psych-010213-115045

Haslam, N., & Stratemeyer, M. (2016). Recent research on dehumanization. *Current
Opinion in Psychology, 11,* 25–29. https://doi.org/10.1016/j.copsyc.2016.03.009

hooks, b. (2014). *Teaching to transgress: Education as the practice of freedom.* Routledge. (Original work published 1994)

Kouchaki, M., Dobson, K. S., Waytz, A., & Kteily, N. S. (2018). The link between
self-dehumanization and immoral behavior. *Psychological Science, 29*(8), 1234–
1246. https://doi.org/10.1177/0956797618760784

Kuo, P. B., Woo, H., & Bang, N. M. (2017). Advisory relationship as a moderator
between research self-efficacy, motivation, and productivity among counselor education doctoral students. *Counselor Education and Supervision, 56*(2), 130–144.

Leyens, J.-P., Demoulin, S., Vaes, J., Gaunt, R., & Paladino, M. P. (2007). Infrahumanization: The wall of group differences. *Social Issues and Policy Review, 1*(1),
139–172. https://doi.org/10.1111/j.1751-2409.2007.00006.x

Lobb, A. (2017). Critical empathy. *Constellations: An International Journal of Critical and
Democratic Theory, 24*(4), 594–607. https://doi.org/10.1111/1467-8675.12292

Macfarlane, B., Devine, E., Drake, T., Gilbert, A., Robinson, M., & White, I. (2017).
Co-authorship in the humanities and social sciences: A global view. https://aut-
horservices.taylorandfrancis.com/wp-content/uploads/2017/09/Coauthorship-
white-paper.pdf

Markham, E. (1915). *The shoes of happiness: And other poems.* Doubleday, Page &
Company.

Mezirow, J. (1993). How adults learn: The meaning of adult education. In D. Flannery (Ed.), *34th Adult Education Research Annual Conference Proceedings* (pp. 179–184). Pennsylvania State University.

Mezirow, J. (2003). Transformative learning as discourse. *Journal of Transformative Education, 1*(1), 58–63. https://doi.org/10.1177/1541344603252172

Newman, A., & Jones, R. (2006). Authorship of research papers: Ethical and professional issues for short-term researchers. *Journal of Medical Ethics, 32*(7), 420–423. https://dx.doi.org/10.1136%2Fjme.2005.012757

Okello, W. K. (2020). "Loving flesh": Self-love, student development theory, and the coloniality of being. *Journal of College Student Development, 61*(6), 717–732. http://dx.doi.org/10.1353/csd.2020.0071

Opotow, S. (1990). Moral exclusion and injustice: An introduction. *Journal of Social Issues, 46*(1), 1–20. https://doi.org/10.1111/j.1540-4560.1990.tb00268.x

Opotow, S., Gerson, J., & Woodside, S. (2005). From moral exclusion to moral inclusion: Theory for teaching peace. *Theory into Practice, 44*(4), 303–318. http://dx.doi.org/10.1207/s15430421tip4404_4

Opotow, S., & Weiss, L. (2000). New ways of thinking about environmentalism: Denial and the process of moral exclusion in environmental conflict. *Journal of Social Issues, 56*(3), 475–490. http://dx.doi.org/10.1111/0022-4537.00179

Patel, L. (2015). *Decolonizing educational research: From ownership to answerability.* Routledge.

Patton, L. D., Sánchez, B., Mac, J., & Stewart, D. (2019). An inconvenient truth about "progress": An analysis of the promises and perils of research on campus diversity initiatives. *The Review of Higher Education, 42*(5), 173–198. https://doi.org/10.1353/rhe.2019.0049

Pettigrew, T. F., & Tropp, L. R. (2006). A meta-analytic test of intergroup contact theory. *Journal of Personality and Social Psychology, 90*(5), 751–783.

Pietrykowski, B. (1996). Knowledge and power in adult education: Beyond Freire and Habermas. *Adult Education Quarterly, 46*(2), 82–97. https://doi.org/10.1177/074171369604600203

Rowan, L. (2019). *Higher education and social justice: The transformative potential of university teaching and the power of educational paradox.* Palgrave Macmillan.

San Pedro, T., Murray, K., Gonzales-Miller, S. C., Reed, W., Bah, B., Gerrard, C., & Whalen, A. (2020). Learning-in-relation: Implementing and analyzing assets based pedagogies in a higher education classroom. *Equity & Excellence in Education, 53*(1–2), 177–195. https://doi.org/10.1080/10665684.2020.1749188

Schwartz, S. H., & Struch, N. (1989). Values, stereotypes, and intergroup antagonism. In D. Bar-Tal, C. G. Grauman, A. W. Kruglanski, & W. Stroebe (Eds.), *Stereotypes and prejudice: Changing conceptions* (pp. 151–167). Springer.

Scott, T. (1997). Authorship. Changing authorship system might be counterproductive. *BMJ: British Medical Journal, 315*(7110), 744–751. https://www.ncbi.nlm.nih.gov/pmc/articles/PMC2127487/pdf/9314763.pdf

Settles, I. H., Jones, M. K., Buchanan, N. T., & Dotson, K. (2020). Epistemic exclusion: Scholar(ly) devaluation that marginalizes faculty of color. *Journal of Diversity in Higher Education, 14*(4), 493–507. https://doi.org/10.1037/dhe0000174

Vasquez, E. M., & Levin, J. S. (2018, January–February). *The tyranny of neoliberalism in the American academic profession.* American Association of University Professors. https://www.aaup.org/article/tyranny-neoliberalism-american-academic-profession#

Warner, E. T., Carapinha, R., Weber, G. M., Hill, E. V., & Reede, J. Y. (2017). Gender differences in receipt of National Institutes of Health R01 grants among junior faculty at an academic medical center: The role of connectivity, rank, and research productivity. *Journal of Women's Health, 26*(10), 1086–1093. https://doi.org/10.1089/jwh.2016.6102

Watt, S. K. (Ed.). (2015). *Designing transformative multicultural initiatives: Theoretical foundations, practical applications, and facilitator considerations.* Stylus.

Watt, S. K., Mahatmya, D., Coghill-Behrends, W., Clay, D. L., Thein, A. H., Annicella, C., & Multicultural Initiatives Consortium. (2021). Being with anti-racism organizational change efforts: Using a process-oriented approach to facilitate transformation. *Journal of College Student Development, 62*(1), 130–133. https://doi.org/10.1353/csd.2021.0011

Waytz, A., Hoffman, K. M., & Trawalter, S. (2014). A superhumanization bias in Whites' perceptions of Blacks. *Social Psychological and Personality Science, 6*(3), 352–359. https://doi.org/10.1177%2F1948550614553642

Weinstein, J. (2004). Creative altruism: The prospects for a common humanity in the age of globalization. *Journal of Futures Studies, 9*(1), 45–58. http://citeseerx.ist.psu.edu/viewdoc/download?doi=10.1.1.390.3921&rep=rep1&type=pdf

Weiss, R. S. (1994). *Learning from strangers: The art and method of qualitative interview studies.* The Free Press.

Westervelt, E. (Host). (2014, November 30). Examining the myth of the 'superhuman' Black person. In *All Things Considered* [Audio podcast episode]. NPR. https://www.npr.org/2014/11/30/367600003/examining-the-myth-of-the- superhuman-black-person

White, S. W., Xia, M., & Edwards, G. (2021). Race, gender, and scholarly impact: Disparities for women and faculty of color in clinical psychology. *Journal of Clinical Psychology, 77*(1), 78–89. http://dx.doi.org/10.1002/jclp.23029

EPILOGUE

Gordon Louie

Prior to the current iteration of this section that you're reading, I had written, revised, scrapped, rewritten, rerevised, amended, and rearranged pieces of text numerous times. Each time I found myself struggling either to encapsulate the sentiments that I wanted to share, convey some nuance that had not already been expressed by the wonderful chapters that precede this epilogue, or effectively give closure to the many thoughtful questions and insights which have been raised throughout this volume. As a testament to how countercultural Being is, I found that each time I tried to write, I would inevitably devolve back to the habit of purely academic writing, stressing over whom I should cite and whether I was sounding "smart" enough (often a proxy for removing oneself as much as possible from the work at hand) to contribute to a text on theory at the expense of writing as my authentic self. Rather than engaging only the head without acknowledging the heart and the hands, my hope is instead to express how being a member of this team and working alongside the authors whose chapters you have read have reshaped my thoughts, feelings, and actions in the work that I do in the context of my own life and experience.

I joined the Multicultural Initiatives (MCI) team as a 2nd-year doctoral student in the higher education and student affairs program at the University of Iowa during the time when I transitioned to being a full-time student again. At the time, the idea of being on a research team took a very concrete form in my mind as a result of prior experiences. I was more concerned with the pursuit of "knowing" than questioning what it means "to know." Though I was familiar with qualitative research and acknowledged the subjectivity inherent in doing research, I ultimately believed that what I was about to embark on would help me further remove these subjectivities rather than lean into them in the research that I produced. I also struggled with the combined demands of work and school, which many part-time graduate students may relate to. There was (and occasionally still is) a pressure to conform to timelines and to believe that a nonlinear path to degree or an "alt-ac" career somehow needs justification and validation. Had I stayed in my full-time role in student affairs at the time, my doctoral journey would have taken at least a better part of a decade to complete. I had already begun feeling the mental toll of having to "switch" my mind between the policy-driven side of my professional life's practice and the theoretical and abstract deep dives in classes as a student. I worried about how these stresses would affect the perceived quality of any work that I produced.

It was in this context that Sherry K. Watt and Kari E. Weaver extended an invitation to me; since my previous professional background had mostly been working with faculty and students in business programs, they were hoping for some insights into broadening the engagement of the team. I can't say that I brought much business acumen to the team's endeavors, but the past few years have been transformative for my thinking and practice. I feel very fortunate to have been able to contribute my time and efforts toward something that I believe has far-reaching potential for systemic and institutional change. In some ways, it is fitting that I am the one tasked with writing this epilogue—as I transition back again to a full-time role in student affairs, I am gifted this opportunity to reflect on how our joint work these past several years has spoken to me most. Bhattacharya (2021) wrote about "shifts" in her journey as an academic; utilizing *ways of Being* has truly "shifted" my conception of the academy and my place within it. Rather than examining shifts over time as she does, I turn specifically to the impact of these shifts on the head, heart, and hands.

Head

Similar to numerous other graduate students with whom I've connected, my return to school and pursuit of a doctoral degree was a culmination of many factors. Most urgently, it was a desire to reach the apex of knowledge in a particular field, to which I had been socialized to believe that *that* was the purpose of a terminal degree. Coming from the humanities, I had an ingrained sense of skepticism about social scientific research methods. Nevertheless, I was eager to learn more and to learn methods that I assumed could help me work toward resolving issues of inequity that I had come to see deeply rooted in my profession.

However, the more methods courses I took, the more I came to see that research is always based on some contingencies. In the very first class that I took in my program, an enduring problem that we consistently wrestled with was the extent to which confounding factors/variables may be present in research—these so-called "selection effects" (Pascarella, 2019). Our conclusion was that even in the most airtight research designs, there is often no guarantee that these may be eliminated completely. The real question was always how opaque or transparent these possible confounding factors or variables were in the research presented. This realization left me intellectually adrift. When I became immersed in the work of the research team, the theory's components provided a direction that truly resonated with me. If knowing is contingent at best, then perhaps what is needed is not more posturing but more humanizing ways of engaging with each other and more explicit acknowledgments of how our experiences, perspectives, and values show up in our research.

Heart

Ever since I was a master's student, critical frameworks and approaches have been core components of my academic training. The controversy surrounding their use in today's political landscape evinces the binary ways in which they were leveraged in the past—that is, as a dividing line of *us-versus-them*. I have certainly done this in discussions with friends, colleagues, and other scholars and harbored the view "if they don't 'get' it, then they're obstructing the work that needs to be done." Even today, this is the mentality that I find easy to revert to when a charged topic comes up. What my time on the team has taught me is that equity work is, by necessity, a thoroughly collective effort. If we are willing to move on without acknowledging some voices or without the investment of all voices, then the effort will not meet its full potential nor its desired outcome(s). This is not to say that everyone should always be in total agreement with others, but the environment needs to be such that everyone can feel open to authentically disagree and feel empowered to shape the direction toward which we are collectively moving.

Hands

In practice, the work of Being has taught me the need to have built-in space for reflection. Tagg (2004) started off his article with a scenario of an instructor encountering two former students—one who failed the class they taught but has persisted in engaging with themes from the class and another who aced the class but remembers nothing. He then posed the question which student can be considered to be more successful. I think often of students with whom I work either as an instructor or staff member. Tagg's (2004) piece makes me wonder how I might have the most impact in the work that I do. Rather than focusing on content, perhaps a focus on process can be equally (if not more) valuable. In advising, a developmental view has been a long-standing approach (Crookston, 1994). Yet, both in my work as an advisor and instructor, I often went along with a more prescriptive approach where the focus was on content. Part of the rationale is that there will always be limited time and unless we normalize Being with the big questions and ideas organizationally/institutionally, there will always be constrained capacities and limited effects to what we might accomplish. However, we need time to make meaning and continue to make sense of what we are presented with. We must disrupt practices that rely on assumed consensus by offering the time and space to reflect and authentically engage.

Remaining Questions

Though incorporating *ways of Being* into my work has been one of the most rewarding parts of my graduate school experience, I find myself simultaneously contemplating the future horizons of this theory and its application. Most pressingly, I wonder whether and how we can practice Being skills with those whom we love and hold most dear. We often talk about being "holistic" in our work, but what are the boundaries of holistic when there is a duality between our professional and personal selves that remains unacknowledged (Palmer, 2004)? I am the child of immigrants, and my parents came of age during the Cultural Revolution in China. It is often said that a generation of youth had their education sacrificed during that tumultuous period. My parents' experiences of living amid this radical movement and expectations of conforming to cultural norms in the United States in which I have been steeped since my youth have created a rift in me. I have found great difficulty in relaying the importance of what I study and what I do to the people whom I love and respect but whose cultural upbringing is drastically different from mine. When we consider issues of social equity and belonging, in what ways are we extending the definitions of these terms beyond the boundaries of those who share a similar understanding of history and culture? I reflect on this tension when I feel limited by cultural boundaries that inherently exist between the time and context I was raised in and how that was different for my parents.

Perhaps two related broad questions are "When we talk about systemic change, whose systems are we changing?" and "Who can participate in this system, and in what capacity?" To people like my parents whose background is so drastically different from someone else's who has spent most or all of their life in the United States, how might they be folded into the conversation, particularly one so reliant on history? This summer, my parents helped me move from Iowa back out West as I began my new professional career. Along the way we stopped by historical sites which, to me, wove a contiguous narrative of Western expansion and colonization that has kept Native peoples at the margins of society. When I heard my father explaining its meaning to my mother, it was much more aligned with how a survey-level history book might have told the tale—an unfortunately bloody but glorious opening of a Western frontier without which they would not have been able to seek the better life that they have now.

How can I even begin to untangle the cultural, historical, and experiential nuances that shape our different views of the world? More to the point, how do I do so without invalidating their lived experience and retaining the respect and deference that align with the cultural norms that are expected of me? There are no quick or easy answers here, and it is undoubtedly the enduring nature of these questions that makes the theory of Being work so crucial. For its applications now as the authors of this volume have expressed through their narratives, questions, and research, and for its continued evolution in the future. One of the consequences of using this approach that has resonated most with me is that I often end up with more questions (albeit refined ones) than I had at the start. Despite the uncertainty that I expressed in the beginning, I have become more comfortable allowing these questions to remain and evoke my personal sense of wonder. There can be a sense of comfort amid accepting uncertainty. We often say on the MCI team that intellectual vertigo can be a disorienting experience, but it may be useful to think of it as learning how to float. When you are dropped into the deep end of a pool, you flail and grab at anything you can to try and get a steady hold, but once you realize that you have to relax for the balance to take hold, it completely shifts how you engage with the water—from how you think about it to how you feel it to how you do it. Similar to this process, it takes willingness to engage, and while there is no uniform way to get there, it certainly is easier with an experienced guide. If you are wading through questions of your own, I hope this volume can be a guide for your journey, and I trust that you are in the right place.

References

Bhattacharya, K. (2021). Becoming a warrior monk: First, second, and third shifts in academia. *Journal of Autoethnography*, *2*(1), 123–127. https://doi.org/10.1525/joae.2021.2.1.123

Crookston, B. B. (1994). A developmental view of academic advising as teaching. *NACADA Journal*, *14*(2), 5–9. https://doi.org/10.12930/0271-9517-14.2.5

Palmer, P. J. (2004). *A hidden wholeness: The journey toward an undivided life*. Jossey-Bass.

Pascarella, E. T. (2019). Assessing the impact of college on students: A four-decade quest to get it approximately right. In M. B. Paulsen & L. W. Perna (Eds.), *Higher education: Handbook of theory and research* (1st ed., Vol. 34, pp. 1–38). Springer.

Tagg, J. (2004). Why learn? What we may really be teaching students. *About Campus*, *9*(1), 2–10. https://doi.org/10.1177%2F108648220400900101

APPENDIX A

*Appendix A is available for download on the Stylus website
(see https://bit.ly/TOBDnLs or QR code on page 234).*

The Theory of Being Brief

The purpose of the theory of Being is to describe a process-oriented approach to dialogue in communities. The theory of Being is inspired by a transformative learning theory (Mezirow, 1991). It teaches the practice of Being, which involves aligning thoughts (head), feelings (heart), and actions (hands) that support the conditions for building stamina necessary to be present with conflict.

The theory of Being offers life-giving ways to face impenetrable social problems that create the possibility of transformational change in communities by shifting the focus of dialogue away from *us-versus-them* to *us-and-them-exploring-it.*

Ways of Being practices support the conditions for building personal, relational, and community stamina.

Theory Components

Personal ways of Being:
- Practices that focus on self-awareness and authentic personal connections to the conflict.
- These practices include *focusing on you, humanizing otherness in self, recognizing defenses, and discerning motivations.*
  - *Focusing on you*: Situating the self in relation to the conflict.
  - *Humanizing otherness in self*: Embracing that difference exists and exploring feelings around incongruities within the self and in relation to the conflict.
  - *Recognizing defenses (PIE model):* Noticing defensive/dissonant reactions as they arise in the self and in relation to the conflict.
  - *Discerning motivations*: Facing the sources of desire or motives from within the self as it relates to the conflict.

Relational ways of Being:

- Practices that sustain being in an active authentic relationship with self and others with an intention, when dissonant during conflict.
- These practices include *listening deeply, humanizing otherness in relationships and idea exploration, exploring defenses, and dissenting wisely and well.*
  - *Listening deeply*: Being present with the expressions of self and others as you listen carefully to what is being spoken (verbally and nonverbally) as you deal with conflict.
  - *Humanizing otherness in relationships and idea exploration*: Embracing that difference exists in relationships and in views on ideas while also exploring feelings around incongruities across relationships in relation to the conflict.
  - *Exploring defenses* (PIE model): Supporting another while expressing defensive/dissonant reactions in the self in relation to the conflict.
  - *Dissenting wisely and well*: Disagreeing while also holding in regard the whole humanity of the self and the other person while in a conflict with each other.

Community ways of Being:

- Practices that face the conflict by shifting a group away from centering on individual survival toward expecting individual and community thriving.
- These practices include understanding the concepts of *third thing and third thinging, balancing dialogue and action, normalizing defenses, embracing trouble as a learning opportunity, and viewing missteps as developmental.*
  - *Understanding the third thing and third thinging*: Centering in-depth examination of the issue as a focal point for the community while exploring the conflict.
  - *Balancing dialogue and action*: Preparing intentionally for dialogue that leads to community action in addressing the conflict.
  - *Normalizing defenses* (PIE model): Acknowledging that defensive/dissonant reactions are natural parts of community deliberations when addressing conflict.
  - *Embracing trouble as a learning opportunity*: Welcoming trouble as an opportunity to learn and grow as a community surrounding the conflict.
  - *Viewing missteps as developmental*: Embracing mistakes and/or missteps as a normal, necessary, and facilitative aspect of learning about the conflict together as a community.

Crosscutting Tools

The theory's key tools are Being *touchstones* (Appendix B), *third thinging* (Appendix C), *open and honest questions* (Appendix D), and *PIE model* (Appendix E).

Key Terms

The theory's key terms are *conflict, Difference,* and *difficult dialogues.*

The *conflict* could be an enduring social problem, a controversial decision, a disorienting dilemma (as Mezirow, 1991, describes), a new/unknown/ unfamiliar or even a fundamentally disagreed upon difference, belief, value, idea, or experience.

Difference is "having dissimilar opinions, experiences, ideologies, epistemologies and/or constructions of reality about self, society, and/or identity" (Watt, 2013, p. 6).

A *difficult dialogue* is "a verbal or written exchange of ideas or opinions between citizens within a community that centers on an awakening of potentially conflicting views of beliefs or values about social justice issues (such as racism, sexism, heterosexism/homophobia)" (Watt, 2007, p. 112).

Primary Theoretical Influences

The primary theoretical underpinnings are pedagogy of the oppressed (Freire, 1970), the principles and practices of the Center for Courage & Renewal (Palmer, 1998, 2009), transformative learning theory (Mezirow, 1991), counseling theory (Rogers, 1950, 1961, 1980), psychoanalytic (Freud, 1979), and engaged pedagogy (hooks, 1994).

Other theoretical influences include psychosocial/identity theory (Erikson, 1963), cognitive-structural theory (Perry, 1970), and ecological theory (Bronfenbrenner, 1979). The theory of Being also stands on the visions of resisting racist ideology expressed by James Baldwin in *Notes of a Native Son* (1955) and *I Am Not Your Negro* (Peck, 2017), Audre Lorde's (1984) *Sister Outsider,* and Toni Morrison's *The Source of Self-Regard* (2019) and her interviews given on television, *The Charlie Rose Show* (Rose, 2015), and in the documentary film, *The Pieces I Am* (Greenfield-Sanders, 2019).

Theory Assumptions

1. *Societal conditions* (racism, sexism, heterosexism, genderism, classism, and so on, and their intersections) are deeply rooted in culture, history,

tradition, and practices of supremacy and domination. Societal conditions are ever-changing and nebulous.

2. *Controversy* is inevitable when facing inequities in societal conditions. Collective exploration of controversy has a greater potential to lead to more just and equitable outcomes for all. Communities need to be continually in a process of dialogue that deconstructs and reconstructs environments for inclusion across Difference. Actions to change societal conditions are disruptive for community members, institutions, and society. States of dissonance, discomfort, and defensiveness are inherently part of the learning process of organizing a community and taking action to change a societal condition.

3. *Transformation* of societal conditions occurs through working at the personal, institutional, community, and societal levels. All spaces within a community are for learning, especially transformative learning. Transforming societal conditions involves people in the community engaging together in dialogues that align their head (intellect and thought), heart (feeling, emotion, and spirit), and hands (practical and real world applications). Change in societal conditions needs to occur rather than retrofitting individuals to fit within a pathological social system that pledges compliance with an ideal and domination as a problem-solving strategy. Change happens when people in the community embrace a learning ethos and face the problem, understand that they have agency, and actively engage their authentic selves in a dialogue about transforming the conditions in which they live.

4. *Process-oriented* practices have a greater potential to lead to transformational change. Process-oriented approaches create sustainable practices that guide ways of interacting around enduring problems whereby communities can continue to employ strategies that address conflict in ways that are nimble and responsive. Ultimately, quality processes, while in dialogue, strengthen communities as they work together to create environments and ways of sustainable interaction that have the potential to result in more just and equitable societal change.

Values of Being

- *Reframes Difference*: Reframes Difference as central and additive, not as necessary and marginalized.
- *Humanizes otherness*: Embraces the view that the human condition brings new arrivals (information, experiences, illness, uncertainty, etc.) and

invites one to embrace otherness as a constant and to welcome it as a state of Being.

- *Normalizes fear, defensiveness, discomfort, and dissonance*: Understands that fear, defensiveness, and discomfort are normal responses to conflict; sees conflict as opportunity; and believes conflict is inherent and beautifully difficult.
- *Repositions otherness*: Situates Difference as an object of collective exploration and wonderment and shifts away from team mentality that protects individual interests and focuses on the societal condition that deforms all.
- *Embraces uncertainty*: Understands that human beings are multifaceted and the inherent problems communities deal with are ever-changing; to address this type of complex uncertainty, uses approaches that are flexible and adaptive rather than linear and reductive.
- *Invites, assumes, values, and knows wholeness*: Expects to nurture health and thriving; intentionally veers away from viewing life as segmented or divided; resists facing conflict as problem-fixing only to survive and solely as curing illness; rejects a focus on deficit; and rather shifts toward a foundation that is focused on promoting health and wholeness.
- *Welcomes paradox*: Embraces conflict with curiosity; expects contradiction, complexity, and disagreement; and values exploration and consideration of varying perspectives.
- *Centers on the community*: Values coalition-building across Difference that is in the interest of the collective; situates individual needs in context of the larger community's interests; recognizes the benefit of dialogue about and inclusion of polarizing viewpoints in order to create better solutions for a community to thrive.
- *Cultivates liberation*: Aspires to be together as a community while upholding central values such as truth, love, kindness, generosity, integrity, and shared power and responsibility; prioritizes collective action and reflection; questions and suppresses traditional uses of patriarchal power such as coercion, extortion, intimidation, shame, retaliation, and patronization; boldly pursues life and thriving even in the face of death and extermination; respects that there is a need to simultaneously consider accountability, responsibility, justice, and defense of life; pursues an offensive strategy rather than a reactionary response that produces primarily a defensive action.

For references, see "Part One Introduction" and chapter 1.

APPENDIX B

Appendix B is available for download on the Stylus website (see https://bit.ly/TOBDnLs or QR code on page 234).

Being *Touchstones*: Intentional Practices for Collaboration

1. *Practicing being present*: Be here. Be present as fully as you are able. Be here with your doubts, fears, and failings as well as your convictions, joys, and successes.
2. *Practicing welcome*: Receive welcome and extend welcome. People learn best in welcoming spaces. We support each other's learning by giving and receiving welcome.
3. *Practicing speaking with intention*: Speak your T(t)ruth in ways that respect the T(t)ruths of others.
4. *Practicing listening with authenticity and depth*: Listen deeply with respect. Help others "hear each other into deeper speech."
5. *Practicing exploration*: Breathe. Everything is an invitation. It is not share or die. Simultaneously, everyone's voice matters and contributes to creating a picture of the issues in the moment as it helps us understand our present reality and identify our work.
6. *Practicing trust*: No fixing, saving, or advising. Respect that the inner teacher is present in us and guides each of us while we learn in the community.
7. *Practicing confidentiality*: Safety is built when we can trust that our words and stories will remain with the people with whom we choose to share and are not repeated to others without our permission. Stories stay, lessons go.
8. *Practicing living the questions*: Let go of right answers. When it's hard, turn to wonder. If you feel judgmental or defensive, ask yourself, "I wonder what brought her/him/them to this belief. I wonder what feelings are arising for him/her/them." And perhaps the most important question: "I wonder what my reaction teaches me about myself."

9. *Practicing pausing*: Offer space and time to ponder. Be open to pausing, silence, and listening to understand before speaking. Be open to hearing from our inner teacher as well as from each other.

10. *Practicing grace and reflection*: Honor that we are all learning together. Embrace missteps as an opportunity to learn—about ourselves, about others and about how we are socialized. Be open to the cycles of ownership, responsibility, regret, grace, reflection, redemption, and forgiveness.

11. *Practicing hope*: Believe that it's possible to emerge from this work with what you need, what the community needs, and with more energy, openness, and perspective so that our community can hold greater capacity for transformation, healing, and wholeness.

Adapted by Sherry K. Watt from Circle of Trust® Touchstones Center for Courage & Renewal (CCR), founded by Parker J. Palmer, https://couragerenewal.org/wpccr/touchstones/—with deep gratitude to Veta Goler and Sally Z. Hare. Each is a facilitator trained by the CCR.

The Practice of *Third Thinging*

A third thing or third thinging is a process-oriented concept (Rogers et al., 1967; Saussy, 2011; Smith, 2005). *A third thing* takes the form of text (poems, quotes, articles, etc.) or another visual means (music, art, storytelling, film, etc.) as a focal point in a dialogue.

A *third thing* allows one person, or the first thing, and another person, or the second thing, to share their experiences about the *third thing*. For example, the first person and the second person are in a dialogue about *the third thing*, which is a tree (see Figure C.1). The first person and the second person can share their experiences with trees. They might have had good experiences (e.g., building tree houses) or negative experiences (e.g., a tree falling on their house during a storm). When *third thinging*, they can share

Figure C.1. Third thing illustration—image of two people (first and second things) on opposite sides of a tree (the third thing).

observations about their own upbringing and about others interacting with trees. The use of *third things* holds each community member accountable by asking each to consider how they relate to the conflict or the focal point of the dialogue.

When a community engages in *third thinging* about a conflict, it is centering a complex problem that is inherently complicated by social constructs such as racism, genderism, sexism, or heterosexism as a focal point in a dialogue. It abandons the notion that the social problem is solely a personal burden and rather shifts the focus to examine the issue as a shared experience. It is not adversarial. In other words, *third thinging* shifts the exploration of complex social problems from an *us-versus-them* perspective to sharing in the exploration from an *us-and-them-exploring-it* angle. *Third thinging* broadens our view of the problem and allows us to see the problem from varying perspectives and responsibilities. The dialogue includes our personal positions but goes beyond our positionality and asks us as whole humans to consider the problem as a shared cultural phenomenon. *Third thinging* "increases the possibility that communities will examine social problems in a way that those with dominant and marginalized experiences will share the burden of creating solutions" (Watt, 2015, p. 34). To sum up:

1. *A third thing* as a noun refers to a focal point for Being, and *third thinging* as a verb refers to an act or a *way of Being.*
2. *Third thinging* as a verb allows *us-them-exploring-it* as a complex problem that the community shares.
3. It is not adversarial.
4. The community is not arguing about it or protecting it. The community is noticing what it does, how it operates, and how it deforms our relationships.
5. It is seen as a problem that we can dissect and take shared action to address.
6. Viewing conflicts as *a third thing* creates a space where a community can see this problem as a transcendent idea. They can view it including and beyond any particular positionality.
7. *Third thinging* allows space for a community to observe the complexities rather than viewing the complex problem as an oppositional idea only.

References

Rogers, C. R., Stevens, B., Gendlin, E. T., Shlien, J. M., & Van Dusen, W. (1967). *Person to person: The problem of being human: A new trend in psychology.* Real People Press.

Saussy, H. (2011). Comparison, world literature, and the common denominator. In A. Behad & D. Thomas (Eds.), *A companion to comparative literature* (1st ed., pp. 60–64). Wiley-Blackwell.

Smith, M. K. (2005). Parker J. Palmer: Community, knowing and spirituality in education. In *The encyclopedia of informal education.* http://infed.org/mobi/parker-j-palmer-community-knowing-and-spirituality-in-education/

Watt, S. K. (Ed.). (2015). *Designing transformative multicultural initiatives: Theoretical foundations, practical applications, and facilitator considerations.* Stylus.

APPENDIX D

The Practice of Asking Open and Honest Questions

The practice of asking *open and honest* questions is a key element of the Circle of Trust® approach developed by the Center for Courage & Renewal where Sherry K. Watt was trained as a Courage & Renewal facilitator. You are invited to use this material in your practice and application of the theory of Being. When you do, please include attribution to the Center for Courage & Renewal and its website, www.couragerenewal.org.

The practice of asking *open and honest questions* is a means for inquiry and discernment that moves us beyond our normal patterns of communication. Usually, questions aim at gathering information to solve problems or effect change in a particular way. They are often little speeches in disguise, ways of spotting a weakness in the other person's position and trying to change their mind, or nudges to move them toward a predetermined goal.

Open and honest questions are intended to help the speaker understand themselves or their situation more clearly by helping them think more deeply about their experience or convictions. Such questions create space for exploratory conversations, generate new insights, forge new relationships between ideas and people, and reveal resources within and among us that can help us achieve a shared goal. They slow the pace of inquiry allowing us to listen and understand while suspending disbelief or judgment, which can deepen the relational trust on which so much depends.

Open and honest questions are not appropriate for all situations—sometimes questions need to be more instrumental. But they can often enrich our interactions in both personal and professional settings.

The practice of asking *open and honest questions* can help us do the following:

- Explore an issue more deeply—both for the person talking and the person listening;
- Step back from jumping to solutions, assigning blame, or approaching someone with a specific end in mind;

- Invite a person to discover their own wisdom and resourcefulness—including insights from prior life experiences;
- Support intrapersonal reflection—including awareness of feelings as well as thoughts;
- Slow down the pace and deepen human connection. It is always a gift to be listened to for understanding without receiving judgment;
- Shift the paradigm from "fixing a broken person" to creating a safe space in which a person can access their own capacities for growth and wholeness.

Suggestions for asking *open and honest questions*:

1. The best mark of an *open and honest question* is that you cannot anticipate the answer, nor do you have an expectation for what the answer should be. For example, ask, "What was easy? What was difficult? What surprised you? What did you learn?"
2. Stay with the person's language. For example, ask, "You said this was an impossible situation. Could you say more about what that means to you?"
3. Rather than only asking questions related to the problem or issue being raised, ask questions directed to the person as well. For example, ask, "What in your life brings you joy? What would a really good day look like for you?"
4. Trust your own intuition. Listen deeply and allow questions to come from your heart, not just your head.
5. Yes/no or right/wrong questions tend to close down inquiry. Instead, ask questions that help open or expand your thinking about the issue or available options.
6. The best questions are often simple and straightforward, without a long preamble or rationale.
7. Ask questions aimed at helping the person explore their own understanding rather than satisfying your curiosity.
8. Offer images or metaphors that might engage the person's imagination. For example, ask, "If you were writing a book about this experience, how might you title the book? Name this chapter?"

Privileged Identity Exploration (PIE) Model

The following list provides definitions of defenses.
Recognizing privileged identity:

- *Denial* is a defensive reaction that denies the existence of the dissonance-provoking stimulus (DPS).
- *Deflection* is a defensive reaction that shifts the focus of the DPS toward another source.

Contemplating privileged identity:

- *Minimization* is a defensive reaction that lessens the issues surrounding the DPS.

Figure E.1. The privileged identity exploration (PIE) model.

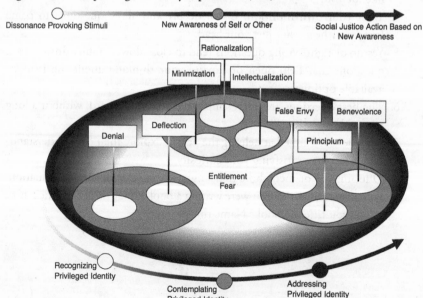

- *Rationalization* is a defensive reaction that generates alternative explanations for the DPS.
- *Intellectualization* is a defensive reaction that attempts to explain the DPS as a data point or with academic theories.

Addressing privileged identity:

- *False envy* is a defensive reaction that compliments or expresses affection toward a person or a feature of a person that represents the DPS.
- *Principium* is a defensive reaction that reports a principle to defend against the DPS.
- *Benevolence* is a defensive reaction that uses an act of charity to situate the self in relation to the DPS.

References

Watt, S. K. (2007). Developing cultural competence: Facilitating privileged identity exploration in student affairs practice. *College Student Affairs Journal, 26*(2), 114–126. https://search-ebscohost-com.proxy.lib.uiowa.edu/login.aspx?direct=true&AuthType=ip,cookie,uid,url&db=eue&AN=507975011

Watt, S. K. (Ed.). (2015). *Designing transformative multicultural initiatives: Theoretical foundations, practical applications and facilitator considerations*. Stylus.

Watt, S. K., Curtiss, G., Drummond, J., Kellogg, A., Lozano, A., Tagliapietra, N. G., & Rosas, M. (2009). Privileged identity exploration: Examining white female counselor trainee's reactions to difficult dialogue in the classroom. *Counselor Education & Supervision, 49*, 86–105. https://doi-org.proxy.lib.uiowa.edu/10.1002/j.1556-6978.2009.tb00090.x

Watt, S. K., Mueller, J. A., Parker, E. T., Neel, R., Pasquesi, K., Kilgo, C. A., Mollet, A. L., Mahatmya, D., & Multicultural Initiatives Consortium. (2021). Measuring privileged identity in educational environments: Development and validation of the privileged identity exploration scale. *Frontiers in Education, 6*. https://doi.org/10.3389/feduc.2021.620827

APPENDIX F

Supplementary Materials for Applying Tools of The Theory of Being

In this appendix, we offer various types of application materials explaining how the theory's tools, such as *third things, open and honest questions*, or a guided activity, can be applicable to in-person or virtual educational environments. The supplementary materials are written by chapter authors and are listed in the order of the chapter's appearance in the book.

Chapter 3, Empathy

Reflective Writing Exercise: Take a few minutes to write whatever comes to mind with the following two questions:

- When I practice empathy, who or what do I pay attention to?
- What do I learn from the process of empathizing?

After answering the questions, take a short break, then go back and read through your answers for each of these questions. When you're done reading, answer two more questions to start the process referred to as *turning to wonder*: What did you feel while reading your answers to the questions? Where did those feelings come from? Continue to practice this process by applying these questions to a recent conversation where you were empathizing with someone's story: What did you pay attention to? What did you learn? What do you feel from listening to your answers to the first two questions?

Open and honest questions: I started the process of naming *intellectual empathy* by thinking about the contexts in which I practice empathy. After recognizing it, I navigated intellectual empathy by placing my identities in conversation with one another. I propose the following general questions to start your own exploration of intellectual empathy via your own identities.

Context of practicing empathy:

- How do you empathize with someone's story when the storyteller holds the same privileged identity as you?

- How do you empathize with someone's story when the storyteller holds the same marginalized identity as you?
- How do you empathize with someone's story when the storyteller holds an identity where you hold privilege and they experience marginalization?
- How do you empathize with someone's story when the storyteller holds an identity where they hold privilege and you experience marginalization?
- What feelings do you associate with each of these scenarios?

Navigating intellectual empathy:

- How do my privileged identities practice empathy?
- How do my marginalized identities want to receive empathy?
- Would my marginalized identities be satisfied with the way my privileged identities practice empathy? Why or why not?

Virtual Application: The chapter starts with a quote from Ta-Nehisi Coates (2011). Go online and read his piece entitled "A Muscular Empathy." Instead of focusing on Coates's application of empathy in race, focus on the essence of how he defines empathy. Place his definition (and the article if you want to talk about empathy and race) at the center of conversation (i.e., make it *a third thing*).

Chapter 4, Shame

Third thing: Tara Brach said, "Don't turn away. Keep your gaze on the bandaged place. That's where the light enters you."

Open and honest question: What occurs in my head (thoughts), heart (emotions), and hands (actions) when I experience shame?

Virtual application: Although it might look different, building relationships in which people feel safe to talk with one another about shame is entirely possible in the virtual context. Questions you might ask yourself:

- How can I hold space for difficult emotions like shame over virtual platforms?
- How do I ensure that I am establishing strong relationships built on trust where we can name when shame arises?
- When I experience shame, where, how, and with whom do I name that experience while protecting myself and others?

Chapter 5, Silence
Third things:

- Desmond Tutu said, "If you are neutral in situations of injustice, you have chosen the side of the oppressor. If an elephant has its foot on the tail of a mouse, and you say that you are neutral, the mouse will not appreciate your neutrality" (Quigley, 2003, p. 8).
- TED Talk, *The Danger of a Single Story,* by Chimamanda Ngozi Adichie
- Song "White Privilege II" by Macklemore and Ryan Lewis (featuring Jamila Woods)

Open and honest question: How does the theory of Being fit into this chapter's discussion of silence as a form of privilege, compliance, and violence?

Chapter 6, Communication

Third thing: Poem by John Fox "When Someone Deeply Listens to You"
Open and honest questions:

- How do you wear your identities?
- What forms/clothing/armor do they take?
- Which/what do you wear when you enter into a difficult dialogue?
- Which/what do you wear when you engage authentically in a difficult dialogue?
- When have you found yourself in an uncomfortable conversation where unspoken power dynamics heightened the tension? How did you respond?
- What environmental factors would help create a space where you could be with your discomfort, move the conversation to a place that felt resolved, or dissolve power inequities?

Virtual application: See Table F.1.

Chapter 7, Resistance

Third Thing: Rumi's poem "The Guest House" can serve as *a third thing* to invite group members to humanize the presence of resistance and show up more fully as themselves to honest conversations. Moreover, educators and other types of group facilitators can invite participants facing relational resistance to humanize resistance through creative expression. For example, at the start of the chapter, the authors described what their respective resistance feels

TABLE F.1

Virtual Applications of The Theory of Being for Interpersonal Communication

Points to Consider	Definition	Examples
Community Agreements	Agreed upon *ways of Being*, relating, and acting while occupying the virtual space that all members cocreate at the start of the interaction	• One person speaks at a time. • Name your intent, but own your impact. • Be present (and question assumptions we have about forms of engagement in a virtual space). • Assume positive intent. • Value and accommodate multiple ways of interacting (speaking, chat, virtual engagement platforms).
Being Present	Active listening, recognizing your own experience, emotions, defenses, and assumptions	• Listen to respond, not to react. • Be aware of the assumptions you make about other people's presence in the conversation. • Take note of when difficult emotions arise and examine that.
Action/ Implementation	Creation of a collaborative plan of action that will ensure organizational and relational change beyond the conversation	• Create a document outlining specific action steps and delegation of responsibilities. • Consider power dynamics, communication styles, and the needs of all parties. • Set deadlines and accountability structures.

like. Participants can identify physical objects, songs, or images to personify and describe resistance within themselves, in relationships with others, or within a group. This tool can translate in person or within our increasingly prevalent virtual environments (i.e., Zoom).

Open and honest questions: Steve Malvaso's narrative and personal meaning-making of *that semester* call for tools to engage resistance and remain present amid controversy. One such tool is to be in continued conversation with resistance at the individual, relational, and community levels. We propose a series of open and honest questions to be in a dialogue with oneself and others about resistance. Each of the meaningful questions seeks to humanize resistance as an inherent part of conflict in Being.

Personal Questions:

- When has your resistance been "an unexpected visitor"? When has it showed up and surprised you?
- What are the contradictions in how your resistance shows up? What are the complexities of my resistance?
- When is your resistance hopeful? What possibilities for transformation might your resistance be suggesting?
- Why might I be resistant to examining my role in a given conflict?
- What is my personal struggle with and through this particular form of resistance?

Relational Questions:

- How does your resistance affect me? What might trigger this reaction?
- How does your resistance interact with others' forms of resistance?
- What does your resistance say to my resistance?
- What do I want others to know about my resistance, and why?

Community Questions:

- What is my responsibility for the collective resistance that is emerging?
- Are we giving a space to resistance at the table in this interaction? Why or why not?
- What might giving a seat to resistance look like?
- What kind of group healing is needed following a situation of resistance?
- Do we need time and space to individually process and revisit resistance?

Chapter 8, Boundaries

Open and honest questions: Milad Mohebali asks: "Janice, if concepts had colors, I wonder what the colors of 'authenticity,' 'unconditional positive regard,' and 'accountability' would be when you are in equity-centered meetings or in professional spaces that (re)center Whiteness."

Janice A. Byrd asks: "Milad, what would it feel like if you were to bring your experience of dizziness to Casey and Jordan?"

Chapter 9, Truth

Third thing: See Figure 9.1.
Open and honest questions:

- What is keeping me from hearing others share their truth?
- Do I see dialogue as a bridge or a debate?

- What are my triggers?
- Do I approach dialogue to win or to learn about self and others?
- What do I need to work on to meet in the middle of the bridge?
- What messages do I communicate to myself?
- What is the origin of these messages?
- What informs my knowledge that has become truth?

Chapter 10, Otherness

Third Thing: In the spring of 2020, Sherry K. Watt shared with us (Saba Rasheed Ali and Duhita Mahatmya) a chapter from Ross Gay's *The Book of Delights*; the following is an excerpt from that chapter. The chapter spoke so deeply to the emotions we felt within ourselves as well as in our relationships with each other and larger communities. We offer this excerpt as both a representation of the chapter and a piece that can invite folks to reflect on the *personal, relational,* and *community ways of Being* with otherness:

> What if we joined our wildernesses together . . . And what if the wilderness—perhaps the densest wild in there—is our sorrow?'
>
> Is sorrow the true wild?
>
> And if it is—and if we join them—your wild to mine—what's that?
>
> For joining, too, is a kind of annihilation.
>
> What if we joined our sorrows, I'm saying.
>
> I'm saying: What if that is joy?

Open and honest questions: We offer questions that focus on inviting in-depth discernment of the roles we play in defining, internalizing, and projecting otherness: If I placed otherness in a room with me, where would it be? How far away is it? Can I reach for it? Can I see it clearly?

Virtual Application: In a virtual space, consider ways that minimize otherness. Sharing *touchstones* and live transcribing of the virtual meeting can help set group rules and make the dialogue more accessible. The work of Henri Lipmanowicz and Keith McCandles (www.liberatingstructures.com/) provides additional in-person and virtual ways to create multiple ways for individuals and groups to engage.

Chapter 11, Research

Third Thing: Edwin Markham's (1915) poem, "Outwitted," provides a unique foundation for exploring the theory of Being in research by figuratively and literally centering humanity and drawing folks in for shared examination that integrates an *us-and-them-exploring-it* orientation. Engaging research from a humanizing approach creates spaces where all involved in the research process can exist holistically in communal examination.

Open and honest questions: We provide the following open and honest questions for consideration during the research process:

- What aspects of this issue (or research focus) make me feel constrained in my full humanity?
- How can my *ways of Being* align with the ways in which I conduct and engage with research?
- What does it feel like being in liberatory research spaces? What does it feel like in dehumanizing research spaces?
- What aspects of my research socialization do I want to unlearn to bring humanity more fully into my (or our) research?
- Where am I situating myself relative to this topic? What would it feel like approaching this topic as *a third thing* for examination?

Virtual Application: It can be difficult to envision humanizing experiences within institutions, relationships, and activities where we have not been able to be our fully authentic selves; where we have been safe to share our beliefs, missteps, and wonderings without fear of judgment and repercussion; and where we feel seen as dimensional and developing. This activity allows for people to wade gently into that conversation.

Picture yourself in a space where you feel that you can speak freely and feel heard. Envision the space fully. Are you indoors, is the space furnished, what does the air feel like, can you smell or hear anything, is anyone else with you? What do you feel like in that space? Next, imagine that you are asked to engage in a research activity in that space (e.g., research meeting, conference, interview, data analysis). Notice if anything changed in what the space looked or felt like, or how you felt in that imagined space. Did any of those changes restrict your feelings of being able to speak freely and be heard? What might these imaginings tell you about what you identify as enabling or restricting your fully authentic engagement in research?

Participants can be asked to share out in various ways depending on the setting and the level of trust between one another, such as noting single words about each space, describing the difference in spaces, describing the ideal space only, and describing the experience of the activity.

⛨ THE THEORY OF BEING AT-A-GLANCE

This handy guide is available to download and print from the Stylus website (see https://bit.ly/TOBDnLs or QR code on page 234). You can use this list of the Being terms as reminders when applying the approach in your own life situations.

The theory of Being offers communities lifegiving ways to be with controversy and take action when facing impenetrable social problems.

Being is the practice *of aligning* thoughts (head), feelings (heart) and actions (hands) when facing conflict.

Key Words

- Conflict
- Difference
- Difficult Dialogue
- Being
- Us-and-Them-exploring-IT instead of Us-vs-Them

Crosscutting Tools

- Being Touchstones
- Open and Honest Questions
- Third Thinging
- PIE Model

Ways of Being

- Personal
- Relational
- Community

You can find fuller descriptions of these terms in Part One Introduction, Chapter 1, and Appendix A.

The Theory of Being Values

- Reframe Difference
- Humanize Otherness
- Normalize Fear and Defensiveness
- Reposition Otherness
- Embrace Uncertainty
- Invite Wholeness
- Welcome Paradox
- Center Community
- Cultivate Liberation

The Theory of Being Assumptions

- Societal conditions are ever-changing and nebulous.
- Controversy is inevitable.
- Transformation requires engagement of head, heart, and hands as well as interaction on personal, relational, community levels.
- Process-orientation is nimble, responsive and offers possibility for sustainable societal change.

https://styluspub.presswarehouse.com/landing/TheoryofBeing

The following biographical statements are ordered on the basis of chapter numbers. In chapters with multiple authors, the authors' last names are listed in alphabetical order. The editors' information precedes the chapter authors' statements.

Editors

Sherry K. Watt, PhD, NCC, LPC, is a professor in the higher education and student affairs program at the University of Iowa. She is also a cocreator of the Multicultural Initiatives (MCI) Research Team. Prior to becoming a faculty member, she worked as a residence life director and a career counselor at the University of North Carolina at Greensboro, North Carolina State University, and Shaw University. She earned a bachelor's degree in communication studies from University of North Carolina at Greensboro and master's and doctoral degrees in counselor education, with an emphasis on student affairs, from North Carolina State University. She is also the founder of The Being Institute (thebeinginstitute.org). Watt is a facilitator prepared by the Center for Courage & Renewal. She is the editor of *Designing Transformative Multicultural Initiatives: Theoretical Foundations, Practical Applications, and Facilitator Considerations* (Stylus, 2015). She has over 25 years of experience in designing and leading educational experiences that involve strategies to engage participants in dialogue that is meaningful, passionate, and self-awakening.

Duhita Mahatmya, PhD, is an associate research scientist in the College of Education at the University of Iowa. As a research methodologist for the college, Mahatmya provides conceptual and analytical support to projects that examine equity issues in K–12 and higher education. Currently, she works with interdisciplinary teams to understand the role of informal learning environments and school-based interventions on academic and psychosocial outcomes of students from historically excluded communities. Her own research interests broadly focus on examining how family, school, and community environments shape the attainment of developmental milestones from early childhood to young adulthood. She has been a part of the MCI Research Team since 2016.

Milad Mohebali PhD, (he/his), is a postdoctoral researcher with the College of Education and the Multicultural Initiatives (MCI) Research Team at the University of Iowa. He also has a certificate in gender, women, and sexuality studies. Mohebali's research broadly involves social justice in education and decolonization. He is particularly interested in examining the role of university in the modernity/coloniality project and the ways that racism works in and through universities. As part of his involvement with the MCI Research Team, he also explores what it means to be in antiracist and anticolonial dialogues that recenter humanization and Otherwise relationalities.

Charles R. Martin-Stanley II, PhD, is the director for Diversity, Equity, and Inclusivity at Mount Mercy University. Martin-Stanley's research focuses on the persistence and retention of Black college men at historically White institutions. More specifically, he focuses on the racial socialization of Black college men and the agency they have within their own socialization into historically White intuitions. In his role at Mount Mercy University, he is charged with creating and sustaining a campus environment where diversity, equity, and inclusivity are welcomed and encouraged. Martin-Stanley uses the theory of Being in teaching faculty, staff, administrators, and students how to engage in difficult dialogues in a thoughtful and meaningful way.

Contributors

Multicultural Initiatives Consortium comprises members of the MCI Research Team over several years led by Sherry K. Watt at the University of Iowa. These research members include Eugene (Gene) T. Parker III, Kira Pasquesi, Janice A. Byrd, Cindy Ann Kilgo, Amanda L. Mollett, Lindsay Jarratt, Laila McCloud, Richard Barajas, Nicholas Katopol, John Mueller, Duhita Mahatmya, DaVida L. Anderson, Steve Malvaso, Becca Neel, Audrey Scranton, Milica Veselinovic, Marius Kothor, Charles R. Martin-Stanley II, Kari E. Weaver, Patrick Rossman, Abilasha Aparajithan, Krista Walker, Alex Lange, Milad Mohebali, Yareli Mendoza, Tabitha Wiggins, Gordon Louie, Nayoung Jang, Kate Lechtenberg, Evan Knoespel, Raquel Wood, Holly Miller, Celine Fender, Olivia Murphy, Chris R. Patterson, Adrienne

Maxwell, Aralia Ramirez, Jeff Lai, Nicole Tennessen, Teri Schnelle, Alyssa Rae Plano, Nicholas Stroup, Lauren Irwin, Brittany Conner, Alison Kramer, Lucas DeWitt, Abbie Williams-Yee, Chad Rhym, Elmira Jangjou, and Mackenzie Kirby.

Saba Rasheed Ali, PhD, is a professor of counseling psychology and the associate dean for research in the University of Iowa College of Education. Her research expertise and publications focus on career development processes for rural and underrepresented youth as well as the role of poverty and social class in career development. She publishes primarily in career and vocational journals including *Career Development Quarterly*, *Journal of Career Assessment*, and *Journal of Career Development*. Ali is also a licensed psychologist in the state of Iowa and brings expertise in rural mental and behavioral health.

DaVida L. Anderson, PhD, (sher/her), works in student affairs leadership and is an adjunct professor. In her current position, Anderson oversees the Behavioral Intervention Team and is responsible for the student conduct system, policy, program assessment, data collection, campus outreach, the student wellness committee, and student crisis response and management. Equity, diversity, inclusion, and empowerment are themes that she incorporates in her work and research agenda. Anderson is also the founder and executive director of Strong Sister, Silly Sister, Inc., a 501(c) (3) not-for-profit organization committed to empowering college women to embrace ethical choices and become their best selves. Through her LLC, she also is a motivational speaker who engages her audiences to embrace and maximize their full potential. In addition, Anderson serves on internal and external boards, committees, and collaborative groups that implement practices that incorporate justice, diversity, equity, inclusion as a value.

Janice A. Byrd, PhD, (she/her) is an assistant professor of counselor education at Pennsylvania State University; she earned her PhD in counselor education and supervision from the University of Iowa. Byrd has previous experience as a school counselor, career counselor, and facilitator of DEI trainings. Her scholarship seeks to examine the lived experiences of Black students within the broader ecological context to critically examine how their personal, social, academic, and career success is interrupted and/or enhanced by school, family, community, and policies throughout all stages of the educational pipeline (K–12, postsecondary, and graduate studies).

Brian Lackman is the associate director of Student Life & Leadership at the University of North Carolina at Chapel Hill. His work in this role is focused around supervising and supporting his team as they craft immersive and impactful leadership educational opportunities for the Carolina community in order to ensure that everyone can craft their leadership identity. His research has focused on the supervision of graduate students, asexuality, and more.

Gordon Louie is the counseling services coordinator for the University of Washington's Runstad Department of Real Estate and a PhD candidate in higher education and student affairs at the University of Iowa. His work broadly examines the internationalization of higher education (and particularly how this connects to the increasing rhetoric of diversity, equity, and inclusion), utilizing *ways of Being* in student affairs and integrating innovative pedagogical practices into college teaching. Prior to his current studies in education, his background was in the humanities and focused primarily on historic preservation and engaging wider audiences in academic research. He hopes to build more sustainable bridges between research, practice, and public engagement.

Steve Malvaso is a student–athlete success practitioner at Johns Hopkins University and is ABD in the higher education and student affairs PhD program in the Department of Educational Policy and Leadership Studies at the University of Iowa. His research focuses on two main areas: college athletics and communication across difference. Within college athletics, he has published articles about interventions associated with student–athlete personal and professional development; his dissertation research is exploring historic and persistent equity issues related to student–athlete academic experiences. Communication across difference concerns both the theoretical and practical evolutions and applications associated with the theory of Being. He has been fortunate enough to work with Watt and her research team since 2015 and has contributed to various ACPA, ASHE, and GEAR UP conference presentations and workshops, journal and book publications, and consulting projects that the MCI Consortium has undertaken during that time.

Amanda L. Mollet, PhD, (she/her/hers) is an assistant professor of educational leadership and policy studies in the higher education administration program at the University of Kansas. Mollet's research explores questions of equity and inclusion from individual, organizational, and ecological perspectives. She primarily focuses on experiences of students, faculty, and staff with historically minoritized sexual and gender identities; extending her dissertation work, her research on asexuality and asexual students' experiences continues challenging existing norms and understandings of sexuality. Additionally, she has a decade of professional experience in residence life, student conduct, and has served in many leadership roles within ACPA.

Parker J. Palmer earned his PhD in sociology from the University of California at Berkeley, and he also holds 13 honorary doctorates. Parker is a writer, teacher, and activist whose work speaks deeply to people in many walks of life. Author of 10 books that have sold nearly two million copies, he is the founder and senior partner emeritus of the Center for Courage & Renewal.

Chris R. Patterson is a doctoral candidate studying assessment and measurement and an assessment consultant at James Madison University, where he is also an assessment consultant. Patterson's background in assessment and quantitative analysis in higher education brought him to the research team that facilitated the uncovering of the theory of Being. Currently, his research centers on critical quantitative methodology and critical assessment. He now practices the theory of Being as a way to connect with research collaborators, clients, and students.

Aralia Ramirez (she/her/ella) is currently an academic affairs practitioner who focuses on increasing students' sense of belonging on campus through her role as the coordinator for the First-Year Experience Program at California State University, Chico. Prior to this position, she worked in student affairs at universities in the Midwest and Southeast regions of the United States, which helped her develop an interest and passion for student leadership, equity initiatives, and equity-minded supervision practices. Her scholarship is focused on student development, retention, and persistence. She is passionate about improving the field of student affairs and hopes one day to develop a cross-campus student–employee leadership training program to help foster community collaboration among students and staff. She also wishes to complete a joint PhD and JD program in education to create positive change within university policies. She received her BA in sociology from California State University, Chico, and MA in higher education and student affairs from the University of Iowa.

Kira Pasquesi PhD, is the Leadership Studies Minor director and instructor with CU Engage and the School of Education at the University of Colorado Boulder. The 16-credit hour academic minor prepares students to lead courageously through a combination of coursework, self-reflection, and leadership application. As an educator, Kira is passionate about community-building in college classrooms and challenging student leaders to navigate the uncertainties of leading with humility. Her research examines the language of diversity and inclusion in higher education, along with critical approaches to university–community engagement.

Audrey Scranton, PhD, is a researcher and educator who focuses on integrating social justice at the personal, relationship, and policy levels in society. She received her BA in sociology and MA and PhD in interpersonal communication studies. These areas of study have provided her with top-down and bottom-up perspectives on what it takes to create equity and inclusion. Her research has spanned topics such as inclusion for first-generation college students, identity negotiation of undocumented immigrants, microaggressions, health communication, and narrative identities. She has worked for equity in a variety of higher education roles, including leadership education, STEM, staff development, curriculum design, critical pedagogy education, community engaged scholarship, dialogue facilitation, teaching, and strategic planning. She hails from the University of Iowa and works at Rensselaer Polytechnic Institute in New York. She currently resides in Denver, Colorado.

Kari E. Weaver earned her PhD at the University of Iowa in the Department of Educational Policy and Leadership Studies, and is currently the director of the Center for Teaching at the Cleveland Institute of Art. Being part of the MCI research collective has allowed her to stay grounded in her own humanity and in her values of community, collaboration, compassion, and continual transformation; she aspires to help facilitate the experiences of being seen, vulnerable, cared for, and challenged toward growth for others. She teaches and researches undergraduate diversity courses, exploring both faculty and student experiences of diversity-related learning. Kari is the author of articles and chapters on curriculum design, queer theory, self-authorship theory, food insecurity, and critical Whiteness. Her writing, research, and teaching center on practices of empathy, transformation, and liberation.

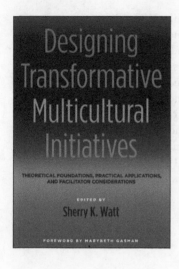

Designing Transformative Multicultural Initiatives

Theoretical Foundations, Practical Applications, and Facilitator Considerations

Edited by Sherry K. Watt

Foreword by Marybeth Gasman

Higher education is facing a perfect storm as it contends with changing demographics, shrinking budgets, and concerns about access and cost, while underrepresented groups—both in faculty ranks and students—are voicing dissatisfaction with campus climate and demanding changes to structural inequities.

This book argues that to address the inexorable changes ahead, colleges and universities need both to centralize the value of diversity and inclusion and employ a set of strategies that are enacted at all levels of their institutions. It argues that individual and institutional change efforts can only be achieved by implementing "diversity as a value"—that is embracing social change efforts as central and additive rather than episodic and required—and provides the research and theoretical frameworks to support this approach, as well as tools and examples of practice that accomplish change.

The contributors to this book identify the elements that drive successful multicultural initiatives and that strengthen the effectiveness of campus efforts to dismantle systemic oppression, as well as the individual and organization skills needed to manage *difference* effectively. Among these is developing the capacity of administrators, faculty, and student affairs professionals as conscious scholar practitioners to sensitively manage conflicts on campus, deconstruct challenging structures, and reconstruct the environment intentionally to include in respectful ways experiences of historically marginalized groups and nondominant ways of being in the world.

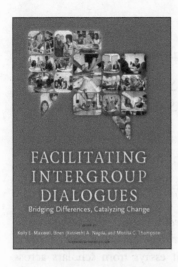

Facilitating Intergroup Dialogues

Bridging Differences, Catalyzing Change

Kelly E. Maxwell, Biren (Ratnesh) A. Nagda, and Monita C. Thompson

Foreword by Patricia Gurin

Copublished With ACPA

Intergroup dialogue has emerged as an effective educational and community building method to bring together members of diverse social and cultural groups to engage in learning together so that they may work collectively and individually to promote greater diversity, equality, and justice.

Intergroup dialogues bring together individuals from different identity groups (such as people of color and white people; women and men; lesbian, gay, and bisexual people; and heterosexual people), and uses explicit pedagogy that involves three important features: content learning, structured interaction, and facilitative guidance.

The least understood role in the pedagogy is that of facilitation. This volume, the first dedicated entirely to intergroup dialogue facilitation, draws on the experiences of contributors and on emerging research to address the multidimensional role of facilitators and cofacilitators, the training and support of facilitators, and ways of improving practice in both educational and community settings. It constitutes a comprehensive guide for practitioners, covering the theoretical, conceptual, and practical knowledge they need.

Difficult Subjects

Insights and Strategies for Teaching About Race, Sexuality, and Gender

Edited by Badia Ahad-Legardy and OiYan A. Poon

Foreword by Lori Patton Davis

Difficult Subjects: Insights and Strategies for Teaching About Race, Sexuality, and Gender is a collection of essays from scholars across disciplines, institutions, and ranks that offers diverse and multifaceted approaches to teaching about subjects that prove both challenging and often uncomfortable for both the professor and the student. It encourages college educators to engage in forms of practice that do not pretend that teachers and students are unaffected by world events and incidents that highlight social inequalities. Readers will find the collected essays useful for identifying new approaches to taking on the "difficult subjects" of race, gender, and sexuality.

The book will also serve as inspiration for academics who believe that their area of study does not allow for such pedagogical inquiries to also teach in ways that address difficult subjects. Contributors to this volume span a range of disciplines from criminal justice to gender studies to organic chemistry, and demonstrate the productive possibilities that can emerge in college classrooms when faculty consider "identity" as constitutive of rather than divorced from their academic disciplines.

Resource materials are available at www.TheBeingInstitute.org to support your continuing practice.

22883 Quicksilver Drive
Sterling, VA 20166-2019   Subscribe to our email alerts: www.Styluspub.com